W9-AOY-771

THE OXFORD
HISTORY OF MUSIC

VOL. VII

SYMPHONY AND DRAMA
1850–1900

BY

H. C. COLLES

NEW YORK
COOPER SQUARE PUBLISHERS, INC.
1973

THIS VOLUME

IS DEDICATED TO

ALL

WHO HELPED TO RETARD

ITS PROGRESS

1911–1932

Revised edition Published 1934 by Oxford University Press
Reprinted by Permission of Oxford University Press
Published 1973 by Cooper Square Publishers, Inc.
59 Fourth Avenue, New York, New York 10003
International Standard Book Number 0-8154-0475-1
Library of Congress Catalog Card Number 72-97077

Printed in the United States of America

CONTENTS

Chamber works after Brahms's symphonic (orchestral) period; duet sonatas, trios, quintets. The clarinet works, particularly the Quintet, Op. 115.

NOTE

ACKNOWLEDGEMENT is due to the following for kind permission to reprint musical quotations from copyright works: Choudens, Éditeur de Musique, Paris (for Bruneau, *L'Attaque du Moulin*). Rouart, Lerolle et Cie, Éditeurs-Propriétaires, 29, Rue d'Astorg, Paris, VIIIe (for Dukas, Symphony in C, and Chausson, Symphony in B flat). N. Simrock, Musikverlag, Leipzig (for Dvořák, String Quartet in G, Pianoforte Quintet in A, String Quintet, and 'New World' Symphony). Novello & Co., London (for Dvořák, Symphony in G major; Parry, 'The Glories of our Blood and State'; and Sullivan, 'The Golden Legend'). Hubední Matice, Prague (for Dvořák, *Dimitrij*). J. Hamelle, Paris (for Fauré, Pianoforte Quartets in C minor and G minor; Franck, Pianoforte Trio, String Quartet, Pianoforte Quintet, and Symphony in D minor). Durand et Cie, Paris (for Fauré, *Danseuse*). S. Bornemann, Éditeur, Paris (for Franck, *Panis Angelicus*). Boosey and Hawkes, Ltd., London, sole selling Agents in the British Empire, for the following works, the copyright in which is owned by Editions M. P. Belaieff (Glazounov, String Quartets and Symphonies; Taneiev, Pianoforte Quartet, and String Quartets). G. Ricordi & Co. (London) Ltd. (for Puccini, *La Bohème*). C. F. Peters, Leipzig (for Wolf's *Phänomen, Gleich und Gleich, Prometheus, Gebet*, and *An eine Aeolsharfe*).

CHAPTER I
MOVEMENTS AND PERIODS

THE mind of the musical historian inclines to oscillate uncomfortably between movements and periods. If he is fortunate he finds his starting-point in the rise of a new movement, it may be through the example set by an artist of genius, or the determined effort of a group towards an ideal shared by its members, or through social and even political changes reacting on the general outlook of civilized mankind and resulting in a fresh conformity of taste. The new movement is then clearly distinguishable from what has preceded it. Its exponents are busied in the choice of new technical methods in which to embody its ideals in sound, and a generation or so is occupied in developing those methods to its own satisfaction. But no sooner does the new movement acquire the definition of assured technique than it begins to lose identity. The movement moves, and in moving becomes something quite different from what its progenitors foresaw. The historian traces it a certain distance; as his volume grows in bulk his mind seeks to put a period to these ramifications. At last in despair he fixes either on some new manifestation as decisive or even falls back on a more or less arbitrary date, and calls a halt there.

This was the problem which Edward Dannreuther had to face in describing the Romantic Movement of the early part of the nineteenth century in the sixth volume of the *Oxford History of Music*. He had the good fortune of a well-defined starting-point, although the movement viewed broadly owed its inception neither to an individual nor to a group. Schumann deep in the study of Jean Paul Richter in his father's bookshop at Leipzig, Berlioz spraining his ankle on the *trottoir* of a street in Paris because his head was too full of the passages for brass

VII   B

instruments in his overture, *Les Francs Juges*, to mind where his feet were carrying him, Chopin allowing his brain to follow his hands on the keyboard till they led him to new expressions of that unsatisfied passion which lies behind mere notes, Weber surprising a Berlin audience nurtured on Spontini with the 'Waldhörner' of the overture to *Der Freischütz*; all these supplied evidence that the movement was afoot. These young artists were all approaching their art from premisses which would have seemed ridiculously inadequate to the generation before them, even to Beethoven trained by the counterpoint of Fux and Albrechtsberger and imbued through the example of Haydn with an undeviating devotion to principles of design.

But the movement moved. Before his death Schumann had come to be regarded as the leader of conservatism in German music. Even Berlioz, laughing at his youthful raptures, could declare that the passage which once made his ankle ache now gave him a pain in the head. Only the shortlived composers, Chopin and Weber, found the romantic impulse sufficiently sustaining throughout their careers, but the latter left a legacy of romantic opera to another hothead, Richard Wagner.

According to Wagner's diagnosis of his own case he turned his back on romantic opera with the completion of the score of *Lohengrin*. We are now all perfectly aware that he did no such thing, that the mighty scheme of *Der Ring des Nibelungen*, the erotic fervour of *Tristan und Isolde*, the happy adventure of *Die Meistersinger* into the Nürnberg of Hans Sachs's day, and above all, the pathetic groping of *Parsifal* in the uncharted territory of religious mysticism, are alike evidences of the mind obsessed by a romantic interpretation of human life. No doubt Dannreuther was equally aware of this. Nevertheless he firmly and faithfully, as became the personal friend of Wagner, drew the line across the page of his history after he had taken cognizance of *Lohengrin*. And in doing so he was a true historian.

His task was to trace, not the influence of the romantic spirit pervading the art of music as a whole, but a specific movement which began in contrast with what had been the general tendency of musical thought hitherto and gradually became absorbed into it.

Among the prominent composers of the early part of the nineteenth century those who have lived were men who fed their art from the life about them, from the evidences of beauty in nature, in literature and poetry. Wagner was at one with them in this, in the storm-tossed seascapes of *Der Fliegende Holländer*, the shepherd on the Wartburg of *Tannhäuser*, Wolfram's apostrophe to the evening star, and the imaginative pageantry of *Lohengrin*. From the moment, however, that his mind turned back from a hero's death to a hero's life, and back again beyond that to the same hero's ancestry, and ultimately to a vision of a primeval cosmogony from which the heroic breed sprang, the position was reversed. In planning *The Ring* Wagner saw his art not as an emanation from life but as the creation of life itself. From letting his art be fed at the breast of natural life he turned to regarding his art as the foster-mother of a spiritual life. His new standpoint may be, indeed certainly is to us, an inherently romantic one, but it is not the romance on which the Romantic Movement, properly so called, had based its action. Its exponents had been content to look on their music as a mirror held up to nature, reflecting countless appearances, hinting at spiritual values beneath the appearances but discreetly draping them in a picturesque imagery. Wagner from *The Ring* onwards saw himself as face to face with reality. Romantic imagery was only the stuff by which the reality could be made evident to human sense. That was his distinction between the music-drama of the future and the romantic opera of his and other composers' past.

About the middle of the century there is a discernible change

in the general attitude towards music itself, which is in some
sort a parallel to this change in Wagner's personal outlook.
Schumann had outgrown the influence of Jean Paul when he
turned to the composition of symphonies and chamber works
in sonata style. His later works in this manner were the most
significant pointers away from the illustrative idea of music,
even though one symphony was called 'The Spring' and another
'The Rhine'. Dannreuther would have been strictly logical had
he divided the Schumann of the Carnaval and the Kreisleriana
from the Schumann of the symphonies, the quintet, and the
violin sonatas, as he divided the Wagner of *Tannhäuser* and
Lohengrin from *The Ring* and *Tristan*. But Schumann's lead
towards the restoration of the classical design was not decisive.
Dannreuther preferred to draw his line in pure instrumental
music between Schumann and Brahms, and here again there
was documentary justification for the division in Schumann's
famous 'Neue Bahnen' article which proclaimed Brahms to be
the leader of a neo-classicism.

The notable revival of the symphonic ideal of music among
composers of both Slav and Latin races, who were very far
from owning Brahms's leadership, is a feature of the later
nineteenth century which lay outside the scope of a volume
devoted to the history of the Romantic Movement. César
Franck, Tchaikovsky, Dvořák, and the others who group with
these representative names, were certainly not anti-romantic,
but must be considered as post-romantic, since in seeking for
a personal expression through the symphonic form they looked
beyond the illustrative function of music, refused to consider
it either as providing a commentary to literature or as becoming
articulate only through association with a verbal commentary.
Music was rehabilitated in their work as a self-contained art.
That implied no self-denying ordinance on their part, no refusal
to give free rein to fantasy or rejection of the enrichments of

harmonic colour and iridescent orchestration which were the legacy of the Romantic Movement. Rather the reconciliation of expression and design gradually emerged as a paramount concern of this post-romantic period. Brahms was generally held by his contemporaries to be reactionary because of the stress which he laid on design, while those who most admired his mastery were inclined to underrate the efforts towards perfection of composers whose first impulse was in the direction of an expression of emotion.

It is the purpose of this volume to examine the several courses of composers in this post-romantic period and to discover relationships between them which are more evident now that the period is definitely closed than they could be a generation ago. It is a period of history rather than a movement which has here to be discussed, although within the period certain movements such as Wagner's creation of music-drama and the return of pure instrumental music to the symphonic ideal stand out with special prominence. Nevertheless its ending is more clearly defined than its beginning.

Because this seventh volume deals with a period and the sixth with a movement there is necessarily a certain amount of overlap between them. In the third quarter of the nineteenth century, that in which Brahms laid the foundations of the return to the symphony with a highly significant series of chamber works, Liszt and his followers were seeking newness in the vigorous pursuit of the illustrative ideal of music. Liszt's music falling within Dannreuther's line of demarcation received liberal discussion by him. It was natural also that he should include the more salient of the Russians of Balakirev's group (notably Borodin), who were strongly influenced by Liszt's creation of the 'symphonic poem' as an orchestral type. Dannreuther refers to them as 'a very late product of the Romantic Movement'. But the Russians of the Balakirev group were something more than this. They raised the question of national characteristics in music in a more acute form than it had ever appeared before. It was largely due to their example that a fever of musical nationalism of which we still feel the effects to-day spread over Europe in the last years of the century. The earlier Romantic Movement which is Dannreuther's chief subject-matter, that in which Weber, Berlioz, and Chopin, the youthful Schumann and the mature Liszt all had a share, had taken comparatively little account of national frontiers. Weber's tunes might follow the lines of the 'Volksthümlicheslied'; Chopin might write Mazurkas and Polonaises, Liszt might gravitate to the Hungarian Rhapsody in his lighter moments, but to none of them had there been any question of music being anything less than an international tongue. The Balakirev group set out to make a Russian music, one founded on the scales and rhythms of the native folk music. Borodin, the scientist, made an intensive study of this raw material in order to discover how to blend it in the European system of tonality without sophisticating it out of all recognition. Moussorgsky, the empiricist, proved himself in the end to be more logical than the scientist. If the implications of this raw material or his own unfettered impulse ran counter to the European system of tonality, then so much the worse for the European system; it must go by the board. Dannreuther accepted Borodin and rejected Moussorgsky. The latter appeared 'wilfully eccentric'. His style 'impresses the Western ear as barbarously ugly'.

Even Rimsky-Korsakov in preparing a performing edition of *Boris Godounov* could write in 1896 of the opera's 'insurmountable difficulties, the fragmentary character of the musical phrases, the harshness of the harmonies and modulations, the faulty counterpoint, the poverty of the instrumentation and the general weakness of the work from the technical point of view'. He had no hesitation in claiming that he had 'improved it from the technical side, making its lofty significance clearer and more accessible to all, while making an end of carping criticism'.

Alas for Rimsky-Korsakov! His well-intentioned effort made rather a beginning than an end of carping, and the controversy over Moussorgsky's meaning and his own interpretation of it still reverberates in our ears.

In Rimsky-Korsakov's preface may be discerned the end of an era. It expresses with confidence a type of criticism which simply could not have been uttered a decade later. What Dannreuther calls 'the Western ear' was a general consensus of judgement on which the European musical system had been slowly built up. It rested on simple conceptions of tonality and rhythm, selected out of an infinite number of possibilities which earlier ages had taken into account. The influence of harmony on the medieval modes had selected two, major and minor, as suitable for development. Their contrast at different pitches had become the principal source of tonal variety. The key system thus engendered proved capable of expansion in two directions, under the influence of that romantic impulse which existed in music long years before the Romantic Movement (as described by Dannreuther) was born, and necessarily survived after that movement had run its course. On the one hand composers took delight in sudden and rapid modulations from key to key as Bach does in the momentous passage of the 'et expecto resurrectionem mortuorum' of the Mass in B minor; on the other they expanded the key itself by the inclusion within its boundaries of chromatic harmonies, as in the *Crucifixus* of the same work. Thus the scope of the keys themselves became wider and their inter-relation more intimate until in certain works of the post-romantics, for example the prelude to the third act of *Parsifal*, the key system had become so intricate a matter that even the trained ear might have difficulty in analysing the composer's harmonic processes into their component parts. Nevertheless the key system held. Wagner was considered the arch-revolutionary of his day, but there is not a single passage in any of his works which is not explicable by the major-minor system of tonality, and the combinations and permutations derivable from it.

Similarly in regard to rhythm, an equally simple time system had been evolved from the complicated proportions of the medievalists. What Purcell wrote of time as being either 'common' or 'triple' into which all other divisions run 'like so many rivulets', might have been said with equal truth two centuries later. The septuple time of Brahms's Variations on a Hungarian Theme (Op. 21, No. 2) is a combination of 3–4 and 4–4; the Allegretto in his Trio in C minor (Op. 101) is written as 3–4, 2–4, 2–4. When Tchaikovsky's 'Pathetic' Symphony first appeared, his use of a genuine quintuple time, one which could not be subdivided into either $3+2$ or $2+3$ beats, was regarded by 'the Western ear' as a marvel of originality. Duple (with quadruple) and triple times, simple or compound, served as the basis for all the rhythmic expansions of *Tristan*, and in only one passage, the climax of the hero's excitement at the coming of Isolde, are they combined into the semblance of a quintuple measure.

Ex. 1.

These conceptions, both tonal and rhythmic, were basic; they are not so now. The composer was expected to regulate his polyphony in accordance with them. Not to do so was to appear wilfully eccentric or woefully barbarous. Eccentricity might be justified by some dramatic purpose or the need for literary illustration of the kind at which the romanticists aimed. Glinka, for example, could set tonality at defiance by the use of a scale in descending whole tones to depict the magician of *Rouslan and Ludmilla*. Liszt, hot in pursuit of 'poetic intention', foresaw the dissolution of the tonal system in one which he described as the 'omnitonique' and which the modernists have labelled 'atonality'. But Liszt was too much a citizen of the great world to drive his theory to its conclusion. That would have been to court the charge of barbarity. Moussorgsky risked more because he knew less, and the risks which he took shook the sympathy of even his warmest admirer. Rimsky-Korsakov undertook to correct him, to expunge the worst provincialisms of his musical speech to bring it into consonance with the usages of civilization. To do so seemed to him an act of piety; his dead friend should not be publicly disgraced by any sign of illiteracy. Piety, if the word may be used of any process governing the twentieth-century outlook, is now against Rimsky-Korsakov. He saw that,

'For some, these defects of workmanship eclipsed not only the merits of the opera, but even the talent of the composer; while for others, their very failings seemed, on the contrary, to be actually qualities and merits.'

The 'some' were of the nineteenth century; the 'others' were the forerunners of the twentieth. Their successors of to-day would go further and declare that there are no such things as faults or failings when a composer says what he means to say. Let his harmonies be as harsh as he will, his counterpoint as defiant of all tradition; none dare call either 'faulty'. The composer's intention and his ability to proclaim it is the one criterion. Gone is the appeal to rules or to any basic conceptions of what constitutes music and what lies outside it.

From this it will be gathered that criticism is very much more

difficult now than then. It will be for the author of the eighth
volume to show the lines which it must follow, and indeed
whether it remains possible at all. The twentieth-century
composer makes his own premisses from which he reaches his
own conclusions; the nineteenth-century composer started from
premisses held in common by him and his hearers; his genius
appeared in the conclusions drawn from them. It is not difficult
to see in what way the concentration on folksong contributed
to a loosening of, if it did not actually break up, the European
system, both tonal and rhythmic. Melodies which owned neither
major nor minor modes must sooner or later receive a harmonization which grew out of their own tonal systems rather than
from that belonging to the system of central Europe. And
similarly melodies which had never known the restraint of
regular time patterns could not be forced into such patterns
without violence to their innate rhythms. Moussorgsky's handling of *The Battle of Kazan* (Varlaam's song) and of the hostess's
song shows the beginnings of both processes.[1]

The disintegrating tendency appeared as the result of many
influences of which this accentuation of local dialect is only
one, though possibly the most conspicuous. Allusion has already
been made to Liszt's sensing of a possible 'omnitonique', and
that pursuit of graphic expression of literary ideas of which Liszt
was the acknowledged apostle was carried a stage further by
the most able of his disciples in the second generation after him.
The 'lustige Streiche' of Till Eulenspiegel, the transcendental
philosophy of Zarathustra, and the madness of Don Quixote,
produced in the tone-poems of Richard Strauss perversions of
the accepted tonal system, which according to the nineteenth-
century standards are 'not music'. What Strauss did as an

[1] It will be worth while here to compare Rimsky-Korsakov's edition
(1896 and 1908) of these passages with 'the original text in accordance with
the autograph MSS.', edited by Paul Lamm and published by the Oxford
University Press, 1928.

intentional suggestion of abnormal psychology was to be accepted
presently as an acquisition of the normal musical language, just
as the whole-tone scale of Glinka's magician was to become a
precedent for a type of harmony based on the equal temperament of the keyboard (twelve semitones to the octave) in the
music of Debussy.

Scholarship also played its part. The revival of ecclesiastical
plainsong and research into the methods of handling the
medieval modes in harmonic and mensural music made it
evident that 'the Western ear' of a few hundred years ago had
accepted with complacence as part of a highly developed type
of music all sorts of progressions which the nineteenth-century
harmonists labelled 'forbidden'.[1] But this revival was even
more important in its influence on current ideas of melodic
structure and rhythm than of harmony. The researches of
Dom Pothier and the monks of Solesmes, brought into prominence by their controversy with the Ratisbon School, put a
wholly new complexion on the rhythmic character of plainsong,
and convinced the world that far from being a crude melody
owing its survival to the conservatism of the Church, it was a
developed art owing its vitality to subtle rhythmic principles
which were not those of mensural music. Mendelssohn's indigna-
tion at the insignificant dullness of the music which he heard
sung to the Holy Week Offices in Rome in 1831 no doubt had
some justification in the manner of its interpretation. His
proposal to re-write the Roman liturgy in the best Mendels-
sohnian style seems laughable a hundred years later, but it is
the monks of Solesmes who have made it so.[2] As research into

[1] Haberl had founded the Palestrina Society in 1879, and the monumental
edition of Palestrina's works in thirty-three volumes was completed in
1894 to celebrate the tercentenary of the composer's death.

[2] Dom Pothier produced *Les Mélodies grégoriennes, d'après la tradition*, in
1881; his *Liber Gradualis* followed two years later. It was in 1904 that
Solesmes received papal authority as editors of the *Editio Vaticana*.

medieval music, both harmonic and melodic, measured and unmeasured, proceeded, its product had a cumulative effect on the work of modern composers. Tradition became an enormously enlarged term, connoting no longer the achievements of the generation immediately before, but rather a body of experience in methods of workmanship some of which seemed to have been blindly ignored in the formation of the musical language based on the major-minor key system and the common and triple times with 'rivulets'. That language had sufficed for Wagner, Verdi, Brahms, Dvořák, Tchaikovsky and César Franck, Parry and Elgar, despite their different characters and aims, the products of their different nationalities, surroundings, and personal temperaments. It was threatened in the nineteenth century itself chiefly by experimentalists such as Moussorgsky and by sensation-seekers such as Strauss.

Debussy's *Pelléas et Mélisande* made its appearance at the Opéra Comique in 1902. It proclaimed a reaction from the principles of Wagner in operatic composition, but more than that it proved that one of the least sensational of composers and one whose ideas were not bound up with national propaganda any more than they were with a student's devotion to the music of a past age, found it necessary to express himself in terms which ran counter to the principles of nineteenth-century music. It was Debussy, in fact, who ruled the line between the two centuries of music.

It is that line which must divide this volume from its successor. The date 1900 marks the end of our period with fair accuracy, even though much which owns the principles of our period, notably the work of English composers, those named above with others, was composed later. It was with the appearance of *Pelléas* that Rimsky-Korsakov's criticism of 'faulty counterpoint' was seen to be belated and Dannreuther's 'Western ear' could no longer be cited as a final Court of Appeal.

How far the music of the twentieth century has already proceeded along its own path may be gauged by the quotation of a simple passage in two-part counterpoint which begins a work by a composer not held to be an extremist of the modern school.

Ex. 2.

The theorist of to-day has no difficulty in justifying this opening of Vaughan Williams's suite, *Flos Campi*, on the ground that each part consistently pursues its own line of melodic modality, but the listener to the music is too impatient even to hear the theorist's explanation. What matter if E flat and E natural, A flat and A natural, are contending at every point! That is what the composer means them to do; it is enough for the modern listener. Yet within this short passage, 'senza misura', is to be found the rejection of every technical principle which the nineteenth century held to be inviolable. Compare it with Wagner's harmonization of the shepherd's pipe (cor anglais) in the third act of *Tristan* and it is at once apparent how far technical standards have shifted.

Ex. 3.

Wagner, the revolutionary of the nineteenth century, is completely subject to a tonal law of which Vaughan Williams, the conservative of the twentieth, takes no account. Between the two there is a great gulf fixed.

The musician of the twentieth century postulates:

(1) That a tune may be made on any series of notes, whether contained in the true (acoustic) scale, in the tempered scale of the keyboard (twelve semitones to the octave), or on a scale constructed *ad hoc*;

(2) That two or more such tunes may be heard simultaneously, each one built on a different scale, and without conforming to any agreed standard of consonance;

(3) That rhythm is capable of infinite variety, and need not be referred to any measurement by regularly recurring accents.

These postulates may not be universally conceded, but it would be a bold critic who dared openly to deny the truth of any one of them. Our concern here, however, is with the practice of the nineteenth century which denied them all. The seventh volume of the *Oxford History of Music* concludes a period; to the eighth will belong another new movement.

CHAPTER II

1853

LOUIS NAPOLEON was declared Emperor and assumed the title of Napoleon III on December 2nd, 1852, exactly a year after the *coup d'état* which had set the stage for him. A little earlier the King of Prussia had put by the offer of a similar title for the confederated German States. The tragedy of Empire was to be played out first in France. England had laid to rest the mortal remains of the Iron Duke beneath the dome of St. Paul's Cathedral and with him her last fears of the Gallic menace. Her German Prince had pictured for her the blessings of pre-eminence in international commerce in the Great Exhibition of 1851. The electric telegraph joined London and Paris. The Crimean War was at hand, in which the new Empire of France and the enlightened monarchy of Great Britain were to combine to maintain the power of Turkey in Eastern Europe.

Europe had shaken from her coat the waters of insurrection which had rained about her in 1849. Government was stabilized for the time being, save in the Italian peninsula, in the affairs of which the new Emperor was shortly to take a hand.

An exact estimate of the effect of this political orientation on the art of music is not to be attempted. At the moment no connexion could be discernible, but since political changes produce new conditions of life, and style in art is largely determined by the conditions in which the artists live, it is not surprising that the middle of the nineteenth century should prove to be an artistic as well as a political turning-point in history.

The musical events which make the year 1853 itself memorable are German ones, and Germany is the country which appears least changed by the political events recalled above. The caution of the Prussian King had delayed the imperial experiment of the North. Francis Joseph's accession was to preserve the equilibrium of the Austrian throne for two full generations to come, and with it the artistic identity of Vienna. The elder Johann Strauss had lately died but the permanence of the waltz dynasty was assured by his son, composer at a later date of *An der schönen blauen Donau* and *Die Fledermaus*. The reputation of Vienna as the cradle of the classics of instrumental music was fading, but was presently to be restored by a fresh infiltration of genius from the North. To the outside observer, especially to the English observer, Germany might well appear to be still the old Germany of the Confederation; that hotch-potch of Kingdoms, Grand-duchies, Duchies, and Principalities amongst which music had been domesticated through two centuries. The art was still to find its domicile for a few decades longer in what remained of the old Court life. That life was to exert a lasting influence on one of the greatest musicians of the rising generation, the one who in fact began to be known to the world in this same year, 1853—Johannes Brahms.

But the old order was changing rapidly. A new spirit of political consolidation was animating German thought. The separation of Germany from Austria, the war of 1866 and the formation in the following year of the North German Con-federation with its parliament meeting in Berlin, the close of the Franco-Prussian War in 1871 with the proclamation from Versailles of King William I of Prussia as German Emperor, are its well-known landmarks. A commercial prosperity which should emulate that of England, an Empire which should far surpass in power that which had been crushed in France, were the new ambitions which were destined to lead up to the catastrophe of 1914. It is the period of a united Germany's rise and fall that is traversed in this volume. The influence of this 'new spirit' on the later phases of the art of both Brahms and Wagner is unmistakable.

VII   C

Certain musical events of 1853 claim attention here. They centre round Liszt at Weimar and Wagner at Zürich. The former was at the height of his power as 'Ausserordentlicher Hof-Kapellmeister', and his ménage on the Altenburg with the Princess Karolyne von Sayn-Wittgenstein was the meeting-place of all the ardent spirits who stood for the new life of German art. Wagner alone could not come there. His participation in the Dresden riots of 1849 had banished him from Germany, but Liszt was the chief upholder of his artistic cause. To him Wagner sent the first copy of the privately printed poem of *Der Ring des Nibelungen* on February 11th of this year.

Performances of Wagner's earlier operas were given at Weimar in March. He organized his successful concerts of selections at Zürich in May. In July Liszt visited Wagner in Zürich and made him acquainted with his own symphonic poems and the 'Faust' Symphony. The intercourse between Weimar and Zürich was very close. There followed Liszt's musical festival at Karlsruhe (October 3rd–5th), where also Wagner could not come, 'the aim of which', Wagner says, 'was to give the public an adequate interpretation of our respective works'.[1] Selections from *Tannhäuser* and *Lohengrin* were played. Hans von Bülow and Joseph Joachim took part in the festival. The latter contributed his own Violin Concerto and Bach's Chaconne for violin alone. Then came the meeting at Basle where 'young Weimar' assembled to greet the exile and to hear the poem of the tetralogy which was to re-create the musical theatre. Besides Liszt himself with his Princess and her daughter Marie, the party consisted of Peter Cornelius, Joseph Joachim, Hans von Bülow, Dionys Pruckner, and Richard Pohl. The first, a young actor turned composer, whose Op. I, *Sechs kleine Lieder, zu eigenen Weisen*, dates from this year, was presently to produce the opera, *Der Barbier von Bagdad*, which would occasion the break-up of

[1] *My Life*, ii. 605.

Liszt's Weimar command. He was a stalwart champion of the cause in *Die neue Zeitschrift für Musik*, originally Schumann's paper, now the organ of the Young German School. We have Wagner's word for it that in this cheerful gathering Joachim alone was a little ill at ease. He 'could not forget my tremendous article on Judaism' and 'consequently felt shy and awkward in my presence'.[1] Joachim's discomfort probably had little to do with Wagner's 'tremendous article'. He was beset by more serious misgivings. A year earlier he had left the Liszt circle to take up the part of Konzertmeister at Hanover, where as teacher of the orchestra he was engaged on his first important work for the advancement of symphonic music. He was himself much engaged in composition. His *Frühlingsphantasie* shows the influence of Liszt, and the Violin Concerto just heard at Karlsruhe was dedicated to Liszt. The latter was a piece of brilliant virtuosity which Joachim later put aside. He still addressed Liszt in correspondence as 'Honoured Master', and he still belonged to the inner circle of the Weimar group, but he already had misgivings. His work at Hanover was bringing him daily experience of the classics of the symphony and of chamber music. A few months before the Basle meeting he had formed a new friendship, through his participation in the Niederrheinische Musikfest, with Robert Schumann. He felt repelled by certain features of the Honoured Master's own symphonic poems. Presently he would have to confess to it, but not yet, not till he saw his artistic faith more clearly. Meantime he came to Basle; Bülow whispered to Wagner that his shyness was the result of that article on Judaism, and Wagner tried to set him at ease with some 'particularly friendly words'.

Bülow and Pruckner were Liszt's most brilliant pupils of the pianoforte. The former was just beginning his career with concert tours; the latter, a lad of nineteen, was still a student at

[1] *Ibid.*, ii. 606.

Weimar. Finally, Richard Pohl was chief spokesman for the party in the Press. He it was who, under his pseudonym 'Hoplit', was describing the recent doings of the group in the *Neue Zeitschrift* under the title of 'Briefe aus Karlsruhe'.

The third of these 'Briefe' appeared in the *Neue Zeitschrift* of October 28th, but it was preceded by a short article with the title 'Neue Bahnen', and the prominence given to this article was explained by the initials R. S. at the end.

Robert Schumann, founder and first editor of the paper, had made a momentary return to journalism after ten years of retirement to announce, not a budding talent to be nurtured and brought to perfection, but a genius whom he declared had appeared already possessed of full mastery. In his journalistic days Schumann had given generous encouragement to every new talent which came his way. Of some of them he had used extravagant language; musicians were inclined to discount his praise. They would do that with the hero of 'Neue Bahnen'. Still there were details in this article which might well be a little irritating to the enthusiasts who had just separated after their meeting at Basle. In his retirement, Schumann said he had marked the appearance of many new and significant talents which betokened new strength to the art of music.[1] Well he might; Brendel, the paper's present editor, was writing of the most significant of them in a series of articles, 'Zur Würdigung Richard Wagners', which had been begun in the *Zeitschrift* on May 9th of this year. 'Hoplit's' third 'Brief aus Karlsruhe' immediately following 'Neue Bahnen' pointed in the same direction. Unfortunately Schumann could not resist a footnote; one which showed that it was not of these talents that he was thinking, and not in them that he observed the art's new power. He mentioned a dozen names. The first amongst them was the

[1] 'Manche neue, bedeutende Talente erschienen, eine neue Kraft der Musik schien sich anzukündigen.'

one member of the Basle gathering whose adherence was insecure, Joseph Joachim, the violinist-composer, who had gone from Schumann's festival at Düsseldorf to Liszt's at Karlsruhe, and thence to Basle to be 'warmly embraced' by Wagner. The rest were either the first product of the Leipzig Conservatorium founded by Mendelssohn ten years since, or those of an older generation whose promise had received Schumann's blessing in the days of his editorship.

Subsequent events have not endorsed Schumann's estimate of the Leipzig group. Ernst Naumann (1832–1910) composed some chamber music, held an organistship at Jena, and did some good work as an editor of the publications of the *Neue Bachgesellschaft* and of the string quartets of Haydn. Ludwig Norman (1831–85) pursued an academic career in his native Stockholm, and is remembered to-day by the world outside as the first husband of the great violinist who was known as Mme Norman Neruda until she became Lady Hallé. Woldemar Bargiel (1828–87) was half-brother of Clara Schumann,[1] composed piano music which gained a fairly wide currency, and ultimately became a professor at the Hochschule in Berlin. Theodor Kirchner (1823–1903) became the composer of voluminous piano music which has been summed up by Dannreuther in a pungent phrase.[2] Julius Schäffer (1823–1902) was brought into personal contact with Schumann through his friendship with Robert Franz. His slender talent issued in some songs and part-songs, and he wrote various brochures on Franz's editing of the classics and kindred matters. Albert Dietrich (1829–1908), Schumann's friend and pupil at Düsseldorf, wrote aspiring works in the larger forms, but is best remembered to-day through his little book, *Erinnerungen an J. Brahms*, published in the year after Brahms's death (1898).

---

[1] Marianne Tromlitz, divorced wife of Fr. Wieck, married Adolf Bargiel, music-teacher in Berlin.   [2] See *Oxford History of Music*, vi, p. 316.

The list might look a little more impressive in 1853 than now, since it was one of active and earnest young men between twenty and thirty. The contention regarding them was at least not capable of disproof, but it might inspire distrust, especially among those equally active and earnest young men who were not included in it. The simple-minded footnote in fact proclaimed Schumann as a party leader, roused a suspicion that the Leipzig party was angling to detach Joachim from the Weimar party, and desired to announce its discovery of a protagonist in the latest of the twenty-year-olds, young Brahms. It did harm; not so much probably to Brahms's personal position, though he may have felt a little embarrassed by the eulogy of the article, as by the stimulus it gave to that tendency of artistic Germany to form itself into mutually antagonistic camps.

Brahms, introduced by Joachim, had already visited Weimar, had been received with peculiar graciousness by Liszt, and had not responded quite as a youngster honoured by a great master might have been expected to respond.[1] He was always *farouche* in a society not wholly congenial to him. Liszt was as eager for the encouragement of young talent as Schumann was, and he had a keener sense of the distinction between big and little. He welcomed Brahms; if Brahms did not appreciate the warmth of the welcome Liszt could afford to let him go. And Brahms had gone back to Joachim at Göttingen, incidentally shedding in Weimar the irksome association with the Hungarian violinist, Eduard Remenyi, who remained to sun himself in the smiles of his greater countryman.

It was amongst the smaller fry, whose loyalties were ready to degenerate into partisanship, that 'Neue Bahnen' worked mischief. Subsequent events, Joachim's defection from Liszt's

---

[1] See the account of an eye-witness of the interview, William Mason (*Memoirs of a Musical Life*), then a pupil of Liszt, reprinted in Florence May's *Life of Brahms* (subsequently alluded to here as May).

party (1857), expressed with what seems excessive conscientiousness in the words, 'I am quite impervious to your music',[1] and
the futile protest against Brendel's conduct of the *Neue Zeitschrift* (1860),[2] which Brahms and Joachim signed, threw up the
earthworks around the opposing camps.

But the main contention of Schumann's article was un-
equivocal, and history has confirmed the rightness of his judgement. He had found something in the compositions of the new-
comer which he had not found in those 'bedeutende Talente'
already esteemed by him. He had no words to say what that
was. He called it 'Magic'. He summoned all the favourite
images of German romantic poetry to describe it: the waterfall,
the cloud, the rainbow, the butterfly, and the nightingale. They
could not help him very much. In the end, no doubt, he knew
that his words had not touched the core of the matter, but he
knew also that the core was there, that there was something
lasting in this music, something stronger than his own fancied
images, and different in kind from all that emphasis on 'ideas'
around and about the music which had sustained the Romantic
Movement and was at this very time finding its outcome alike
in the music-drama of Wagner and the poetic-music of Liszt.
People misinterpreted Schumann's words and imagined that,
in hailing Brahms as the one who should come, he claimed him
as his own disciple. They could not credit him with a largeness
of view which founded its faith on the fact that the new-comer
was not a disciple either of himself or of any one else.[3] That
misunderstanding even cramped the otherwise open mind of

[1] Moser's *Life of Joachim* (English translation), p. 167.

[2] May, i, p. 250. Kalbeck, i, p. 419.

[3] 'Ich dachte, die Bahnen dieser Auserwählten mit der grössten Theil-
nahme verfolgend, es würde und es müsse nach solchem Vorgang einmal
plötzlich einer erscheinen, der den höchsten Ausdruck der Zeit in idealer
Weise auszusprechen berufen wäre: einer der uns die Meisterschaft nicht in
stufenweiser Entfaltung brächte, sondern, wie Minerva, gleich vollkommen
gepanzert aus dem Haupte des Kronien spränge. Und er ist gekommen . . .'

Richard Pohl in the finely impartial analysis of Brahms's early published works which, as 'Hoplit', he subsequently contributed to the columns of the *Neue Zeitschrift*.[1] He realized that Brahms was no mere disciple of Schumann but he saw also signs of what he conceived to be some of Schumann's defects in the early Brahms. On that account he held that Brahms ought not to have been acclaimed as the mature artist. He found inconsistency of style and was at some pains to show that after all Brahms was not a Minerva springing fully armed from the head of Jove.

The three Pianoforte Sonatas (C major, F sharp minor, and F minor) with the Scherzo in E flat minor and the first version of the Trio in B major (published 1854 as Op. 8) are all that remain of the self-dependent music of Brahms at this date. The other concerted chamber music mentioned by Schumann, and discussed as possible matter for publication in Brahms's correspondence both with Schumann and Joachim,[2] was withheld, and what Brahms withheld he subsequently destroyed. It is possible that had Brahms relied solely on his own judgement, the Sonata in C alone would have seen the light, but to a certain extent be deferred to his mentors.[3] His dedication of the Sonata in F sharp minor to Clara Schumann shows him at least reconciled to its publication, and he made considerable alterations in the Finale of the F minor Sonata, now by far the

---

[1] *Neue Zeitschrift*, Dec. 14, 1855, quoted by May, i. 189.

[2] The withheld works included:

Phantasie in D minor for pianoforte, violin, and violoncello—*Largo and Allegro.*

Sonata in A minor for pianoforte and violin.

String Quartet in B flat major.

The Sonata in A minor was given to Senff for publication as Op. 5, but its place was ultimately taken by the Piano Sonata in F minor.

[3] He wrote to Joachim (Oct. 17, 1853), 'Opus 4 (i.e. the Sonata in C ultimately Op. 1) is the only one I am really satisfied with', and this he dedicated to Joachim.

most widely admired of the three, before allowing it to go to press.[1]

The Sonata in C, his first favourite, shows at once the immeasurable distance between Brahms's mind and the best contemporary work of the kind. To quote its opening motive tells nothing; to give any conception of the quality of the principal theme would require the transcription of the first thirty-six bars, in the course of which the plain statement of the opening motive has been followed by a supple rhythmic development covering a wide range of keys and mounting by a series of tonal climaxes to the point at which further progress is checked by the emphatic partial cadence on a chord of B major. Contrast with this Schumann's tight repetitional treatment of similarly terse figures in his own F sharp minor Sonata, his First Symphony (B flat), and elsewhere. Brahms is moving in an altogether freer world of musical thought. The passage from this to the more lyrical second subject section is abrupt, but the abruptness is designed. The exposition leaves one asking what relation can be found between the two groups of opposed ideas. The development, beginning with the second group, answers the question decisively in a long colloquy beginning at the fortissimo where the two salient themes appear simultaneously; it is sustained with unflagging power up to the moment where the first theme reappears in triumphant recapitulation and with richly expanded harmony.

In this movement the young Brahms picks up the normal language of the sonata (that language which we think of as characteristic of Beethoven's middle period), and handles it with an assurance unparalleled in history, save by Mozart's handling of the simpler idioms of his day.

The Andante and Scherzo are interludes, as in the classical, pre-Beethoven form, the former a decorative set of variations

---

[1] See Brahms's letter to Schumann, Nov. 16, 1853.

on an old German *Minnelied*,[1] the latter (E minor, 6–8 time) an
impulsive, bull-in-a-china-shop movement, of a type which
remained characteristic of one side of Brahms throughout his
life, as witness the corresponding movement of the Fourth
Symphony. It has for Trio the first of those long-phrased soaring
tunes by which Brahms is everywhere known, a tune to be
compared with the second subjects of the Pianoforte Quartet in
G minor, and the Violin Sonata in G major. The Finale returns
to business, recalls the opening motive of the first movement,
transforms it into a new and bustling rhythm (9–8 time), and
builds it into a wholly fresh idea of a kind which in mood and
shape anticipates to some extent the Finale to the Violoncello
Sonata in E minor (Op. 38). Indeed a comparison of these two
Finales would provide a measure of Brahms's advance in technical subtlety in the dozen years between the two publications.
There is justification here for 'Hoplit's' charge of inconsistency,
especially in regard to the third subject (the movement is in a
free rondo form), a *Volksthümlicheslied*, harmonized like a part-
song, which never becomes anything more than an interpolation
and a strangely irrelevant one. But however out of keeping with
the idiom of the pianoforte sonata, this theme and others like
it are essentially part of Brahms. The square-cut stockish
German folksong was bone of his bone. His shorter vocal pieces
(part-songs and single-voiced songs) are full of its influence and
in them it finds its proper place. The *Academic Festival Overture* (Op. 80) shows him at a later stage of his life able to weld

---

[1] Friedländer (*B. Lieder*, Eng. ed., p. 248) declares that this song was
written, both words and music, by Zuccalmaglio, who published it on three
different occasions, first in the collection *Bardale*, Brunswick, 1829.

Brahms believed in the genuineness of this and other 'folksongs' in
Zuccalmaglio's collections and made it the last (No. 49) of his series of
Deutsche Volkslieder (published 1894). In a letter to Simrock he drew
attention to the coincidence by which *Verstohlen geht der Mond auf* had
found place in his Op. 1, and in what he then thought would be his last
publication.

together securely traditional examples of such tunes and make them a part of his own symphonic design.

Schumann had called these sonatas 'veiled symphonies' ('verschleierte Symphonien'). In the larger movements a polyphony wider than two hands can compass on the keyboard is often implied, sometimes felicitously (see the D major passage in the development of No. 1), sometimes clumsily, by filling both hands full of as many notes as they will hold (and much more than small hands can possibly hold). In the slow movement of the same sonata the decorative details surrounding the *Minnelied* (notably the triplet[1] in the first variation) are suggestive of instrumentation. The whole of the slow movement to the F sharp minor Sonata, which includes a long passage requiring three staves for its presentment, looks like a condensed orchestral score. It is impossible to think of the D flat passage in the middle of the first movement of the F minor Sonata as anything else than a long violoncello solo accompanied by syncopated string figures.

Such things present the curious paradox of a composer thinking orchestrally in an orchestral age, but unable to write for the orchestra. Schumann, both in 'Neue Bahnen' and in personal correspondence, pressed on Brahms the duty of writing a symphony, and Brahms dutifully tried, and failed. His letters of 1854 are full of reference to his symphony. He got his friend, Julius Otto Grimm, to help him with the technical matters of orchestration,[2] but he could not be happy about it. The ideas were there in abundance; the substance was presently thrown into the form of a sonata for two pianos which he played with

---

[1] An essay might be written on Brahms's use of these triplet figures striking across the texture of his music. The device had a peculiar significance for him and constantly appears when his mood is one of a brooding solemnity. Compare the Intermezzo (Rückblick) of the F minor Sonata. The drum rhythm in the second movement ('Denn alles Fleisch') of *Ein deutsches Requiem* is the most eloquent example of all.

[2] See letter to Joachim, July 27, 1854.

Mme Schumann;[1] the first two movements of it ultimately issued in the Pianoforte Concerto in D minor.

Brahms at this stage was primarily a pianist. He could think orchestrally at the piano, but he could not think apart from the piano. It was to take the next twenty years to make the orchestra his own. When the process was completed and the result appeared in the First Symphony (1876), it was found to be his own orchestra, just as the piano in 1853 was his own piano, something quite unlike current fashions in instrumental handling and therefore open to the criticism of those to whom the orchestra had become the vivid dramatic instrument of Wagner and the picturesque toy of Berlioz.

To look back on the momentous year of Brahms's arrival with his subsequent achievements in mind, is to endorse the wisdom of the decision to publish the three piano sonatas together as the first-fruits of his contribution to pure instrumental music, with the songs beside them, including at least one masterpiece in the profoundly beautiful setting of *Liebestreu*,[2] to offer their commentary on the lyrical inspiration of Brahms's melody. Together they assert him as the new-comer, completely assured in his conception of what his music was to be, daring and even ruthless in adapting the technical means to that conception, and, moreover, growing in his ability to fit the means to the end even in the short interval between the first two and the third Sonata.

The Sonata in F minor is the one by which pianists almost invariably choose to represent the early Brahms to-day, and their choice is natural because, while its ideas are no less commanding than those of the first, and on the whole more

---

[1] Dr. Mandyczewski, Brahms's intimate friend of later years, assured the writer that the MS. of this sonata, like everything else which Brahms did not wish published, was destroyed. What is now the third movement of *Ein deutsches Requiem* is said to have been the Finale of the projected symphony (see May i, p. 167).

[2] Composed in January 1853, words from Reineck's *Lieder*, Friedländer.

genial than those of the second, their sequence has an inevita-
bility not found earlier, and the style of writing has largely
outgrown the ungainliness which has thrown the F sharp minor
Sonata into the shade. There is, moreover, an inner unity
between the several movements of the F minor Sonata not
found in the other two, despite the fact that the C major Sonata's
first movement and Finale and the F sharp minor's slow movement and Scherzo, are linked by transformed themes. That
useful device hardly appears in the F minor Sonata as a link
between two movements, except in so far as the Intermezzo
'looks back' on the long-drawn tune of the Andante. Brahms
chose to particularize that Andante with Sternau's sentimental
lines about the lovers in the moonlight, but that does not
separate it from its context as the *Minnelied* separates the slow
movement of the C major. The unity is found essentially in an
emotional sequence, though a technical attribute of it may be
discerned in the distribution of keys. All the four greater movements (all, that is, except the Intermezzo) gravitate towards the
key of D flat major, the first movement in what has been
described as the 'violoncello solo', the Andante in its central
section and more remarkably in the coda, the Scherzo in its
Trio, and the Finale in the first appearance of that majestic
march tune which sweeps aside all other thoughts and whirls
the music forward to its exhilarating climax in F major.

A word may be said here about Brahms's use of the process
known as the transformation of themes. The device of binding
together various musical episodes by the use in all of them of
the same melodic idea transformed rhythmically to suit varying
moods is practically as old as the conscious composition of
music. It is found in the Masses of medieval composers upon
plainsong or folksong themes.[1] The fugal devices of augmenta-

---

[1] Compare for example Kyrie and Sanctus of Palestrina's Mass *Assumpta
est Maria.*

tion, diminution, inversion, and retrogression are modifications of the process. One may trace it through the Allemandes and Courantes of Handel's Suites for the harpsichord to the early works of Beethoven (see Finale of the Concerto in C minor).

But in the nineteenth century it was brought into special prominence by the composers who sought to link their music closely with literary ideas. The *idée fixe* in Berlioz's *Symphonie Fantastique* is a salient example, and the deliberate attempt to transform the dreamlike melody of the earlier movements into a travesty of itself in the scene of the Witches' Sabbath is of the most literal kind. It requires no great imaginative faculty to transform themes in this way, and, where music is associated with a literary idea or a dramatic scheme, the device has a very obvious utility. It can serve to recall the same idea in different circumstances, to make a contrast the more pointed by the very fact of a likeness with a difference, and its pliability was no doubt the chief cause which led to its adoption by Liszt and his followers as a structural feature.

Liszt particularly wished to do two things, to emphasize the connexion between music and literature in his symphonic poems, and to gain a closer unity of design in the various sections of works which did not proclaim themselves as 'programme-music', such as the Sonata in B minor and the piano concertos. The transformed theme could be helpful in both directions but in the latter its possibilities were limited. An English writer[1] has put the matter in a nutshell by saying that in such a transformation 'the feeling is new but the form is familiar; this is the direct opposite of the idiom which sustains one emotional mood with an ever-varying form. The latter is development of an idea.' Where a theme is developed by processes which gradually enhance its interest and beauty, transformation sinks into insignificance. The examples men-

[1] Miss Margaret Glynn, *Evolution of Musical Form*, p. 173.

tioned from Handel and Beethoven use both processes. At the outset of Handel's Courante following the Allemande in the Suite No. 4 in E minor and in the coda of Beethoven's Concerto in C minor we feel a certain stirring at the discovery of an old friend in a new guise, but it is the development of the new guise which is really essential, and that follows speedily in both cases.

Brahms's uses of transformed themes in the first two piano sonatas have been spoken of by his admirers as showing a youthful leaning towards the heresies of Weimar which he spurned as soon as his better nature asserted itself.[1] That is quite untrue. It is possible that the two instances were suggested to Brahms by Liszt's example, and a certain stiffness in the handling of the second (Sonata in F sharp minor) seems evidence that he was trying his hand at what was for him a new experiment. He must have discovered that it would not by itself carry him very far, but he never made any recantation of it as a means of expression. On the contrary he kept it as a weapon in his armoury with which in later years he made many a skilful thrust. Sometimes he used it to heighten the excitement of a finale and nowhere with more brilliant success than in the F minor Piano Sonata itself and the Piano Quintet, Op. 34, in the same key, or with a stronger sense of rhythmic contrast than in the Second String Quartet, Op. 51, No. 2. At other times it stilled tʰ ʾounding energy of his movement to a mood of calm reflectiveness as in the Third Symphony (Op. 90). Or again it could just provide a connecting link between a number of episodes strongly opposed in feeling, as in the first movement of the Second Symphony, or still more subtly in the slow movement of the Clarinet Quintet, his last big work of concerted chamber music. But in these later instances the transformation initiates some new and stimulating development; it calls no

[1] See Fuller-Maitland, *Brahms*, p. 72.

attention to itself as an achievement; on the contrary it impels the interest forward. The moment in which Brahms transforms a theme is the signal that he is just going to do something; when Liszt transforms a theme he generally proclaims aloud, 'See what I have done.'

Thematic transformation leads naturally to the much larger matter, variations, a form in which Brahms was shortly to prove himself one of the greatest, if not actually the greatest of the masters. Only Bach's 'Goldberg' and Beethoven's 'Diabelli' variations dispute the supremacy of Brahms's sets on themes by Handel, Paganini, and Haydn. It happened that his first publication of this kind, apart from those variations occurring in the piano sonatas (Opp. 1 and 2), appeared in the following year (1854) as *Variationen über ein Thema von Robert Schumann*, Op. 9. It happens too that this is almost the only considerable instrumental work of Brahms about which it is necessary to know the circumstances of its composition if the music is to be understood. By so much is it Schumann rather than Brahms in spirit.

Early in 1854 Schumann's mind collapsed, and on February 27th he attempted suicide by throwing himself into the Rhine. He was placed in a private asylum at Endenich, where he remained until his death on July 29th, 1856. The event was the first stab of human sorrow which had come to shake the boyish confidence of the young Brahms. Hitherto his moods had ranged between what Schumann himself had humorously called the 'wing flapping' of the young eagle to the misty moonlight romances of the slow movements in the sonatas. But here was something real that touched him nearly. From a nature more susceptible to volatile emotion, some poignant slow movement filled with clamorous lamentation might have been expected. But not so Brahms. He devoted himself very largely at this time to giving such practical support and comfort to Schumann's wife as a younger friend, regarded almost as a son by both of them, could offer. Clara Schumann's troubles were intensified by the fact that she was then expecting her seventh child. She occupied herself by composing variations on one of her husband's melodies,[1] dear to both of them. This theme Brahms also took, and on it wrote sixteen variations which he sent to her and subsequently published with a dedication to her. He did with it instinctively what he was to do again later with each of the themes adopted as texts from other composers; he absorbed its character and allowed that character, as it were, to control his own invention.

The plain strength of Handel, the meteoric virtuosity of Paganini, and the steady propriety of the Choral *St. Antoni* pervade Brahms's works on these several themes (Opp. 24, 35, and 56); Handel culminates in the resplendent fugue, each of the Paganini Books in a brilliant rhapsody, St. Anthony in a cumulative 'ground bass' which, like the tune itself, belongs to an age far older than Haydn though its musical matter is, as in the other cases, pure and unadulterated Brahms. Brahms's variations in each case comment on the type of mind and its characteristic musical forms represented by the theme. In these three sets, too, it is to be observed that he preserves the actual phrase form and the general harmonic form of the theme through each variation save in the Finales. They are 'strict' variations.

---

[1] *Bunte Blätter*, Op. 99, is a collection of fourteen short piano pieces, three *Stücklein*, five *Albumblätter*, and six other pieces variously named. This is the first of the *Albumblätter* and the fourth in the whole series. It is dated 1841. It is complete as given both by Brahms and by Clara Schumann at the head of their variations. Clara Schumann's variations, published as her Opus 20, are seven in number. All are purely decorative, that is to say, the theme appears in more or less its original form in each with well contrived pianistic figures surrounding it. Variation III is in F sharp major with quasi-chromatic harmony; Variation VI introduces a canon at the fifth below, and Variation VII ends with an extended coda in the major key.

The Schumann set (Op. 9) are less strict, and the tune itself, especially the drooping first phrase, is kept more constantly present in the texture of the variations. The majority of the numbers display some ingenious transformation of the tune, setting it off with skilfully devised pianistic figures. Only numbers 2, 5, and 10 suggest that deeper polyphonic treatment of the variation form which became Brahms's own. In Variation 2 the bass of the theme, changed to a cantering 9–8 figure, stands out while the tune is sunk in the inner parts of syncopated chords above the bass figure. Variation 5 takes up what had been a figure of accompaniment in Variation 4 and develops it freely with only incidental reference to the theme. Variation 10 is a subtle interweaving of motives from both tune and bass, with a hidden allusion of the kind which Schumann loved, to another theme from Clara Schumann's early *Romance Variée* (Op. 3).[1] The last two, Variations 15 and 16, in the keys of G flat major and F sharp major (the same thing on the pianoforte but having a different 'feel' to the mind of the composer) are full of Schumann. The former might have been labelled 'Der Dichter spricht'; in the latter the broken sighs of the tune above the inexorable tread of the bass are too poignant, one is tempted to feel, to be the offering of consolation which the work as a whole was intended to be. At any rate they are a convincing proof of how Brahms had been affected by the tragedy of his friends.

The appearance before the public of this work (the first composition of Brahms written since the publication of Schumann's article 'Neue Bahnen') must have done much to confirm that false impression of discipleship which clouded most of the early estimate of Brahms. The special conditions could scarcely be taken into account. All that was evident was that the young man had chosen a theme by his Master and had written music on it which in style and in mood recalls that Master's manner at

[1] For analysis of this variation see Fuller-Maitland's *Brahms*, p. 89.

many points. For us who look back on Op. 9 with the knowledge
of all that Brahms subsequently did with the variations form
up to the Finale of the Fourth Symphony, it is easy to discern
his own musical language underlying his thoughts on Schumann.
For that is what these variations are. We cannot speak of them,
as we can of the Handel, Paganini, and Haydn sets, as pure and
unadulterated Brahms. For the moment he had cause to set
bounds to his own invention and to project himself into the
minds and hearts of his suffering friends, and that he could so
far forget himself in them merely means that these variations
provide no measure for the extent of his own originality. The
re-study of them along with the piano sonatas compels the
student to-day to connect their promise with the fulfilment in
the long series of piano, chamber, and orchestral works to which
they were the prelude.

The listeners of 1853–4 had not this knowledge of subsequent
events as a basis for their criticism, but they had the advantage
of hearing the sonatas played by the composer, and his playing
was as individual as his composition.[1] The choice of the piano
sonata as his first medium of expression enabled Brahms to
appear in Leipzig and elsewhere as his own interpreter. His
personality, his performance, and his work together made a
signal impression on the musical society then encountered for
the first time. In this he was in line with that classical tradition of which Bach, Mozart, and Beethoven are the leading
examples. They all established their positions primarily as
players of their own music. The increased complexity of the
mid-nineteenth-century world was producing a division of
labour amongst musical artists as in other occupations. The
new race of composers who could not play and of players who
could not compose had established itself. Berlioz to be heard

[1] See 'Hoplit's' notice in the *Neue Zeitschrift* of Brahms's first public
appearance in Leipzig on Dec. 17, 1853, quoted by May, i, p. 140.

at all required his hundred-handed orchestra; Wagner was per-
ceiving that nothing but a specially constructed theatre, completely staffed with every class of interpreter from artist to
scene-shifter, could suffice for the display of his many-sided
genius. Liszt had turned to serious composition only when he
had exhausted the possibilities of the pianist's career; with Anton
Rubinstein composition for the instrument of which, like Liszt,
he had supreme mastery, was no more than the efflorescence of
his versatile nature.[1] Joachim and von Bülow looked on composition as the possible crown to honourable careers primarily
devoted to the interpretation of other men's work. There was
also the long line of virtuosi, who either did not compose at all
or had better not have done so.

Brahms was unique in his generation, a composer first and
foremost, but one who could speak for himself at the keyboard,
and had done so from his earliest years. He had to learn to let
others speak for him, to master a technique in composition by
which his music should be no less himself when interpreted by
other pianists or confided to instruments which he could not
himself play. This was the meaning of those years following his
first appearance in which he was so deeply occupied with piano
variations on the one hand and chamber works for strings with
or without piano on the other. His own technique as a pianist
was a highly individual matter. Passages in these sonatas,
which were child's play to him, proved almost insuperably
difficult to other gifted pianists, and not merely to pianists with
small hands. Brahms's own hands were small.[2] Untrained in
any acknowledged school of virtuosity, he had developed that

---

[1] See *Oxford History of Music*, vi. 312.

[2] For a first-hand account of Brahms's methods at the piano, both as
player and teacher, see the 'Personal Recollections' which form a preamble
to F. May's *Life*. See also 'Some Personal Recollections of Brahms as
Pianist and Interpreter', by Fanny Davies, *Cobbett's Cyclopedic Survey of
Chamber Music*, i. 182.

complete cohesion between brain and hand possible only to the creative mind intent on self-expression. In the subsequent variations and chamber works, he submitted to a sterner mental discipline, that of adapting his thought to the technical capacities of others and using the common stock of resources for the expression of his own ideas. Not that he ever fell back on the common stock of ideas, or padded his works with the conventional figures, either of accompaniment or of ornament, which spring from the hand of the virtuoso on the instrument. All through his life his conception of piano style remained something entirely his own. It is that which gives unique character to those last lyrical pieces (Opp. 116–119) and assures them their place in piano literature beside the preludes of Chopin. They are the outcome of a long experience, and to Brahms experience of every side of life came slowly and was not acquired without pain. The contradictions of a nature at once ardent and shy, proud and humble, genial and forbidding, above all *frei aber einsam*,[1] accounted for his peculiar difficulty in making his art readily communicable. That he took infinite pains to do so, however, without for a moment swerving from the ideal to which he was devoted, is shown by what took place in the years following 1853. When his mastery was complete, but not before, he sought Vienna and made it his home.

[1] Motto used by Brahms and Joachim in their correspondence with each other.

CHAPTER III

BRAHMS AND CHAMBER MUSIC

THERE was a general tendency in the middle of the nineteenth century to regard concerted chamber music as a backwater of the art. The Weimar party was little concerned with it. The richer opportunities for graphic expression afforded by the orchestra absorbed the attention of its adherents. Even the masterpieces of Beethoven were, apparently, very imperfectly known by Liszt and by Wagner when they were in Paris together in the autumn of 1853. Both wrote of the impression made on them by the playing of the Maurin-Chevillard[1] Quartet of the Quartets in E flat major and C sharp minor,[2] and Wagner declared frankly, 'This was the first time that I really became intimately acquainted with the C sharp minor Quartet because I had never before grasped its melody'. Berlioz, at about the same time, that is at the age of fifty, was making similar discoveries, not in Paris, where Wagner was so pleased to meet with Beethoven, but in London, where he found that the Beethoven Quartet Society[3] was in the habit of giving complete cycles of Beethoven's works in this kind. It seemed as though the great composers of that generation had to leave their native countries in order to discover the highest manifestations of their art.

Meantime the fact that concerted chamber music was assidu-

[1] Pierre Alexandre François Chevillard, violoncellist, father of the famous conductor, founded 'La Société des Derniers Quatuors de Beethoven' in 1835. Jean Pierre Maurin led the Quartet at this time. See Wasielewski, *Die Violine und ihre Meister*.

[2] See Liszt's letter to Joachim, Nov. 2, 1853, and Wagner's *My Life*, ii. 608.

[3] The Beethoven Quartet Society was founded by Mr. T. M. Alsager, a Manager of *The Times*, in 1845. See *Grove's Dictionary of Music and Musicians*, ed. III, vol. i, p. 73. The party heard by Berlioz consisted of Ernst, Cooper, Hill, and Rousselot. See Berlioz's *Soirées de l'Orchestre*, quoted in *Cobbett's Cyclopedic Survey*, i. 123.

ously cultivated by the pupils of Mendelssohn and by the 'bedeutende Talente' who proceeded from the Leipzig Conservatorium, would not encourage the advocates of the new music to any strong belief in its future. Brahms's concentration on it probably served to strengthen the impression that he was to be counted with these second-class talents rather than with the prime movers of musical composition. Even Schumann was a little impatient at Brahms's continued refusal to 'allow trumpets and drums to sound'.[1] Indeed only Joachim, who was daily steeping himself in the classics of chamber music, and who refrained from the composition of string quartets himself, thoroughly understood the isolation of Brahms's position. He realized that in addressing himself to concerted chamber music Brahms was not tackling the smaller problem first, using it as a stepping-stone to greater things, as Schumann seemed to imagine; rather that he was going straight to the heart of the special work which he, and he only at that moment, was qualified to accomplish.

The first version of the Trio for piano and strings in B major (Op. 8) is now the only surviving example of the evidence on which Joachim formed his conviction of Brahms's mission, and it is not difficult to perceive from it that its extraordinary fertility of invention was the quality which produced that conviction. Faults of style there might be; weak passages slackening the movement, which at a later stage of his mature craftsmanship Brahms himself would not tolerate. He subsequently re-wrote the work, joined new subsidiary material to the principal subject of the first movement, greatly reduced the length of the discursive Adagio, and by the invention of a completely new second subject to the Finale altered the course of its development materially. But that only proved what fertility was present in it. It meant that when years later Brahms

[1] Letter to Joachim, Jan. 6, 1854.

returned to the consideration of his young work, he found that
its ideas still had germinating power, enough to stimulate him
to the composition of what is virtually a new work on the old
themes.[1]

It was this power which from the first decisively separated
Brahms's chamber music from the best product of the Leipzig
School, Niels Gade for example (whose chamber works Joachim
occasionally played), which never rose above the level of momentary acceptability. From the first Brahms belonged to an entirely
different category, and in the middle of the century there was no
one else who could conceivably share it with him. There was
indeed in Paris a young Belgian organist who had made his first
essay in concerted composition with some trios for piano and
strings. He was eleven years older than Brahms, but many
years were to pass before the world would have cause to consider
the name of César Franck seriously in this connexion. There was
also a boy from a village in Bohemia, who, in the year after
Schumann's death, found his way to the Organ School at
Prague, and whose genius Brahms himself was to discover and
foster in Vienna some twenty years later. Antonín Dvořák in
fact profited by that re-creation of the status of chamber music
which Brahms effected single-handed in the third quarter of the
century through his own works.

Historically Brahms is as important in the domain of concerted chamber music as is Wagner in that of the musical drama.
The nature of Wagner's art and the peculiarities of his personal
temperament made the latter by far the more spectacular figure
in the 'fifties, but the group of chamber works which Brahms
wrote in the years between Schumann's death and his own

[1] Professor Tovey has made a detailed comparison of the two versions
in his article on Brahms in *Cobbett's Cyclopedic Survey*. See also the
author's comments in 'The Chamber Music of Brahms' (*The Musical
Pilgrim*, 1933).

migration to Vienna may fairly be compared, for their far-reaching effect on the condition of the art, with their contemporaries, the music dramas of Wagner.

One episode in Brahms's career undoubtedly had a formative effect on his style, although his mind had been firmly set in this direction before he encountered it. For the three autumn seasons of 1857–9 he was engaged as pianist to the small provincial Court at Detmold. There he joined with Konzertmeister Karl Louis Bargheer (1831–1902) and other principals of the Court Orchestra in playing wellnigh the entire repertory of classical chamber music. In particular this experience deepened his knowledge of Mozart and of Schubert. He had been nurtured on Beethoven. That less assertive attitude towards art which the two Austrians shared was foreign to the brusque North German temperament of Brahms, as it was completely alien to the views of the Weimar school. In the comparative seclusion of his life at Detmold, a late example of that kind of life to which the chamber music forms owed their existence and their eminence, Brahms gained power to speak calmly and to think temperately. His intimacy with Mozart and Schubert did this for him, and it is at any rate partly accountable for that change of style so clearly discernible between the piano sonatas and the first String Sextet, Op. 18 in B flat.

This was the first[1] of the group of chamber works which belongs to the period between the death of Schumann and Brahms's first visit to Vienna (1862). The group includes also the two Quartets for piano and strings (Opp. 25 and 26) and the first draft of the Quintet (Op. 34) as a work for strings with two

[1] The Serenade in D (Op. 11) was first planned as an octet for stringed and wind instruments for members of the Detmold Court Orchestra (1858). It ultimately appeared in its orchestral form at Hamburg in 1859. The second Serenade in A (Op. 16), without violins, was sketched at about the same time. Thus Brahms's orchestral writing, like Haydn's, is seen emerging from his experience as a chamber musician.

violoncelli. The second String Sextet in G, Op. 36, the Violoncello Sonata in E minor, Op. 38, and the Trio for piano, violin, and horn,[1] Op. 40, though appearing a little later, may be considered with these as to some extent the outcome of the Detmold experience.

The Sextet in B flat is mature. It is a surprise to be told that it was subject even to the slight after-thought suggested by Joachim of a preliminary statement of the opening theme by the first violoncello (bars 1–10). Each one of the four movements is couched in a form of perfect symmetry and those of first Allegro and final Rondo are developed at leisure. Their themes, in themselves gracious and supple, full of activity yet never strenuous, follow one another with the utmost naturalness. There are few arresting moments but not a single dull one. Each movement seems to have been thought of whole, not plotted out as a series of events with connecting links. The undulating arpeggio theme with which the first movement opens sets a tone and a time for the whole first movement. The themes which follow it, widely though their contours vary, fall in with its swinging measure and cause much of the movement, especially all that part which belongs to the second subject section, to approach the style of the slow German Waltz or *Ländler*. This movement belongs to the mood of the piano duet Waltzes (Op. 39), the *Liebeslieder Waltzer*, and much else in the later Brahms, a mood of gracious lyrical charm saved from insipidity by the subtle interweaving of rhythmic phrases.

It is ideally followed by the Andante, a set of six variations on an original melody (D minor, 2–4 time) which gets a peculiar distinction from its chordal accompaniment in emphatic

[1] August Cordes, first horn player at Detmold, stimulated Brahms's interest in the horn and its capabilities just as at a later stage Richard Mühlfeld of Meiningen inspired him to compose for the clarinet. At Detmold Brahms played Beethoven's horn sonata with Cordes, 'whose rich mellow tone drew from Brahms enthusiastic expressions of admiration' (May, i. 215).

spondees. Each part of the melody here quoted (Ex. 1 *a* and *b*) is repeated with scoring for the full sextet of instruments. This metre is not usual with Brahms but is more prevalent in Schubert.[1] The strong outline of the melody and the harmonic progressions marching through a well-defined cycle of keys make it a splendid subject for Brahms's favourite 'strict' type of variation, each number gaining a character of its own from the consistent handling of new figures developed in accordance

Ex. 1. (*a*)

[1] Cf. the Andantes of Schubert's Quartets in A minor, E, and D minor (*Der Tod und das Mädchen*), spondee and dactyl; also that of the Symphony in C.

with the main structural scheme of the theme. Number 3 with rapid scale passages on the two violoncelli is the one of greatest energy; Numbers 4 and 5, both in D major, the one choral-like, the other a viola solo on a drone, get furthest from the outline of the theme, which is recalled almost in its simple form in the last number. Brahms was fond of playing these variations as a separate piece on the piano and the set is quite complete in itself. But it gains an additional significance from its place as slow movement in the sextet. The normal function of the slow movement in the sonata cycle is to provide mental relaxation

after the first Allegro by an appeal to the softer emotions. Here
the process is reversed; the theme and variations are bracing
after the suavity of the *Ländler* rhythms in the first Allegro.

The Scherzo and Trio (F major, 3–4 time) following the variations is comparatively conventional, a sample of a type which
Beethoven evolved and Schubert adopted. Fresh and stimulating
though its ideas are, they are proportioned so precisely on a plan
laid down by previous generations, that comparatively little
of the movement proclaims its authorship unmistakably. Perhaps the only passage which no one but Brahms himself could
have written is the broad unison passage in the development
section of the Trio.

Ex. 2.

Since one of Brahms's greatest achievements lies in the new freedom of thought which he was presently to bring to the scherzo in
chamber music and symphony, his acceptance here of the usual
type, with the regular balance of sections and the repetitions inherited from the minuet of the eighteenth century, is noteworthy.

Brahms was the last composer who showed himself able to say something new with the rondo finale of the classical tradition. His attitude to it here may be compared with that of Beethoven in the Piano Sonata in E (Op. 90), save that Beethoven's coda to the Rondo of Op. 90 is an inspiration with which Brahms's rather obvious animato to a fortissimo ending cannot come into competition. Modern composers writing chamber music primarily for public performance in the concert-room have become increasingly obsessed with the idea of climax. Their finales must outstrip everything already said in energy and brilliance. For them the rondo form is too reflective, since its essence lies in the perpetual return to the starting-point. Brahms here has made the Scherzo the highest point of energy and brilliance. Deliberately he turns back to a mood of reflection and unfolds a calm melody of a kind which can restore that sense of leisured well-being which had belonged to the opening Allegro. The prevalence of emphatic spondees in those sections which provide contrast with the fluent principal theme suggests a point of contact with the slow movement.

Ex. 3.

The passages by which the returns to the principal theme are effected are contrived with great subtlety and afford the highest evidence of Brahms's perfect craftsmanship. About such things here and henceforward there can be no question of 'padding'. The power to delay or to withhold an event is as essential to the artist's equipment as the power to create one. Indeed the delay and the withholding are parts of the creation. The assertion that an intermediate passage, which may not be very eventful in itself, is a piece of padding used to fill out the form, is a sure sign of superficiality in the criticism of a master of Brahms's calibre. Not what the passage contains in itself, but how it affects coming events, is the measure of its value, and viewed from this standpoint Brahms's judgement is found to be very rarely, if ever, at fault.

The two Piano Quartets (Opp. 25 and 26) and the Quintet (Op. 34) may all be accounted greater works than the Sextet, for their wealth of ideas, the wider range of expression which each covers, and, especially in the case of the Quintet, the consummate execution of a large design. The 'young eagle', who flapped his wings in the piano sonatas and grew his mature plumage in the Sextet, soars in the Quintet straight into the eye of the sun.

The Quartet in G minor for piano, violin, viola, and violoncello was first tried over by the Detmold party during Brahms's last season there (1859). It was two years later that Dietrich found Brahms at Hamburg working on the Quartet in A major for a similar group of instruments, and this was played privately with Joachim at Hanover in February 1862. These two quartets were to effect Brahms's introduction to the musical circle of Vienna in November of that year.[1] Meantime the Quintet was

[1] On Nov. 16, 1862, Helmesberger's Quartet concert in the Vereinsaal consisted of: (1) Mendelssohn, String Quartet in E flat, (2) Brahms, Piano Quartet in G minor, (3) Beethoven, String Quartet in C sharp minor, Op. 131. Brahms played the piano part in his own work. He gave a concert of his own in the same hall on Nov. 29. The programme consisted of:

the close contemporary of the second piano Quartet and was completed in its first form as a string quintet in the summer.[1]

All these works involve a technical consideration which does not arise in the case of the sextet, the balancing of two contrasted bodies of tone, the piano and the strings. A glance at the first subject section of the Quartet in G minor shows how this consideration conditions the composer's thought. The two bodies speak antiphonally. What the piano proposes the strings amplify. Not until bar 50, where the violoncello bursts into song with piano accompaniment, do the strings take the initiative; once taken they keep it through that series of broad lyrical melodies which hold chief place in the second subject group. The piano responds to them in its turn, emulating their legato, but the melodies are as inalienably theirs as the several elements in the first subject group are the property of the piano. This sense of duality may be illustrated from almost any page of Brahms's music for piano with strings. The two bodies of tone rarely coalesce into a single mass. One may be used as decoration or as accompaniment to the other, but their identities are preserved. There is no 'filling up'; every note and phrase has to be unerringly placed in music which thus grows out of the confluence of the two forces. The first movement of the Quartet in A major affords a striking instance of this avoidance of massed tone. With such a theme as the first (Ex. 4), announced 'poco forte' by the piano, one foresees from the outset an obvious climax in which all available instruments will be sawing and hammering at its rhythm in fortissimo chords. Schumann could

(1) Brahms, Piano Quartet in A (with Helmesberger, &c.), (2) Brahms, Variations and Fugue on a theme by Handel, (3) Bach, Organ Toccata in F arranged for piano, (4) Schumann, Fantasia in C, Op. 17.—Kalbeck, ii. 23, 25.

[1] The C minor Piano Quartet (Op. 60) seems to have been projected even before the others (see Kalbeck i. 297, and May i. 207). It was then in C sharp minor. It did not appear until the autumn of 1875, and through what stages it passed is not definitely known.

Ex. 4.

scarcely have avoided such a climax; Tchaikovsky, far from avoiding it, would have lived for that as the supreme moment. But what one foresees does not happen with Brahms. Here is the climax of his development, and when its vigour has spent itself the piano slips quietly into its recapitulation sotto voce an octave lower than at first.

Ex. 5.

Brahms has defeated expectation. It was of this movement in
particular that Hanslick made his notorious misjudgement,
from which he recanted later, that Brahms's themes were
'workable rather than original or significant'. All themes are

workable to a musician of Brahms's technical ability, but not all are worth working. A second-rate musical mind would have found this one worthless, and proved it to be so in the handling; only the insight of Brahms could discover its significance, and in discovering it his originality is declared.

A comparison of the recapitulatory sections of these two first movements will show how Brahms's handling of the most conventional procedure of sonata form is liable to modification by the character of his subject-matter. The conventional procedure is a restatement in relation to one key centre (the tonic) of all the material which formerly was distributed between two key centres, and that is what Brahms does in the A major Quartet, where the themes are positive assertions demanding symmetry in their presentation. Having reaffirmed them, he extracts a new significance from the chief of them in a coda of ruminating after-thoughts. In the G minor Quartet there is no such regularity. The order of the two melodic ideas belonging to the first subject group is reversed in the recapitulation. The second of them steals in in G major to be succeeded presently by the first played fortissimo in G minor. Then with unexpected abruptness the lyrical second subject arrives, its exhilarating upward sweep heightened by its position in a new key (E flat major). Thus the wayward impulse of this exquisite movement is unchecked, development is carried further in the process of repetition, and it is left to a profoundly thoughtful coda fully to re-establish the key.

The different sequence of movements in the two piano quartets exemplifies further their contrast of character. Again it is the second (A major) which proceeds along the more normal lines of the classical design. An elaborate slow movement (E major) developed from one of the richest of Brahms's long-drawn melodies follows the first Allegro, and is succeeded in turn by an exuberant Scherzo and Trio (A major), each part of which is in

a fully articulated 'first movement form'. The middle movements of the G minor Quartet do not accord with classical
precedent. They consist of an Intermezzo ('allegro ma non
troppo', C minor, 9–8 time) with a Trio (A flat) which carries on
the same rhythmic impulse ('animato'), and an 'andante con
moto' (E flat, 3–4 time) with a swinging march tune (C major) as
its central episode. While formally the Intermezzo with Trio
seems to stand in the place of Scherzo and Trio, the wistful
tenderness of its melody, the delicacy of the scoring with muted
violin and the 'una corda' effects on the piano, give it the
emotional place of a slow movement despite its flowing tempo.
Its music is all in a half light; the interlacing triplet figures veil
the melody as the overhanging branches of a winter forest veil the
light. The broad melody of the Andante (violin and violoncello
in octaves) steps out once more into the open. The quaver
movement of the piano part, like the springy turf of the hillside,
supports its easy gait, till the muscles are braced for the tramp
on the high road, the march. Nominally a slow movement, it
fulfils the purpose of the Scherzo. It restores the full tide of
energetic life which was checked by the subdued Intermezzo.

The Finales of both these quartets show the influence of those
'Hungarian' dance tunes which had been in Brahms's head ever
since his early tours with Remenyi.[1] The gipsy[2] tunes with
their swift decisions and wayward impulses had made an instant
appeal to Brahms, opening to him ways of musical speech

[1] The *Ungarische Tänze*, arranged for piano duet; books I and II were
published in 1869; books III and IV did not appear until 1880, but some
of them were played in public as piano solos by Mme Schumann in 1858
when Brahms was at Detmold. (See May i. 222.)

The Variations on a Hungarian Song (Op. 21, No. 2) had been played
by Mme Schumann in the previous year.

[2] The music of the gipsy bands is not really Hungarian, as the later
researches into the native Magyar folksong made by Béla Bartók and
others have decisively shown. (See *Grove's Dictionary* (3rd ed.), vol. iii,
p. 289.)

foreign to his native slow-moving North German tongue. The Hungarian Dances for piano duet, which immediately became his most popular work, were admittedly arrangements; in the Finale to the G minor Quartet labelled 'Rondo alla Zingarese', he talks the language like a native. The shapes of the themes (a three-bar phrase predominates), the accents, the ornaments, the scoring, are all in keeping. There is no hint of 'the brooding Brahms'[1] here, though everything of Brahms's inimitable dexterity in handling material according to its own character. The Rondo is in fact the gipsy band of Budapest with all its glitter and *abandon* raised to the highest power of artistry.

The Finale of the A major Quartet, also a rondo in fact, though not so described, is gipsy only in its principal theme and what relates to it. The episodes between the several recurrences of this theme are the Brahms we have known in the sonatas and earlier chamber works, brooding at moments, soaring at others. The gipsy rhythms have become absorbed into his own language.

The Rondos of the Sextet in B flat and of the Quartet in G minor lie as far apart from one another as Hamburg and Budapest. The Finale of the A major Quartet bridges the distance and reconciles the tongues. Now and henceforward[2] the gipsy idiom is not an acquired accomplishment; it becomes the instinctive expression of one side of Brahms's nature, not to be isolated from others or given a label to acknowledge its source. Its combination with his native Germanic way of thought goes far to account for those subtleties of crossed rhythms which are among the most fascinating characteristics of the Viennese Brahms.

This period of Brahms's chamber music composition is magnificently rounded off with the Quintet for piano and strings in

[1] Hans von Bülow's phrase.
[2] Compare Finales of String Quartet in A minor, Op. 51, No. 2, and of the Violin Concerto, Op. 77.

F minor. It and the C minor Piano Quartet, begun with the others, seem to be the last works of the kind about which the composer had serious doubts. To those who know the Quintet only in its ultimate form, it must seem curious that these particular doubts should have arisen. While actually engaged on the piano quartets Brahms conceived this as a work for string quintet with two violoncelli, possibly attracted to that combination by the example of Schubert's Quintet in C major (Op. 163). It proved to be the wrong one, and it is noteworthy that Brahms never attempted a work for that combination again. The two String Quintets[1] which he produced at a much later period of his career are both designed for the more usual combination of two violins, two violas, and one violoncello. But his difficulty was not the small technical one of balancing a particular group of stringed instruments. It was rather that he was tempted to write for the homogeneous string quintet music which cries out for that duality of expression already described as existing in the combination of piano and strings. When the work was tried over, Brahms found that he had chosen the wrong medium, but curiously enough he did not instantly recognize that the right one was virtually that in which he had been lately working. Dissatisfied, he threw it into the form of a sonata for two pianos, and though he played it publicly in that form he must have realized that the matter was too big to be left there.

The string quartet and the piano together proved to be so right that the hearer of to-day wonders how anything else was ever thought to be possible. That quickened arpeggio after the first ruminating statement is inconceivable as anything but the percussive piano asserting its identity while the strings exclaim at its restiveness.

[1] Op. 88 in F published 1883, and Op. 111 in G published 1891. Both were played before publication, which, however, followed almost immediately on production as was generally the case with Brahms's later works.

Ex. 6.

Throughout the four movements the eloquence is found to depend very largely on the delicately devised contacts of the two tonal groups. Without that eloquence the elaborateness of construction might be felt to be oppressive.[1] As it is, though

[1] Apparently it was so felt on the occasion when Brahms and Tausig played the Sonata together in Vienna (1864) (see May, ii. 214).   The published edition of the Sonata (1872) contains a passage which differs materially from the Quintet in its final version for piano and strings.   It is

the analytical mind will discover niceties of workmanship in the growth of new ideas out of the elements of preceding ones, the hearer is not held enchained by the intellectual processes of thematic development. The first movement is one of the greatest examples of sonata form in the whole of music, because, while it is filled with strongly contrasted events, the events never crowd on one another. The whole rhythmic movement is as

worth quoting as a glimpse into Brahms's workshop, and one moreover which seems to have escaped the attention of commentators.

These five bars, and the corresponding passage in the recapitulation, Brahms reduced to four in the piano quintet by cutting out the first of them. The interest of the change is enhanced by the fact that it shows him to have been alive to the temptation which beset him to worry a cross-rhythm as a dog worries a rat.

supple as that first undulating arpeggio, from which the hearer
is prepared to swear at the end that everything has sprung. An
unusual distribution of keys results from the fact that the
second subject group first arrives in the key of C sharp minor.
It gives rise to an expansive handling of that group in the
recapitulation section which prepares the way for a wonderful
recovery of energy in the coda. There is no moment that is
either tautologous or irrelevant. Nothing is done to comply
with formal requirements, but everything to allow the fecund
ideas to fulfil themselves in a perfected form.

The gently romantic 'andante, un poco adagio' (A flat) has
neither the energy of invention found in the Andante of the
G minor Quartet nor the deep poetic wonder of the Adagio of
the A major Quartet. Taken by itself it is a slighter matter than
either of these, but it fills its place as the moment of relaxation in
the aesthetic scheme of the Quintet. It is followed by the first
of Brahms's wholly free and original Scherzos. The quick triple
time measure of the Beethoven tradition is abandoned. Three
themes in strongly contrasted rhythms make up its principal subject-matter. They appear in rapid succession, the third coming
in a fortissimo outburst, all the instruments for once massed
together on it, with a frank exuberance heightened by contrast
with the mysterious murmurings of the two preceding themes.

Ex. 7.

3.

Here, Brahms shows his hand at the outset, yet loses nothing by his confidence. The subsequent movement, even the central Trio which is closely related to the third theme, develops spontaneously out of these ideas and is presented in a form which defies classification as it defeats expectation at every turn. With this Scherzo Brahms triumphantly proclaims his emancipation from the last of the 'classical' conventions. The absence of coda is significant. The Scherzo is repeated, 'da capo sin al fine'; the semiquaver figure reiterated (and stretched out by viola and violoncello) in a way which suggests some influence from the theme of the first movement, while the G strings of the two violins give a snarl to the D flat C,[1] and contradict any feeling of ending in C major despite the major chord. Indeed the Scherzo does not end at all. It reaches its highest point of energy and ceases. The snarling D flat C finds its answer in the quiet F–G flat with which the violoncello introduces the 'poco sostenuto' of the Finale. Brahms has placed no attacca or other warning direction to secure continuity here, but if ever there were two movements which are closely linked without any obvious display of material shared between them, they are these. At

[1] Professor Tovey says 'the savage flat supertonic acciaccatura (D flat C) at the end of the Scherzo comes straight from the end of Schubert's Quintet, and from nowhere else in the whole history of final chords' (*Cobbett's Cyclopedic Survey*). Here we must differ: Schubert's use of the effect is merely a last moment flash of inspiration, producing an unusual cadence in C major. Brahms's is not a last chord or a cadence in C major; this D flat C was foreseen in the first bar of the first movement and surely comes from nowhere else but the principal theme of the work to which it belongs.

first the hearer is conscious only of the opposition between the physical activity of the Scherzo and the complete withdrawal into a mood of hesitant reflection induced by the violoncello's upward phrase imitated by other instruments.[1] With the arrival of a new melody descending in octaves on violin and violoncello from a high D flat above a pulsing rhythm on the pianoforte, he realizes that here is a second slow movement, giving vent in its few bars to a more generous flow of the romantic spirit than the gentle Andante had admitted. At the close, where the bass of the piano settles down on the D flat C against the rising figure on the violoncello, it is found that this 'poco sostenuto' is more than merely a slow introduction to a rondo finale, more than a point of contrast between two vigorously rhythmic movements. It is in fact that which shows the relevance of the parts in the design of the whole quintet, though without any conscious quotation from other movements. It gives the key to the affinity between the first movement and the Scherzo, fulfils the promise of the Andante, and prepares the ear for the completion of the scheme in the last Allegro.

The violoncello brushes away reflection with the crisp rondo-like theme delivered 'tranquillo' against the chattering semi-quavers of the piano. A dropping semitone at the climax of the tune, much dwelt on in the immediate development but less conspicuous as the movement gathers impetus, shows that the mood of the 'poco sostenuto' is not yet outgrown. But the long crescendo in rhythmic energy of which the movement is composed soon leaves it behind. While rondo is the basis of the form, as in the other works of this group, the transformation presently of the principal theme into a new rhythm (6–8 time) so alters its character that the music has little of that repetitional character

[1] Professor Tovey (ibid.) points to this passage as giving the only sign in the whole work of its original form as a quintet with two violoncelli. The pianist's left hand momentarily supplies the part of the second violoncello.

which belongs to the rondo proper. The new version arrives 'presto, non troppo' in C sharp minor, and the identity of the sequence of keys (F minor, C sharp minor) with that of the exposition of the principal themes in the first movement, is noteworthy. The new time and the new key together put a sharper edge on the contours of the theme, and from that transforming moment Brahms never looks back. The music surges forward and at the height of the climax the second theme, which formerly had appeared as a plaintive contrast to the principal one, strides in fortissimo to complete the triumph. There is a long decrescendo in which the two themes are combined. Then just when a point of repose is nearly reached there is a revival with a return to the syncopated rhythm of the Scherzo, and an exclamatory coda 'agitato' ends abruptly in a sudden downward rush of strings.

This group of works, the Sextet in B flat, the two Piano Quartets, and the Quintet, have been dwelt on with some particularity here, not only because they are those with which Brahms asserted his mastery, but because they are actually the only master-works of chamber music belonging to the time round about 1860. Concerted chamber music still remained essentially a German art, but the New German spirit, as represented by Weimar, was unfavourable to it. The Scandinavian pupils of the Leipzig Conservatoire, Gade and Svendsen, had carried home the Mendelssohn tradition to their native countries, there to unite its formal principles with pleasant suggestions of 'local colour'. The one published his Octet for strings in 1849; the other his in 1867.[1] Chamber-music parties still find the occasional performance of their several works an agreeable diversion, while most of the output of German composers of that time has now sunk into oblivion. Brahms alone showed that the sonata form,

[1] Svendsen's Octet in A was played and acclaimed at the festival in Weimar in 1870.

whatever group of instruments the scheme might embrace, was still plastic. Instead of handling it as a set of pieces, of contrasted mood pictures, scored for whatever set of instruments happened to take his fancy at the moment, he began with a musical thought which could find expression only through the right instruments and be completed only in the evolution of the right form. And, as the rapid analysis undertaken here has attempted to show, the thought spans the whole course of such a masterpiece as the Quintet in F minor, so that what was adumbrated in the opening theme of the first movement is only fulfilled in that last downward rush of strings. It was in the power of sustained musical thought and in the power to choose the right medium (form and instrumentation) for his thought that Brahms grew from the early piano sonatas up to the Quintet in its ultimate form.

Having reached his full stature the only question which arises is, how much thought had he to give? Brahms's limitations are obvious. His appetite for adventure was never large, and as life progressed and circumstances forced him increasingly into a position of conservatism, he avoided risks. He could never, like Michelangelo, have produced a David from an imperfect block of marble, or, like Beethoven in the *Grosse Fuge*, have attempted the impossible with four stringed instruments. We shall never know how many failures he destroyed. The long series of great works, in every form save opera which he has left us, all bear the mark of this limitation. He speaks that which he knows. They contain no daring escapades of the kind which could make succeeding generations hail him as their pioneer or deride him as a speculator. Brahms is certain and safe. The certainty is his glory. Is the safety to be accounted his shame? Moreover in the fashioning of his ideas Brahms had a tendency to fall back on certain turns of expression or figures of speech, which, reappearing in later works, suggested that in them he was treading again well-trodden paths. The prevalence of the arpeggio theme and particularly of arpeggios formed from two components of a triad,[1] the use of a dropping seventh to give a declamatory ending to a phrase,[2] the carrying on of a melody by repetition of its figures with differently placed accents,[3] are devices which by the frequency of their use are apt to harden into mannerisms. Add to the reminiscences of himself some few of tunes by other composers and the charge list is completed. Save for the first, the lack of venturesomeness, it amounts to very little. The others dwindle into insignificance the moment we attempt to trace them through the twenty-four scores of sonata-type works in the various groupings of concerted chamber music, every one of which has distinctive beauties of its own embodied in some fresh aspect of design.

The numerous publications of the years immediately following that of the Piano Quintet in F minor (1865) include the second Sextet (Op. 36 in G), the Sonata for violoncello and piano (Op. 38 in E minor), and the Trio for piano, violin, and horn (Op. 40 in E flat). After that there are no more chamber-music publications till 1873, when the two String Quartets in C minor and A minor appear together as Op. 51. But we know that Mme Schumann[4] was given a private hearing on the piano of the Quartet in C

[1] See Ballade in D major, Op. 10, No. 2; Sextet in B flat, Op. 18 (1st movement, 2nd subject); String Quartet in A minor, Op. 51, No. 2 (opening theme); Symphony in C minor, Op. 68 (1st movement, introduction); Symphony in F, Op. 90 (Motto theme).

[2] See Piano Quartet in A, Op. 26 (1st movement); Pianoforte Quintet in F minor, Op. 34 (1st movement); String Quartet in C minor, Op. 51, No. 1 (1st and 4th movements); Symphony in C minor, Op. 68 (1st movement).

[3] This characteristic seems to spring more particularly from the Hungarian rhythms; see Piano Quartet in A (Finale), String Quartet in A minor (Finale), and compare these with the second subject of Symphony in F (1st movement).

[4] 'Johannes has been playing me some magnificent movements from a Requiem of his own and a String Quartet in C minor.' Mme Schumann's diary, quoted by May, ii. 48.

minor as early as September 1866 and that the Horn Trio had received its first public performance at Oldenburg nearly two years earlier than that (January 1865), so that these may be grouped together as belonging to the early years of Brahms's Viennese life. Many and varied experiences in choral and orchestral music separate them from the later series of chamber works which may be said to begin with the third and last String Quartet, Op. 67 in B flat, composed, played, and published in the year of the First Symphony (1876).

The first Allegro of the Sextet in G has a good deal in common with that of its predecessor. A quietly swaying 3–4 time, a murmuring quaver accompaniment, set a mood at the outset which is never disturbed by any strong contrast. It almost seems as though Brahms, contrary to his usual custom when he wrote in pairs, was making a second essay in the emotional tracks of the first. But this movement, beginning with a theme poised on two chords (G and E flat) as against the tonic-dominant structure of the principal subject of the Sextet in B flat, is all a little more recondite than the first. The hearer is less likely to find that 'divine familiarity' with the second Sextet, the feeling that 'such beautiful and obvious sequences of notes must have been existing in the world long before they were written down'.[1] The beauties must be sought out. Moreover this opening theme extends its influence through what follows into the Finale, though there is no precise quotation, and the Finale itself is à movement of strikingly contrasted features cunningly brought into close relationship, as unlike the reposeful Rondo of the Sextet in B flat as anything can possibly be. In this case the Scherzo precedes the slow movement and, though the latter is once more a theme with variations, similarity with the earlier work goes no further. Both Scherzo and the theme for variations are strikingly new. The Scherzo suggests a dance of elves

[1] Fuller-Maitland, *Brahms*, p. 67.

(G minor, 2–4 time) interrupted by one of heavy-footed human beings (G major, 3–4 time), the elves resuming their revels as soon as the last human footstep is out of earshot, an exquisite fantasy. The theme of the Adagio, a diatonic melody springing from two rising fourths (counterpart of the rising fifths of the first movement) set off against a chromatic accompaniment made hazy by conflicting duplet and triplet quavers, leads to rhythmic subtleties in the succeeding variations of a kind which could never have come from the stalwart spondees of the first sextet's slow movement. A comparison of these two sets will illustrate how Brahms, in writing variations to his own themes, preserved the same principle which governed his treatment of the themes of other composers. The variations remain true to their originals. They are developed from the character of the theme and not only from its shape.

Practically every one of Brahms's subsequent works reveals some new handling of the Scherzo idea. That of the Horn Trio is the only one which bears any traces of the pattering three crotchets in one beat of the Beethoven type. It is worked out in a full sonata form with Trio and repeat. The first movement which it follows, though one of a haunting lyrical beauty, is slighter in style and more subdued in feeling than any other of Brahms's first movements. The full-dress character of the Scherzo is accounted for by its place in the scheme. The Violoncello Sonata in E minor has neither slow movement nor Scherzo, but a demure Minuet with its delicately poised Trio, at first hesitant, then confiding, fills the place of both. Later, wistfulness often takes the place of humour and joviality. It is unmistakably present in the 'allegretto molto moderato e comodo' (F minor, 4–8 time) of the String Quartet in C minor, and still more in the Quartet in A minor where a doleful quasi Minuetto (A minor) rhythm alternates with a gossamer Allegretto (2–4) in the major key. The Scherzo with Trio (not so called) of the Piano Quartet in C minor comes much nearer to Brahms's early type as exemplified in the pianoforte sonatas and the Scherzo in E flat minor. Its character seems to be a heritage from the early inception of the work. After this the word 'Scherzo' disappears from Brahms's vocabulary[1] save in the case of the Trio in C major, Op. 87, the rhythm of which suggests a comparison with the corresponding movement of Schubert's String Quartet in G, and incidentally shows the much greater flexibility of Brahms. In the later works the scherzo idea is either worked in as a contrasting episode[2] in the course of a slow movement, or replaced with a movement bearing such directions as 'Presto non assai',[3] 'Un poco presto e con sentimento',[4] 'Un poco allegretto',[5] all of them indications of that withdrawal from the ebullitions of high spirits which belong to the Scherzo proper.

Brahms showed considerable hesitancy about committing himself to string quartet writing, and in spite of the distinctive beauties of each of the three works which he has left in what is generally held up as the ideal type of chamber music composition, it may be questioned whether he ever felt quite at ease in handling it. The C minor Quartet in its first and last movements bears some traces of his desire for more notes, not in the places where he uses double stopping, generally with admirable effect, but in the places where he denies himself that luxury. It is

[1] He never used the word in his Symphonies, and although the 3–4 type makes an unexpected reappearance in the 'allegro appassionato' of the Second Pianoforte Concerto (B flat), Brahms's rather inexplicable remark to Billroth about the 'simple' character of the first movement requiring something more strongly passionate to separate it from the equally simple Andante at any rate shows that he was conscious of an exceptional aesthetic scheme underlying the sequence of movements in this Concerto.

[2] See the Quintet for strings in F, Op. 88, and the Sonata for violin and piano in A, Op. 100.

[3] See the Trio in C minor, Op. 101, and the Clarinet Quintet, Op. 115.

[4] See the Sonata for violin and piano in D minor, Op. 108.

[5] See the Symphonies, No. 1 in C minor, No. 3 in F, and the String Quintet in G, Op. 111.

wonderful how the four instruments cover the ground, but the development section of the first movement leaves us wondering whether five or six instruments might not cover it more satisfactorily with less effort. The ideas seem too big for the means through which they are presented. As with the First Piano Concerto and later with the First Symphony, so with the first String Quartet, Brahms seems to have been a little overburdened by a sense of responsibility. In that state his intellect became over-active and its working was apt to obscure the natural geniality of his temperament.

In the Second Quartet, as in the Second Symphony, this wrought-up condition of mind has spent itself, the tense muscles are relaxed, and the result is a work of delightful spontaneity, never flagging from its first undulating arpeggio theme to the last ecstasy of the whirling 'Hungarian' Finale. The A minor Quartet is an undoubted masterpiece, but he did not follow it up. The string quartet combination never became for Brahms what it had been for Beethoven, the medium in which the intimate diary of his own inner life could be written. It remained for him the purest of the forms of instrumental chamber music, and a little too pure for daily use. The only other specimen which he left is the work in B flat (Op. 67) which Professor Tovey describes as a 'Haydnesque comedy'. The phrase can be accepted as a polite way of saying that it is comparatively insignificant in Brahms's output. Or the work may be regarded as the composer's recreation after the momentous effort of the First Symphony, his holiday task and a very happy one.

In 1876, with the Symphony in C minor, Brahms at last 'allowed trumpets and drums to sound' with no uncertain voice.[1] The panoply of the musician's armoury was now com-

---

[1] Brahms had never neglected the orchestra. The two Serenades and the First Piano Concerto (Op. 15 in D minor) show his distinctive handling of it in the years immediately following Schumann's death. Later the group

pletely at his command. Three more symphonies, three concertos for solo instruments with orchestra, and two overtures
were to follow in the twenty years of life which remained to
him. While these activities never diverted him for long from
the composition of concerted chamber music, that kind of music
was no longer the main preoccupation of his life. Much of his
chamber music habit of mind passed into his style of orchestration. It may even be maintained that what used to be complained
of as poverty in his orchestration and is now admired as a
refinement peculiar to himself, is the result of that habit. He
thought of the orchestra more as a large chamber music party
than as the single instrument with a myriad tone qualities which
Wagner proved it to be with the production of *The Ring* in this
same year as the Symphony in C minor appeared.

Brahms's subsequent chamber works were composed in groups
and each succeeded a bout of work on the grander scale. After
the overtures, *Nänie*, and the Second Piano Concerto (a work of
symphonic proportions), he returned to his first love, and the
Trio for piano and strings in C major (Op. 87) and the Quintet
for strings in F (Op. 88) appeared simultaneously at the end of
1882. The summer holiday of 1886 passed beside the Lake of
Thun, that is the year after the production of the Fourth
Symphony, was particularly prolific. Its group contains the
Sonata in F for violoncello and piano (Op. 99), the Second
Sonata in A for violin and piano (Op. 100)—its predecessor in G
(Op. 78) had followed the Violin Concerto six years before—and
the Trio in C minor for piano and strings (Op. 101). The last
Violin Sonata, that in D minor (Op. 108) dedicated to Hans von
Bülow (Brahms in later life never dedicated his major works

of choral works, *Ein deutsches Requiem*, the male voice cantata, *Rinaldo*,
the Alto Rhapsody, the *Schicksalslied*, and the *Triumphlied*, had all contributed to the widening of his orchestral experience, and in the Variations
on the Choral *St. Antoni* he had produced a masterpiece for orchestra
alone three years before the production of the long-awaited symphony.

without special reason),[1] was also the product of a holiday at Thun (1888), and from Ischl two years later came a magnificent finale in the Quintet for strings in G (Op. 111).

This was not actually his last chamber work; the famous clarinet group was still to come, but it may be called a finale in the sense that it was the last of its line, a return to that attitude towards chamber music from which Brahms had begun, the final reassertion of his faith in it as a vehicle able to bear the weight of his deepest thoughts and sustain the highest flights of his exuberant energy. In the ripeness of his experience, his symphonies and concertos all accomplished, and after a long period in which the duet sonatas and trios had shown his increased tendency to reserve the chamber forms for the more lyrical types of expression, he comes back in this Quintet to take his stand on his old ground.

Its predecessor, the Quintet for strings in F (Op. 88), is an unequal work. Its prosaic opening hardly prepares the way for a middle movement of rare imagination and power, one of those in which slow movement and scherzo are fused together. Nor does the athletic Finale seem at all the inevitable complement of what has gone before. But the Quintet in G is a work the stature of which can be measured against that of the Piano Quintet in F minor. Beginning with a violoncello theme beside which that of Strauss's *Ein Heldenleben* (written more than ten years later) seems pale and nerveless, the unflagging sweep of Brahms's first Allegro is succeeded by a profoundly moving Adagio, an Allegretto of a delicious simplicity, and a Rondo in which the gipsy rhythms issue in a wholly happy ending. Here, once again, is the whole Brahms concentrated in a masterpiece of chamber music, and for the last time.

[1] The Violin Concerto had very naturally borne a dedication to Joachim and the Second Piano Concerto one to Brahms's old master, Edward Marxsen. These are the only dedications of concerted instrumental works later than the string quartets.

The Quintet in B minor for clarinet and strings (Op. 115) is one of the most beautiful pieces of chamber music ever written, but it cannot be called the whole Brahms. It is entirely the expression of a single mood of wistful melancholy. There is no hint of the self-pity of Tchaikovsky's 'Pathetic' Symphony (in the same key), but the drooping themes, the quiet endings of each movement, the refusal of any of those vivid contrasts either of tempo or tonality which belong to the great chamber works above discussed, mark it as the work of a man of decreasing physical vitality, an old man content to watch life pass, to ponder and reflect. Yet in the year of that spring visit to Meiningen (1891), when the quality of Richard Mühlfeld's clarinet impressed him so deeply, Brahms was only fifty-eight and the illness which caused his death in his sixty-fourth year was still far distant. The Quintet and the Trio for piano, clarinet, and violoncello were the immediate outcome of his new friendship with Mühlfeld. The two Sonatas for clarinet and piano (Op. 120), actually his last works of concerted instrumental music, were not written until his summer visit to Ischl in 1894. The Trio and the Sonatas may be attributed to the desire awakened in him by Mühlfeld to write for the clarinet; they might never have been written but for Mühlfeld. The Quintet is a work which must have been written anyhow, though probably not in exactly the same terms. It is the epilogue of Brahms's chamber music life, as surely as the piano sonatas are its prologue.

Brahms was very susceptible to the characters of certain instruments and, as suggested earlier in this chapter, his pre-eminence in chamber music is largely due to his instinct for an ideal union between the chosen medium (the group of instruments) and the form of the music. The Horn Trio (Op. 40) affords the first decisive example of this susceptibility as the Clarinet Quintet is the last. The writing for the violin and the violoncello in the duet sonatas proclaims it at innumerable points. All the subject-matter of the Horn Trio is conditioned by the abilities and disabilities of the horn. Though the clarinet does not demand the same deference, and many of its exquisite melodies are discussed on equal terms between it and the violin, the wealth of its range, the contrast of its registers, its capacity for sudden flights of eloquence through arpeggio figures (most particularly in the arabesques of the slow movement) are characteristics which condition the form of the Quintet.

So strongly does the instrument impose itself on the style of the music that it is something of a shock to find the words 'oder Bratsche' in brackets on each title-page of the clarinet works, just as 'oder Violoncell' is on that of the Horn Trio. The clarinet sonatas[1] indeed have been a godsend to viola players, whose repertory is singularly meagre, and even if Brahms had not sanctioned the transference, the fine performances viola players have been able to give would have been their sufficient justi-fication. But what can be done where the instrument, clarinet or viola, is combined only with the piano, cannot be equally satisfactory where other strings are concerned, as in the Horn Trio and the Clarinet Quintet. Brahms's sanction there must be taken not as an expression of indifference to tone quality but merely as saying, better the substance of the music than silence. And be it remembered that to him the primary use of chamber music was domestic; its performance by players for their own delectation as much as for that of a possible audience. Public concert-giving was on the increase during his life, and the public chamber concert, which in his youth had been a rare and special occasion, had by the end of the century become the normal condition of performance. Brahms's chamber music was written less to be set before an audience than to be shared among friends, and the clarinet works are his last communication to his friends.

---

[1] Brahms also arranged the two clarinet sonatas for violin and piano, and in that form they are occasionally played in public.

CHAPTER IV

CHAMBER MUSIC

1870–1900

THE struggles of English and French musicians to acclimatize concerted chamber music in their own countries during the latter part of the nineteenth century are in some respects similar. In neither country was there any national tradition to build on. The English had quite lost sight of theirs, and the French had never had one. It is significant that Hubert Parry, who as an undergraduate at Oxford in the 'sixties was the first English composer of modern times to address himself seriously to the delicate art of writing string quartets, wrote much later in the third volume of this work that Purcell's 'Golden' Sonata 'still dimly echoes in the ears of men' and that 'after Purcell's death in 1695 English music in its most characteristic forms, whether sacred or secular, progressed·no further'. The full history of that earliest school of chamber music composition and performance in England, represented in the sixteenth and seventeenth centuries by the fantasy for a consort of viols, must still remain unwritten while a great part of its product remains unexplored.

In the middle of the nineteenth century the English and French alike were stimulated by the classical traditions evolved by Germany, but the English were the more ready frankly to acknowledge the debt. Indeed, so eager were they to pay it in full that for a generation or more they were unwilling to acknowledge the existence of any chamber music outside the German classics, and least of all would they tolerate home products.

It was mentioned at the beginning of the last chapter that associations were formed both in Paris and London for the performance of classical chamber music and more particularly for the quartets of Beethoven. Such movements set on foot by a few enlightened musicians and enthusiastic amateurs were little regarded by the wider public. That public could only be reached through the concert-room. Édouard Colonne began a series of chamber concerts in Paris in 1867, and in these last years of the Empire chamber music associations abounded.[1] This was a little later than the beginning of the famous 'Monday Popular Concerts' at St. James's Hall, London, which for upwards of forty years were to be the chief means of familiarizing the London public with the masterpieces of chamber music.

In both countries young composers were eagerly emulating the masters, and they encountered a common experience. They discovered that audiences newly awakened to the enjoyment of masterpieces had no attention to spare for the efforts of novices, whether native or foreign. Charles Camille Saint-Saëns (1835–1921), that most indefatigable of composers, grasped the situation with a resourcefulness beyond the ordinary, and began giving concerts of his own works in Paris at the age of 25.[2] He too was one of the first to storm the defences of one of the classically minded societies of Paris by appropriately writing a Trumpet Septet[3] for the Society called 'La Trompette' which Émile Lemoine had founded in 1860. It required nothing less than the fall of the third Empire and the military disasters of the Franco-Prussian War to open the doors of Parisian concert-rooms to the efforts of less pertinacious composers. Again Saint-Saëns was to the fore, and it was largely due to him that the Société Nationale de Musique was founded in 1871, the

[1] See *Cobbett's Cyclopedic Survey*—article 'French Chamber Music since the Revolution' by Henry Prunières.

[2] Saint-Saëns produced his Quintet for pianoforte and strings, Op. 14, at his own concert in 1860.

[3] Saint-Saëns's Trumpet Septet, Op. 65, is scored for trumpet, pianoforte, and quintet of strings with double-bass. It was also arranged by him as a trio for pianoforte and strings.

programmes of which were to consist exclusively of works of all classes by living native composers. Assisted to success by the new nationalism and particularly by the desire, not unnatural in the circumstances, to repudiate all things German, the Société Nationale began a new era in French music. Two names amongst those of its first committee are outstanding. They are those of César Franck and Gabriel Fauré, and to these two, more than to any others, French chamber music in the last quarter of the century owes its distinction, it might almost be said its identity.

Meantime, since Queen Victoria's Government remained stable, British composers had to wait longer for recognition. Alexander Campbell Mackenzie (born 1847) led the way in Edinburgh, where he initiated a series of Classical Chamber Concerts in which he was one of the leading violinists. For these concerts he composed several chamber works and secured the publication of one of them in Germany (1874), a Quartet for piano and strings.[1] It attracted the attention of Hans von Bülow, who not only offered his friendship to Mackenzie on the strength of it but played the work in Germany once. Subsequently it secured no less than three performances at long intervals at the Monday Popular Concerts. But Mackenzie did not follow up his advantage with further work on similar lines.

It was not till 1883 that Parry's finest chamber work, the Quartet for piano and strings in A flat, received a solitary performance at a Monday Popular Concert.[2] His more assiduous contemporary, C. V. Stanford, did not even receive this modest meed of appreciation until, in 1886, he gained admission with his Sonata in A for violoncello and piano, and followed it in the

[1] The Quartet was republished in England by the Oxford University Press in 1931.

[2] For an account of the manner in which the programme annotator (J. W. Davison) prejudiced the reception of Parry's Quartet in 1883, see the writer's article on 'Parry's Chamber Music' in *Cobbett's Cyclopedic Survey*, ii. 209.

same series (March 1887) with his Quintet in D minor for piano and strings. These composers, however, failed to impress themselves on their generation as their French contemporaries were doing, not from any inferiority in ability, but simply because their generation would not listen long enough to become impressed. The British public rigidly maintained towards them the attitude of 'aut_Caesar aut nullus'; either a masterpiece, and one which by some magic could be known for a masterpiece before it was heard, or nothing. By the time the public was ready to relax this severity there were younger claimants to attention, and the early works of Mackenzie, Parry, and Stanford were considered out of date. Some day the best of them will be revived as 'classics'. Here it is only necessary to note as an historic fact that the movement towards chamber music composition was contemporaneous in the two countries, that the French was furthered by political disaster and the English smothered beneath political prosperity.

The case of César Franck (1822–90) is peculiar. He was not, like Saint-Saëns, a man quick to seize on opportunity. He was well on in middle life when the opportunities afforded by a post-war nationalism began to open up. The outstanding fact of his career is that after beginning composition with four trios for piano and strings, which, whatever may be said of their merits, hardly give promise of conspicuous genius, he settled down as an organist in Paris and composed little beside church and organ music of variable quality until after the Franco-Prussian War. All the works which have contributed to give him an assured place among the outstanding musical figures c the century came to birth when he was past the age of fifty. Amongst these are three works of concerted chamber music, the Quintet for piano and strings in F minor (1879), the Sonata for violin and piano in A (1886), and the String Quartet in D (1889), with the two resplendent piano solos described as

'*Prélude, Choral, et Fugue*' and '*Prélude, Aria, et Finale*'. On these, together with the Symphony in D, his pupil and biographer, Vincent d'Indy, has principally based his claim that Franck is the one true and legitimate successor of Beethoven in the development of pure instrumental music. We have learnt to discount such claims,[1] but this one was seriously maintained without bringing ridicule on the innocent head of the Master, and was steadily upheld, at any rate until d'Indy's death, within the walls of the Schola Cantorum, where pupils were trained in the principles of the Gregorian Chant and in those of modern composition as formulated in the works of 'Bach, Beethoven, and César Franck'.

In his study of Franck[2] d'Indy draws an intimate picture of the man, one which shows at once his modest shrinking from publicity and his assured adhesion to his own artistic principles. Another of his pupils, Paul Dukas,[3] has insisted that Franck's classicism was not the filling up of a prearranged formal pattern in the manner of the imitators of Beethoven, but the creation of an organism strong enough to carry the weight of his own classical thought. This is a claim which can be maintained for the best of all the composers who have worked along the lines of the sonata form since Beethoven. It has already been suggested that it is as applicable to the Quintet for piano and strings in

[1] Hanslick in the *Neue freie Presse* declared that no composer had yet 'approached so nearly to the great works of Beethoven as Brahms in the finale of the C minor Symphony', and there were enthusiasts who chose to allude to that symphony as 'the tenth'. Hans von Bülow invented the appellation of 'The three B's'.

In England Joseph Bennett nicknamed Parry 'the English Bach', and as late as 1920 George Bernard Shaw inaugurated a new periodical (*Music and Letters*) with an allusion to the firm of 'Elgar, late Beethoven'. That kind of eulogy was then seen to be rather a bad joke.

[2] *César Franck, L'Artiste et son Œuvre*, by Vincent d'Indy, 1906. English translation by Rosa Newmarch.

[3] *Chronique des Arts*, No. 33, p. 273, 1904, quoted from by d'Indy in the above.

F minor of Brahms as it is to the Quintet in the same key which some twenty years later announced Franck's accession to power. The two have frequently been compared and contrasted, and too often with a bias, personal or racial, in favour of one or other. It was d'Indy's contention that the followers of Beethoven, in what he was pleased to call 'les trois nations artistiques', had all disregarded the message of Beethoven's last period which had entered the gentle heart of César Franck in the quiet of his organ loft at St. Clothilde. He alone had perceived that the processes of fugue and of 'la grande variation' ('n'ayant rien de commun . . . avec le "thème varié"') were the renovating principles of sonata form. In d'Indy's view, Brahms, whose power he had no desire to underrate, had remained cumbered by that heavy symphonic baggage from which Beethoven had freed himself, and therefore potentially all subsequent develop-ment of the art, in the last sonatas and quartets.[1] Franck had accepted the revelation of freedom and had proved his accept-ance by no longer arranging his musical ideas into self-contained compartments. Though his larger instrumental works, apart from those which illustrated a 'poetic' idea such as *Les Djinns* (piano and orchestra) and *Le Chasseur Maudit* (orchestra), continued to exhibit the traditional distinctions of movements, normally first Allegro, slow movement, and Finale, their unity was attested by the fact that a theme once stated was never to be considered completely worked out and laid aside until the work had come to rest in its last chord. This was acclaimed as Franck's new principle of 'cyclic form'. To some extent it had been anticipated by Liszt's plan of transformed themes which it has been shown can scarcely be attributed to Liszt's invention,

[1] 'Brahms lui-même, malgré un sens du développement qu'on peut, sans exagération, rapprocher de celui de Beethoven, ne sut point tirer parti des précieux enseignements laissés pour l'avenir par le maître de Bonn, et son copieux bagage symphonique ne peut être regardé que comme une continua-tion et non comme un progrès.'—D'Indy's *César Franck*, p. 68.

and it has been suggested in the discussion of Brahms's chamber
music in the last chapter that the return to a theme is by no
means the only, or the most subtle, means of securing unity of
design to a large work. But Franck's use of the device was very
much his own, more systematic than Brahms's, more imaginative
than Liszt's. It might be a fairer estimate of his contribution to
the evolution of musical form to describe him, not as the only
legitimate successor of Beethoven, but as the reconciler of the
two schools of thought into which German music in the middle
of the century had divided. Franck, a Belgian, naturalized a
Frenchman in the fatal year of 1870, founded a new school of
French music on the reconciliation of German enmities.

It is, however, the impulse of Franck's music rather than any
technical peculiarity of form which has given it a perennial
attraction beyond that of most of his contemporaries. Of the
three qualities which d'Indy attributed to him:

(1) Noblesse et valeur expressive de la phrase mélodique;
(2) Originalité de l'agrégation harmonique;
(3) Solide eurythmie de l'architecture musicale;

the first two can be immediately recognized by all hearers.
Franck never, like Brahms, asks for patience from his hearers;
rather, like Schumann, he launches at once an arresting statement or an appealing sentiment, which cannot fail to gain their
confidence. The Quintet gives a conspicuous instance of this.
Any one who fails to be brought under the spell of the opening
bars, the dramatic descent of the first violin, and the ruminating

Ex. 1. *Dramatico.*

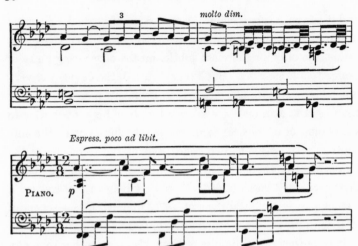

answer of the piano to its challenge, need go no further, for he
will find nothing better. The 'noblesse et valeur expressive'
are declared at once. From this springs the principal theme of
the Allegro, which may be quoted as an example of Franck's
habit of compressing themes rather than expanding them. Here
the compression is rhythmic. The first impulsive phrase is reduced to a short, tightly gripped rhythm continued by a process
of laying bar to bar:

Ex. 2.

Later in the course of the development this theme undergoes further compression in the use of smaller intervals. The piano introduces this form of it.

Ex. 3.

It may be taken as the occasion to note the high value set by Franck on semitonic melody, a feature in which he is most clearly opposed to Brahms, the basis of whose melody is frequently the arpeggio of a chord. Where Brahms would tend to widen his intervals, Franck tends to contract his. This example suggests that the semitone itself is not small enough for him, and that the B double flat is repeated because the keyboard does not allow him to divide the whole tone into more than two parts.

But before this point is reached Franck has created a fascinating expository section by the accumulation of melodic ideas growing naturally from one another and issuing in one which seems to be the very pith and essence of his thought. It may be compared with that which has become known as the 'Faith

VII   G

Theme' in his symphony. It takes a similar place of central importance,[1] and recurs in varying forms through all three movements. Again here in the alternation of A and A sharp, E and E sharp, Franck's emphasis on the expressive value of the semitone is declared, and the general plan of the tune is a salient instance of his fondness for melodic outlines which circulate round a single note like the intonations of plain-chant around the recitation. The sequential system of harmony too (bass notes rising by minor thirds till the point of departure, C sharp, is regained) is a good example of Franck's way of giving stability to those original aggregations of harmonic progression which d'Indy rightly points to as typical of his style.

Ex. 4.

---

[1] The traditional nomenclature of sonata form is more than usually inadequate when applied to Franck. His expositions are not like those of the German classics built on the antithesis of two key-centres. The frequent modulations are decorative rather than structural, so that there can be little justification for labelling this, actually the sixth or seventh tune in order of appearance, a 'second subject'.

It may be noticed, while this passage is under contemplation, that this Quintet is to a large extent piano music with a colouring of strings. Practically all the harmonic structure rests with the piano. Through long passages the strings are playing in unison or octaves, not from any lack of contrapuntal capacity on Franck's part, but because that is the method which best fulfils his thought. There is a complete freedom from 'cleverality'; he says what he wants to say with singular directness and cares nothing for the look of the score. The habits of a lifetime as a keyboard performer no doubt influenced him in this matter and to a certain extent hampered him. While his writing for the piano is that of a highly accomplished pianist, he is apt to add his string parts to his piano music rather like solo stops drawn on his organ. It must be admitted that there is not that close correspondence between the thought and the medium of expression which made Brahms's Quintet in F minor issue inevitably in the combination of piano and strings, but it can be said that there are few moments throughout its three movements where the strings are used with anything less than complete effectiveness.

Indeed Franck's instinct for effect in tone-colouring of every kind, and the pleasure which he took in it, is the most surprising thing about him. It scarcely seems proper to his role of quiet recluse without worldly ambitions that he should take so much pleasure in effects of such naïveté and in their apt disposition. It was an innate sense, not an acquisition; something which it has been suggested came to him through his ancestry of Flemish painters, but whether or not this is so, it is certain that without it Franck could never have attained, as he did posthumously, his position as head of a distinctively French school of composition.

As an instance of design and decoration playing closely into one another's hands, the second presentation of the principal theme of the slow movement of the Quintet may be quoted. The first violin is repeating the drooping melody already given out 'lento, con molto sentimento' above the piano's accompaniment of repeated chords. The lower strings add a dark-hued theme introducing a rhythm and a chord progression which is to become salient throughout this movement and the Finale. The piano arpeggios, legato and pianissimo, supply a shimmering background. The passage might be described as a successful three-colour process, but it is none the less an essential part of the structure (Ex. 5). The Quintet has been criticized for its too great consistency of mood. If Brahms was over-given to brooding, how much more Franck! Even the bustle which the violins set up at the outset of the Finale becomes no more than a background for the reiteration of these sombre ideas, and there is no scherzo to provide relief. Franck's was not a resilient nature; he was not over-strong in what is regarded as the first of modern virtues, a sense of humour. His lack of humour is shown in other ways besides his reluctance to include a scherzo in his designs, particularly in a tendency to drop into banality

Ex. 5.

either by over-emphasis of a serious idea or the introduction of
a trivial one into his brighter moments.[1]

But the Quintet, though it lacks scherzo, humour, and brightness, may be accounted one of Franck's strongest works for
that very reason. It nowhere exhibits his weaker side, but, like
the two great piano pieces, concentrates on the deeper feelings
of a nature which, though it sought joy as a duty, found solace
in 'divinest melancholy'.

Only two of Franck's 'cyclic' works contain scherzos, the
Trio in F sharp minor, Op. 1, No. 1, and the String Quartet in D,
his last chamber work and the only one which was received with
general acclamation during his life. Of the former d'Indy
observes that it follows step by step in the track of Beethoven's
Scherzos of the Quartets Nos. 10 and 15. To the less partial
observer this may not appear equally evident or equally desirable.
What is more interesting to note is the fact that in Opus 1
Franck's personal method of developing his themes in 'cyclic'
fashion is displayed in its completeness, and that the designs of
his first and last works have this feature in common. In Opus 1,
for example, we get the second subject of the first movement
worked into the second Trio of the Scherzo accompanied by a
fragment from the theme of the first Trio. In the String Quartet
we find the opening theme embedded in the texture.

Trio for Pianoforte and Strings.   Op. 1, No. 1.

Ex. 6 a.

2nd subj., 1st mvt.

[1] The Finale of the fine *Variations Symphoniques* for piano and orchestra,
culminating in the brightness of Franck's favourite key of F sharp major,
gives instances of this last.

2nd Trio to Scherzo.

String Quartet.
Ex. 6 b.
Poco lento.

molto cantabile.

The difference between the two, however, lies in the composer's handling of the mechanism. In the early work he appears interested in it for its own sake; in the mature one it has become habitual. The Scherzo of the Quartet is self-existent, a movement of the most delicate texture in the happiness of which Franck for a moment forgot to brood. The 'molto cantabile' theme on the violoncello is not forced in; it just occurs.

The Scherzo of the Quartet follows the spacious first movement with complete spontaneity, and the two together give promise of a masterpiece which is not completely fulfilled by what follows them. Slow movements are apt to be something of a temptation to the church organist. He passes too much of his daily life in the improvisation of such things, and any theme must serve for the mood of 'dolce molto cantabile' which he has to induce in himself and his hearers.[1] The Larghetto of the String Quartet opens directly with its principal theme, but it is one which gives a hint of the organist's fingers feeling their way

[1] Cf. what is said below of Franck's songs, p. 411.

to an idea not fully formulated beforehand in the composer's head. The result is a little desultory, despite the incidental beauties of chromatic part-writing for which Franck was never at a loss, and despite a passionate climax of tone as its central feature.

The beginning of the Finale prompts the suggestion that by the time he wrote the Quartet Franck may have heard his pupils call him Beethoven's successor once too often. The quotation of the principal themes of each of the previous movements with a turbulent unison passage separating each quotation, and as it were placing them in inverted commas, can come from nowhere else but the Ninth Symphony. But this formality completed, Franck gets into his stride and evolves from the materials a movement of great energy and power. Beethoven made his initial quotations to dismiss them with his 'nicht diese Töne!' Franck makes his in order to recall them all as separate entities before fusing them into one in the peroration. The last few pages beginning from the violoncello's low C are the apotheosis of Franck's favourite method of thematic combination. The viola murmurs the theme of the Scherzo, the violins combine that of the first movement, and the first violin soars presently to the melody, 'largamente e con passione', of the slow movement.

The most cursory glance at Franck's chamber music must include some reference to his Sonata for violin and piano in A. Following on the composition of the *Variations Symphoniques* for piano and orchestra, it belongs to his most prolific period, when he was occupied with the *Prélude, Aria et Finale* for piano, and the Symphony. It carried his fame abroad more quickly and more decisively than any of the works for larger combinations, because it instantly found its ideal interpreter. Eugène Ysaÿe was able to do for Franck with this Sonata something of what Joachim did with the longer series of Brahms's works.

Born at Liége (Franck's birthplace) in 1858, Ysaÿe was just beginning his important work as professor of the violin at the Brussels Conservatoire, and was combining with it tours as a virtuoso of high rank, when Franck presented to him this Sonata so ideally suited to his impulsive temperament and calling out all that intimate sense of beauty freed from conventional propriety which was the great charm of Ysaÿe's playing.[1] The Sonata is too well known to require detailed description here. It must suffice to point out that in it the composer is less held by the traditional procedures of sonata form than in the Quintet, the Symphony, or the String Quartet. Its gentle opening movement slips into existence unostentatiously through a melody undulating tentatively from the violinist's bow. Hints of greater things to come are thrown out and they find fulfilment in the more energetic second movement introduced by the surging arpeggios of the piano. There is no suggestion here of the organist feeling about for an idea, and the Recitativo-Fantasia, which takes the place of a slow movement, is inspired by the contact of the two instruments as directly as anything in Brahms's duet sonatas. Moreover the final issue of events in the flowing canonic tune of the last movement, alternating with episodes from what has preceded it, is the most triumphant attainment of Franck's constant ideal, light emerging from darkness, joy from sorrow.

After Franck's death the example set by him was exalted into a cult by the pupils who had fought loyally to obtain even the slightest recognition for him in life. Vincent d'Indy (1857–1931)

---

[1] It was first played in Brussels by Ysaÿe and Mme Léontine Marie Bordes-Pène, to whom Franck dedicated the *Prélude, Aria et Finale*.

Later Ysaÿe found another ideal collaborator in the pianist, Raoul Pugno (1852–1914), whose special predilection in piano music was Mozart. It was the playing of Franck's sonata by these two artists which enabled English audiences to form an appreciative estimate of Franck, unfettered by the partisanship which had surrounded him in Paris.

took up the position of high priest of the cult, and his whole life as teacher, writer, and composer was devoted to celebrating the mysteries. But his numerous chamber works, finely constructed though they are, must be considered (to adapt his own phrase) as a continuance of, rather than a progress in, the Franckian manner. Two short-lived composers made distinct contributions to the art. Ernest Chausson (1855–99) left a small group of works, amongst which a Concerto for violin, piano, and string quartet attracted attention because of the peculiarity of the combination, and held it because of the warmth and spontaneity of the music thus presented. His romantic *Poème* for violin and orchestra endeared him to concert violinists and their audiences, and these works showed that, however much he might owe to the technical foundations of his master, he did not allow system to take the place of inspiration. Guillaume Lekeu (1870–94), a Belgian, had scarcely passed out of his pupilage when his life was cut short by typhoid fever. He owes his posthumous fame chiefly to the Sonata in G for violin and piano which he had written for Ysaÿe and which Ysaÿe made it his business to place beside the Sonata of César Franck. It is the vigorous and aspiring effort of a youth who might well have attained to greater things had maturity been granted to him. Outside the immediate circle of his pupils, Franck's influence appears sporadically, notably in the elaborate Quintet for piano and strings of Florent Schmitt (born 1870) which recalls Franck's Quintet in the shape of its themes, and especially in the insistence on the semitone.

With the appearance of Claude Debussy's String Quartet (1893) French chamber music entered on a new phase of development, one of great historical importance which lies beyond the scope of this volume. With it Debussy shook off the influence of Franck's 'organ class', and struck out a line of his own, which, despite the fact that its direction was pointed by his early travels in Russia, we now think of as typically French. It became the line along which French music of the early twentieth century was mainly to travel. We shall not attempt here to trace its course. Rather this epoch must be rounded off with a more particular mention of Franck's younger contemporary, Gabriel Fauré (1845–1925). Though Fauré outlived Debussy by seven years, he belongs indisputably to the nineteenth century. Less versatile than Saint-Saëns, and more facile than Franck, Fauré produced a fairly long list of chamber works, in which his two quartets for piano and strings (Op. 15 in C minor, 1879, and Op. 45 in G minor, 1886) are of outstanding merit. Their form is based on an easy acceptance of classical procedure, and they show a composer untrammelled by that tendency to theoretical reflection which is Franck's or that love of displaying technical ingenuity which beset Saint-Saëns. Both quartets begin with a broad theme given out in unison by strings with piano accompaniment, the lyrical impulse of which is quite unmistakable (see Ex. 9 a and b). Essentially a song-writer, this method of presentation is the one most natural to Fauré. He has been well compared with Schumann, with, however, the necessary qualification that as Schumann is always Schumann so Fauré always remains Fauré.[1] Like Schumann, Fauré is ready to vary this forthright expressiveness with some stroke of ingenuity which comes the more happily because its coming is unsuspected beforehand, and departs the more graciously for not having been worked out to its utmost limits of usefulness. Such are the two forms of the theme in the Scherzo of the C minor Quartet,

Scherzo. C mi.
Ex. 7.
(a)

[1] Vuillemin, *Gabriel Fauré et son Œuvre*, p. 49.

and the engaging problem in mixed rhythms which gives
distinctive colour to the pastoral tune in the Adagio of the
G minor Quartet.

Adagio. G mi.

Ex. 8.

The 'fifths' in the latter may be held to be a small sample of
that tendency to claim freedom which has made Fauré's followers
point to him as a pioneer.[1] But Fauré's pioneering never went
very far off the beaten track either of harmony or of part-
writing. His own genial personality appears without affectation
or pose in all his music, but it is not a compelling personality.
The limitation of interest lies in the fact that while we quickly
distinguish the voice of Fauré in the melody, the works are not
clearly distinguished each from each as different parts of himself. Even the two Piano Quartets have some of the bewildering
likenesses of twins. The opening themes contain a similarity of
phrase which may not be instantly apparent in the different
settings of the first statements (Ex. 9 a and b). But when the
phrase marked (a) is under development, as in the following
passages, it is not easy to distinguish, apart from the evidence

[1] Koechlin, *Gabriel Fauré*, 1927.
Koechlin gives a complete tabulated list of Fauré's works, published and
unpublished, with dates of composition, &c., similar to that which d'Indy
compiled for Franck.

C mi.

Ex. 9.

(a)

G mi.

(b)

of the key and time signatures, to which work each passage
belongs.

Quartet in C minor.

Ex. 10 a.

Quartet in G minor.

Ex. 10 *b*.

The twins both have 'Tweedle' written across them and one
must look behind to discover the termination '-dum' or '-dee'.
Unreflecting, spontaneous, and débonnaire, Fauré may occasionally descend to the commonplace, but never to vulgarity. His
works seem more important as a factor in that new seriousness
of attention to purely musical designs, which French musicians
began to display in the last quarter of the nineteenth century,
than for their intrinsic qualities. They must always hold a
place among the classics of French instrumental music, though
not among the world's masterpieces. That place has been well
indicated by a countrywoman.[1]

'La tonalité, les accords, les rythmes, les formes, sont ceux que
Gabriel Fauré a trouvés quand il a commencé de servir la musique:
entre ses mains, ces choses usuelles sont devenues précieuses.'

The quotation may well bring us back a little shamefacedly
to that contrast in the fortunes of French and English composers
with which this chapter started. Those who know Parry's
Quartet for piano and strings in A flat have no difficulty in
finding stronger terms in which to appraise its quality than

---

[1] Nadia Boulanger, *Revue Musicale*, Oct. 1922.

those applicable to the similar works of Fauré, and the Trios in
E minor and B minor, with the String Quintet in E flat, all
written at about the same time, bear out the high estimate which
Dannreuther placed on Parry's work. C. V. Stanford's longer
line of chamber music composition includes four published
string quartets, a piano quintet and quartet, three trios, and
several sonatas. His accomplishment was fully equal to that of
Saint-Saëns, his mind was a finer one and his output more
consistent. Yet the English public has never accorded to the
founders of its modern music anything like the place which the
French have eagerly claimed for theirs. While unappreciated at
home it is not to be expected that English composers should be
so much as heard of abroad, and while the names of Fauré and
Saint-Saëns are commonplaces on London concert programmes,
the appearance of a work by Parry or Stanford in Paris would
be regarded as a nine days' wonder. It is scarcely less, when one
of their chamber works is heard in London at the present day.

The Russian composers of the end of the century rapidly
became a far more potent influence than these comparatively
tentative efforts in Western Europe, although the first generation
of them, those briefly summarized by Dannreuther as 'a very
late outcome' of the Romantic Movement, inclined to regard
chamber music as a 'pis aller' for orchestral music. Tchaikovsky's
first and most popular String Quartet (Op. 11 in D major) was
written for a concert given by him in Moscow (1871), for which
he could not afford to engage an orchestra,[1] and his letters show
him to have been fully conscious of certain disabilities in his
handling of this most sensitive medium for musical expression.
Nevertheless, as Dannreuther says, 'with Tchaikovsky Russian

---

[1] Tchaikovsky had previously written a String Quartet in B flat in the
year (1865) that he entered the Moscow Conservatoire under Nicolas
Rubinstein. He subsequently destroyed all but the first movement.
See *Life and Letters of P. I. Tchaikovsky*, English translation by Rosa
Newmarch, p. 61.

music became cosmopolitan',[1] and the Quartet in D is said to
have been the first of his works to sell widely abroad. It was
followed fairly rapidly by the two others (Op. 22 in F and Op.
30 in E flat minor), and these three together, which preceded
Borodin's by several years, were the first intimation that the
Russian outlook was not completely bounded by national opera,
the ballet, and the programme symphony. Whatever criticism
may be made either of their texture as pieces of compressed
orchestration, or of their style as exhibiting that patchwork
conception of sonata form which the Russians had derived from
Schumann and from Liszt, they leave no doubt of Tchaikovsky's
seriousness in tackling the problems of a self-contained musical
design. True, the most successful moments occur in the slighter
middle movements where those problems hardly present themselves. The Andante, a deliciously sentimental little reverie on
a folksong, which brought tears to the eyes of Tolstoy, has given
the Quartet in D a distinction above its fellows. But though
Tchaikovsky wept with Tolstoy over the Andante, it was the
Second Quartet as a whole which held his special affection. He
referred to it subsequently with the opera, *Eugen Oniegin*, and
the Fourth Symphony as 'a labour of love, an enjoyment',[2] and
it is certainly as free as anything Tchaikovsky ever wrote from
the least hint of 'programme', dramatic or picturesque. Moreover, it is the one of the three which least suggests that the
refusal to colour the outline with woodwind and brass was an
act of deliberate self-denial.

Tchaikovsky's string quartets were followed in 1882 by the
more famous Trio for piano and strings in A minor. The fact
that the Trio was dedicated to the memory of Nicolas Rubinstein has given opportunity to biographers to enlarge on the
'elegiac' nature of the work. The title, 'Pezzo Elegiaco', of the

---

[1] *Oxford History of Music*, vol. vi, p. 329.
[2] Letter to Mme von Meck, Oct. 15, 1879 ; see *Life*, p. 355.

first movement and the direction 'Lugubre' on the last page are their justification, and there is no denying that Tchaikovsky intended the beginning and the end of the Trio to be an expression of his grief at the loss of a friend, while the whole was a tribute to the memory of a great artist. But the work as a whole cannot fairly be called elegiac. The 'Pezzo Elegiaco' is followed by a set of eleven variations on an Andante theme in E major, the chief merit of which is its pliability. The variations adapt it to innumerable rhythms amongst which a pretty 'tempo di valse', an over-elaborated fugue, and a sprightly 'tempo di mazurka' are conspicuous. Between the fugue and the mazurka, Variation IX with muted strings marked 'lamentoso', and arpeggiando figures on the piano, is no more than a recall to the mood of mourning which the composer seems to have forgotten in the interest of thematic metamorphosis. Indeed, one slow movement amongst a set of ten more or less vivacious ones is the least which might be expected even without the incentive of a personal bereavement. Nor is the bulk of the 'Variazione Finale e coda' conceived in a mood of depression. It begins with yet another metamorphosis of the theme, 'allegro risoluto e con fuoco', in A major, rather Schumannesque in character,[1] which pursues a buoyant, not to say flamboyant, course until forcibly arrested by the reappearance 'sempre fortissimo' of the theme of the 'Pezzo Elegiaco' (see examples below). From that point there is a long decrescendo both of rhythmic energy and of tone to the 'lugubre' ending.

The Trio indeed as a whole is typical of the kind of emotional scheme in which Tchaikovsky constantly worked, and in that scheme some expression of lamentation and sorrow is most frequently to be found. The fact that here, as in the 'Pathetic' Symphony, that mood comes last certainly emphasizes its presence, and in the latter case the imaginative biographers, in

[1] Compare the Finale to the *Études Symphoniques*.

default of a dedication to a departed friend, have discovered a foreboding of the composer's own end.[1]

The Third String Quartet, dedicated 'à la mémoire de F. Laub',[2] had given opportunity for the display of similar feelings, but as they were expressed with rather more refinement, notably in the 'andante funebre e doloroso' of the slow movement, and as the quartet ends brilliantly, 'vivace e fortissimo', it had not the same *réclame* as the Trio and the Symphony.

For Tchaikovsky music was primarily the embodiment in sound of a personal emotion, and in his gamut of emotions grief was prominent to the point of morbidity. It was his pre-occupation with emotion which made him impatient with the music of Brahms on the one hand, and the tenets of his country-men, the Nationalists, on the other. The search after beauty for its own sake and the attempt to reach a communal ideal (the soul of a people in the sounds of an individual) seemed to him alike mere pretentiousness. He desired that his own music should be the most direct expression of himself, no more. Never-theless he could be a singularly clear-sighted critic of himself, and in the very letter in which he protests against what he calls Brahms's 'pretension to profundity' he can continue:

'. . . I have suffered all my life from my incapacity to grasp form in general. I have fought against this innate weakness, not—I am proud to say—without good results: yet I shall go to my grave without having produced anything really perfect in form. There is frequently padding in my work. To the experienced eye the stitches show in my seams but I cannot help it.'[3]

In the string quartets, more particularly the two later ones, he had taken the greatest pains to sew neat seams and had

[1] When the 'Pathetic' Symphony was produced in England shortly after the composer's death an absurd story gained some credence that immediately after finishing it Tchaikovsky had committed suicide.

[2] Ferdinand Laub, leader of the quartet which had produced Tchai-kovsky's Opp. 11 and 22.

[3] Letter to the Grand Duke Constantine, Sept. 21, 1888. *Life*, p. 567.

succeeded far more than in the Trio. One might think that in
the latter he had abandoned the attempt, but it too was an
effort at self-discipline, strange though it may seem. It was
undertaken with the set purpose of mastering an aspect of style,
not only new to him but at first antipathetic, the combination of
piano with strings. In the letter in which he announced the
undertaking to Mme von Meck he said nothing of the desire to
commemorate Nicolas Rubinstein but much of his 'wish to
conquer all difficulties'.[1] When he tells her that it is finished[2] he
is fearful for the result.

'. . . I am afraid that having written all my life for the orchestra,
and only taken late in life to chamber music, I may have failed to
adapt the instrumental combinations to my musical thoughts. In
short I fear I may have arranged music of a symphonic character as
a trio instead of writing directly for my instruments.'

Here he has diagnosed his own disease with precision. Almost
any page of the score could be taken as an illustration of it.
That in which the Finale begins to work up to the climax where
its course is arrested by the 'elegiac' theme will serve as a
peculiarly obvious case of 'arrangement'. The drums are rolling

Ex. 11.   Tchaikovsky Trio.

(piano, left hand, dominant pedal); the strings are running about. As there are actually only two of them the pianist's right hand must supply the deficiency, while the actual strings must answer their own entries. At the height of the crescendo they must all make as much noise as they can on two bars of diminished seventh chord, the poverty of which only a blaze of full orchestra could disguise,

Ex. 12.

and next, the strings must pretend to be brass and the piano act for strings and woodwind, as they approach the dénouement.

Ex. 13.   STRINGS.

PIANO.

This shows Tchaikovsky to be utterly devoid of that sense of duality which has been pointed to as the formative principle of all Brahms's music for piano and strings. He made no further attempt to master the combination, and the Trio, save for the unimportant sextet (*Souvenir de Florence*) written near the end of his life, closes his contribution to chamber music, and, so far as style is concerned, closes it in defeat.

Of the nationalists known as 'the Five' only two, Borodin and Cui, devoted serious attention to chamber music, and the works of the latter have not lived. Borodin began his musical life as an amateur violoncellist and at the age of sixteen he was occupying himself in quartet playing.[1] He had, therefore, early acclimatized his mind to the style of the four strings and the experience had acted for him, though in a smaller way, very much as Brahms's Detmold experience had. Borodin's fastidious taste made his output of music of all classes the smallest left by any of the masters of his age, but the two string quartets declare a mastery beyond that of Tchaikovsky's three. The early experience, moreover, will account for a peculiarity in the First Quartet described on its German title-page as 'angeregt durch ein Thema von Beethoven'. A subsidiary episode from the Finale of Beethoven's Quartet in B flat, Op. 130 (the movement which replaced the *Grosse Fuge*), seems to have been running in Borodin's head. He nowhere quotes it strictly as a subject for either development or variation, but its bass hovers in the viola part of his 'moderato' introduction, and what may be called a Russianized version of it over a drone bass becomes the theme of his principal Allegro (Ex. 14 *a* and *b*). Its influence can further be traced both in the Andante and in the Russian dance Finale.

Reminiscences of other men's music are notoriously the bane of players who would be composers, but that is not the case of Borodin, a composer who had also played. To his keenly imaginative and clear-thinking brain such a memory was an

[1] Brando (Biography, 1922), quoted in *Cobbett's Cyclopedic Survey*, tells of certain youthful essays by Borodin in chamber music composition, notably a Trio and a Pianoforte Quintet. His mature work contains no example of the piano combined with strings.

Ex. 14.   BEETHOVEN.

incentive to originality. The Quartet as a whole is unlike
Beethoven and entirely typical of Borodin. A noteworthy technical feature is the device of extending the scheme of tonal effect
by an ingenious use of harmonics. This was new in 1878, and to
musicians trained in the solemn traditions of German chamber

music, it appeared not quite respectable. Fiddling in harmonics
had been the prerogative of meretricious virtuosity ever since the
days of Paganini. But Borodin uses his harmonics for two special
effects, neither of which could have been obtained otherwise. The
first is in the first Allegro, where the following passage, not in itself
a very significant one perhaps, is treated in descending sequence:

This could have been scored in a dozen ways all of them simpler
than that of making the violoncello produce the high E as an
harmonic from the A string. At first sight it appears to be an
affectation. But the harmonic adds to the ethereal character
of the chord, and its purpose is perceived in the descending
sequence which gradually comes down from the heights, till
the motif loses its unearthly light and fades away in the lower
registers of second violin and violoncello.

The other and much more elaborate use of harmonics is in the
Trio to the deliciously dainty Scherzo, where violoncello and
first violin become elfin pipers above the rustle of the woodland
leaves (second violin and viola muted). The piquancy of the
tone colour is evident from the following:

Lightness and aptness of texture are apparent throughout Borodin's two quartets quite apart from such special effects as these. Unlike Tchaikovsky, he never seems to be thinking how he can get in all the notes. It is comparatively rarely that he wants more than four notes at a time, and where an instrument is required to play chords they are in positions which come easily off the strings.

The Second Quartet (D major) is generally considered to be his *chef d'œuvre*, and its suave opening is a good specimen of his effortless style.

Ex. 16.

The theme propounded by the violoncello and taken up by the
first violin is gently unfolded. The features of these sixteen bars
all contribute something to the subsequent process of thematic
development. Amongst them may be noted those touches of
chromatic variety in the harmony of bars 9 and 13 which present
in their simplest form examples of the type of progression
through which Borodin constantly gives a distinctive colouring
to his scores. This movement, and indeed the whole Quartet,
dispels the Western notion, made prevalent by Tchaikovsky,

that Russian music proceeds by the violent alternation of hectic
excitement and morbid exhaustion. In movements founded on
the dance (the Scherzo of this Quartet, and still more the Finale,
give instances of it) Borodin is inclined to keep the energy going
by the reiteration of short exclamatory figures suggestive of the
primitive excitation of the Gopak, and of that physical energy
which has now become familiar to us in the Diaghilev Ballet's
sophistication of the peasant dances. But this is only one side
of Borodin's art, and in the first movement of this Quartet it is
entirely in abeyance. Rather it exhibits the quietly thinking
artist who has arrived at a personal manner of expression by
a fusion between his scientific study of the principles of folk-
music and his practical experience in playing the classics. He
reproduces neither; both help to liberate that distinctive charm
which is his own. After the lively measures of the Scherzo comes
a reflective slow movement described as 'Notturno' which, if
it nowhere cuts very deep, restores the meditative mood in the
high-pitched violoncello tune of its opening. A few bars from
the coda are quoted here as illustration of the extension of
those harmonic progressions noted above as typical in the
opening theme.

Ex. 17.

The extreme meticulousness with which phrasing and nuances
are marked in the first violin part will not escape attention.

The brilliant Finale, founded on two contrasted phrases, one
in light quavers, the other in heavy crotchets, is the only movement which tempts one to think of the orchestra, and the
temptation is chiefly due to an obvious likeness between its
theme and that which begins Borodin's Symphony in B minor.
The crotchet theme would be the more 'pesante' if double-basses
paced it out instead of the viola and violoncello on their fourth
strings. Nevertheless, here too Borodin preserves a pure quartet
texture throughout its vivid development, and the Finale
rounds off the work with the feeling that the attractive design
has been admirably accomplished. Alas! that save for a few

fugitive movements, these two Quartets are all that Borodin, 'the national genius after Glinka',[1] contributed to Russian chamber music. There were only seven years of life before him after the composition in 1880 of the Quartet in D.

Rimsky-Korsakov has given a detailed description[2] of that change in the outlook of Russian musicians towards their art which is characteristic of the 'eighties. It is the change from what he calls the Balakirev circle of the 'sixties and 'seventies to the Belaiev circle of the 'eighties. M. P. Belaiev was a wealthy amateur whose patronage, beginning with a lively interest in the genius of Alexander Glazounov, blossomed into the institution of his famous Friday Evenings of Chamber Music (1883), the Russian Symphony Concerts in St. Petersburg, and, presently, the publishing house of his name established at Leipzig. The acquisition of such a Maecenas[3] necessarily meant a flood of music of all sorts, and more particularly of chamber music, not all of it of the first importance and some of it bringing into prominence the names of composers of whose works otherwise the world might have been well content to remain in ignorance.

The contrast between the two circles can best be appreciated from the words of Rimsky-Korsakov himself, who was a member of the first and became the musical leader of the second. He writes:

'Balakirev's circle consisted of musicians of feeble technique, amateurs almost, who were pioneering by sheer force of their creative talent. Belaiev's circle, on the contrary, consisted of composers and musicians technically trained and educated. . . .

---

[1] Dannreuther, *Oxford History of Music*, vol. vi, p. 322.

[2] Rimsky-Korsakov, *My Musical Life*, translated from the revised second Russian edition by Judah A. Joffe, New York, 1923; see p. 242 et seq.

[3] 'He was a Maecenas; but he was no gentleman-Maecenas to squander money on art to suit his whims while really advancing it nowhere. . . . He became a concert impresario and publisher of Russian Music without counting on any personal benefit; on the contrary he gave to the cause enormous sums of money, concealing his name moreover to the utmost of his ability.'—Rimsky-Korsakov, *My Musical Life*, p. 243.

'Balakirev's circle recognized well-nigh exclusively the orchestra, the piano, the chorus and vocal solos with orchestra, ignoring chamber music, vocal ensembles (excepting the operatic duet), the chorus *a cappella* and the solo for bow-instruments; Belaiev's circle had a broader outlook on these forms. Balakirev's circle was exclusive and intolerant; Belaiev's was more indulgent and eclectic.

'Balakirev's circle did not want to study but broke new paths forward, relying upon its powers, succeeding therein and learning; Belaiev's circle studied, attaching as it did great importance to technical perfection, but it also broke new paths, though more securely, even if less speedily.

'Balakirev's circle hated Wagner and strained to take no notice of him; those in Belaiev's circle had their eyes and ears open with eagerness to learn and respect.'

Rimsky-Korsakov's personal influence must also be taken into account:

'I was the general teacher of the members of the circle [i.e. Belaiev's] who had in the majority of cases graduated from the Conservatory under my guidance, or had at least received some measure of instruction from me. Glazounov had not studied much under me and soon came into the relation of a younger friend. Liadov, Dütsch, Sokolov, Wihtol and others became my pupils in free composition, after having been pupils of Y. J. Johansen up to fugue inclusive. Somewhat later I began to guide my pupils from harmony on; accordingly men like Tcherepnin, Zolotariov, and others were my pupils entirely. . . . In the 'nineties Glazounov and Liadov began to share the leadership with me; upon M. P. [Belaiev]'s death, in accordance with his last will and testament, they formed with me a Board of Trustees to manage the publishing business, the concerts, etc.'

We can see in all this the revolutionary movement of 'the Five' being tamed, its hair cut, and its claws pared. The earlier generation had begun by composing symphonies and operas and had been content to discover principles of their art in the process of creation; the younger are led carefully through a conservatoire course proceeding from harmony on to fugue, instrumentation, and free composition. The tale of the Leipzig Conservatoire of 1850 producing Schumann's 'bedeutende Talente' is repeated in St. Petersburg forty years later, and this product need detain our attention no more than the earlier one.

Glazounov (born 1865) alone among those named by Rimsky-Korsakov calls for special consideration here. His talent was the initial cause of the formation of Belaiev's circle; it was essentially a musical talent, neither dramatic nor illustrative of literary ideas, and from early years Glazounov expressed himself with equal ease and directness through the orchestra and the string quartet. All his chamber music is for strings, and the earlier group of quartets is divided from the later by the Quintet in A, Op. 39, which, like Schubert's and like the original form of Brahms's Piano Quintet, is written for two violins, one viola, and two violoncelli. Before the Quintet came the little Quartet in D, Op. 1, that in F, Op. 10, with more distinctly folksong-like themes, repetitional phrases, Borodinesque in manner, the Five Novellettes, Op. 15, actually a suite of short pieces in contrasted styles, the Slavonic Quartet in G and the Suite in C, a second essay in the fashion of the Novellettes.

The first two of these, as the work of a lad of about 18, are remarkable for their easy control of form resulting from an innate sense. Did ever an Opus 1 appear with so concise and perfectly modelled a slow movement as Glazounov's little pastoral Andante of 51 bars? The suites similarly show shapeliness in small compass to be among the first of Glazounov's virtues, but they also display more immediately attractive qualities. The fourth movement of the Suite in C is a theme with a set of variations each couched in a distinctive mood and described as 'Tranquillo', 'Mistico', 'Scherzo', 'Penseroso', with a lively 'Alla Polacca' for ending. The 'Alla Spagnola' and 'All' Ungherese', first and last of the Novellettes, and the 'Orientale' movements, one in each suite, show that Glazounov's propensity for local colour was not confined to that of his own country. The Slavonic Quartet in G contains an 'Alla Mazurka' which is as true to type as the best of Chopin's for piano, while its Finale, 'Une fête slave', spurning the fastidious delicacy of the Polish dance, ends the work with a truly Russian orgy of energy. Glazounov in his first phase of chamber music indeed seems to be the fulfilment of Dannreuther's commentary on the work of his predecessors:

'There is no need that the young Russian composer should hark back to partially exhausted formulae. The laws of musical design, the principles of good sense and proportion will make themselves felt, whatever may be the material to which they are applied.'[1]

The String Quintet and the two more highly wrought string quartets after it, Op. 64 in A minor and Op. 70 in D minor, show the composer to have outgrown his childish pleasure in dressing up, whether as a native peasant or as a foreigner. These works are often spoken of as marking a reaction towards classicism and owing something to the influence of Brahms. Rather we should describe them as an advance to a purely musical outlook, the one which Brahms had steadfastly maintained for half a century in face of all exhibitions of literary, poetic, descriptive, and illustrative music through which romanticism had wandered. There is no technical influence from Brahms apparent in the mature Glazounov, and it must be confessed that he is deficient in the greatest of Brahms's gifts, the power to create compelling and stirring melody. But in his pursuit of his aim he displays a like power with Brahms of discovering uncommon beauty and interest in a theme which to the ordinary mind would at first appear unpromising, such a figure for example as the four notes which form the initial idea of Op. 64—

Ex. 18.

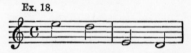

---

[1] *Oxford History of Music*, vol. vi, p. 328. It is a general comment. No individual is alluded to in the phrase 'the young Russian composer'.

or the rather bald subject given out in fugue at the outset of
Op. 70.

Ex. 18 a.

The sonata form movements proceeding from these beginnings
are not mere patterns in sound but organic growths, and that
is the difference between the handling of the master and that
of the tiro in form. Nevertheless a composer who publishes his
Op. 70 in his thirty-fifth year[1] prompts us to some misgiving,
especially when the bulk of the list consists of large-scale
instrumental works. Can any man in the complex conditions
of modern art expect to hold on at such a pace through
the whole course of life? Did Glazounov's Maecenas make the
running a little too smooth for him over the first part of the
course?

Belaiev died in 1902 and Glazounov's pace slackened.[2] The
music of the new century was already passing into experimental
phases to which he could not contribute anything, and he
had not the stamina of Brahms, who, in face of other drastic
changes of fashion a generation earlier, had held doggedly to his

[1] Brahms in his thirty-fifth year published *Ein deutsches Requiem*,
which is his Op. 45. He was 53 when his First Symphony, Op. 68, made its
appearance.

Mendelssohn's Op. 91, his setting of Psalm XCVIII, was first performed
on New Year's Day, 1844, and he was then in his thirty-fifth year.

[2] Glazounov's Eighth Symphony was produced by Stanford at the Leeds
Festival in 1907 and little has come since. Mrs. Newmarch's suggestion
(*Grove's Dictionary*, 3rd ed., vol. ii, p. 391) that 'his life seemed the realization of a fairy tale set to music, until the political troubles of his country
threw his life and his art into the shadows' does not cover all the facts.
His output had slackened off before the political troubles made their
appearance.

course so that ultimately he not only justified himself, but
stimulated that phase of symphonic revival through the length
and breadth of Europe of which Glazounov's symphonies,
string quartets, &c., form a part.

Another figure in Russian music, who has some importance in
this revival, is Serge Ivanovitch Taneiev (1856–1915). A pupil
and intimate friend of Tchaikovsky, he remained outside the
circumferences of both Rimsky-Korsakov's 'circles', and the
composition of chamber music was the chief occupation of his
creative career.[1] He was a brilliant pianist and it is significant
that he chose to make his début in Moscow (January, 1875) by
playing Brahms's 'ungrateful' Piano Concerto in D minor.[2]
He possessed a natural aptitude for contrapuntal device and
great assiduity in testing the amenity of his themes to contrapuntal development. Rimsky-Korsakov declares that Taneiev's
methodical habits ought to have resulted in dry and academic
composition but admits that that was not invariably the case.[3]
These characteristics made it inevitable that Taneiev in the
'eighties should be called a 'Brahmsite', and, not unnaturally,
considering what the appellation meant to his contemporaries,
Taneiev rather resented it. He was disdainful of the dilettantism
of the Balakirev circle and impatient of the mutual admiration
of the Belaiev circle, an aloof person who, though he can have
had little sympathy with Tchaikovsky's manner of wearing his

[1] Apart from chamber music an operatic trilogy on the *Oresteia* was
Taneiev's most important work.

[2] See *Life and Letters of Tchaikovsky*, p. 175.

A little later Taneiev played Tchaikovsky's own Concerto in B flat minor,
for which the composer, if not the concerto itself, proved 'grateful' in the
following words:

'The chief feature of his playing lies in his power to grasp the composer's
intention in all its most delicate and minute details, and to realise them
precisely as the author heard them himself.'

[3] See *My Musical Life*, p. 322 et seq., for a fair if not wholly sympathetic
account of Taneiev's artistic personality.

heart on his sleeve in his music, yet not only loved him as a man but admired his strength as an artist, his freedom from cliquism, and his ability to express himself in direct and uncompromising musical terms.

Taneiev's quartets show his own determination to express himself by a process of clear thinking. Of the six which survive the earliest is said to be that called No. 3 in D minor (Op. 7). It consists of two movements only, a rather conventional first Allegro and a set of eight variations on a charmingly Mozartian theme (6–8 time) concluding in a reference to the theme of the first Allegro. The variations are not only ingenious but beautiful. It is noteworthy that though less strict than are most of Brahms's in preserving the harmonic structure and phrase form of the theme intact, yet they belong more to the classical method, to which Brahms adhered, of treating the whole form of the theme as the subject for variation than to Tchaikovsky's easy-going one of merely changing the rhythms of the tune.

The Quartet No. 1 in B flat (Op. 4) has five movements, a delicate Intermezzo being placed between the Presto (Scherzo) and the Finale. It is dedicated 'à mon maître, M. P. Tchaikovsky', and it is not only by such directions as 'semplice, ma con intimissimo sentimento, tranquillo' alternating with 'appassionato' in the slow movement, that the composer is seen to be actuated by a stronger emotional impulse here than usually elsewhere. The themes are for the most part broader and more significant, the style generally less conscious. In this work Taneiev seems to be reaching out towards the spirit of his master.

The other four quartets are in the customary four movement plan. No. 2 in C undoubtedly shows a certain idiomatic likeness to Brahms in the handling of such cross rhythms as the following:

Ex. 19.

If we are seeking influences, however, that of Liszt appears to be the stronger in the portentous motif given out first on the violoncello and threading its way through various combinations of tone, till it reaches a grandiose climax in the recapitulation. This climax is one of the few places where Taneiev suggests that he would be glad of more instruments than he has got. The Fuga which provides a virile climax to the last movement is a good specimen of Taneiev's skill in such things, and there is a delightful humour in the way he allows the energy to evaporate in the final coda. The coda is evidence that despite Taneiev's use of scholastic.counterpoint, his musical outlook is not bounded by it.

Some influence from Czech folk-music is said to underlie the thematic material of the Quartet No. 4 in A minor, dedicated to the Bohemian-Czech String Quartet.[1] The hearer will be little conscious of any variation from Taneiev's normal style, though the opening theme of the first Allegro is set forth rather in the manner of a quotation.

Ex. 20.

A motto theme of two rising fifths with which the 'adagio' Introduction opens is also worked into the whimsical Divertimento; the Introduction (8 bars) is repeated entire at the beginning of the Finale and the rising fifths form the basis of the lively 'presto' theme of that movement. This use of thematic links between movements had become almost habitual among the more reflective composers of the late nineteenth century, of whom Taneiev is certainly one.

Thematic metamorphosis rather grows on Taneiev, as the following samples from the lighter and generally charming Quartet No. 5 in A (Op. 13) will show:

Ex. 21.

1st movement.

Allegro.

---

[1] M. D. Calvocoressi writing in *Cobbett's Cyclopedic Survey of Chamber Music*.

The names of the Czech Quartet are given on Taneiev's title-page (published 1900). They are Hoffmann, Suk, Nedbal, and Wihan.

2nd movement.

It is, as has been suggested earlier, a device the interest of which very soon palls unless backed up by a vigorous invention. It equally pervades Taneiev's Quartet No. 6 in B flat (Op. 19), generally accounted his finest work and undoubtedly the most spacious in design. The reiteration in the Finale of the figure arising out of the opening phrase,

Ex. 22.

and its subjection to an elaborate contrapuntal treatment, which it hardly seems to deserve, become artificial in effect, and one is inclined to wish that the work had ended with the spontaneous and diverting Giga which precedes the Finale.

A study of Taneiev's quartets in short shows us a finely tempered musical mind, superior, it may be too superior at times, to those kinds of effect which immediately captivate attention, and just lacking in that inevitableness, the power of spontaneous creation through quite simple means, producing in the hearer the sense of 'divine familiarity'[1], which belongs to the greatest artists alone.

The two quintets for strings are of a piece with the quartets, but the chamber music for piano with strings, a Quartet in E, Op. 20 (published by Belaiev in 1907), and the Quintet in G minor, Op. 30 (Édition Russe, 1912), belong to a different category. Here we find Taneiev completely at ease in handling that texture which had so baffled Tchaikovsky and which most of his countrymen had avoided. He had no temptation to confuse the issue with the style of the orchestra. Indeed, Rimsky-Korsakov tells us that orchestration was the one phase of technique in which Taneiev was deficient until Glazounov took him in hand.[2] The fuguing in the Finale of Taneiev's Quartet can be contrasted with that in Tchaikovsky's Trio as an example of how piano and strings may be combined without losing their identities or attempting to perform one another's functions. The fact that Taneiev oddly introduces his theme in augmentation on the piano with the words 'quasi tromba' need not be taken as evidence that he is thinking orchestrally.[3] Taneiev knows exactly what he wants from his own instrument and its

[1] See Chapter III, p. 65, Fuller-Maitland's phrase about Brahms.

[2] Taneiev dedicated his First Symphony to Glazounov.

[3] It is in fact a thoroughly pianistic direction, like Hans von Bülow's quasi flauto, &c., in the Waldstein Sonata. Tell a pianist to think of a trumpet or a flute and he will phrase in a certain way, using a particular kind of 'touch'. The result is not a bit like either a trumpet or a flute; the direction is a stimulus to the pianist's imagination causing him to produce an effect characteristic of his own instrument.

participation in these works is an ameliorating influence. Though
analysis may show that the thematic development is as close
as in the string quartets, a less conscious effort of mental
analysis is demanded from the hearer. The invention moves
more easily; one is more certain that the composer is enjoying
his own work. The declamatory opening of the Quartet by the
piano and the impulsive entrance of the strings attest the freer
tone of mind at the outset.

Ex. 23.

PIANO.

STRINGS.

The motif marked (*a*), arriving first merely as a kind of flourish
to the phrase, is that on which a great deal of the subsequent
form depends.

The two slow movements, 'Adagio più tosto largo' in the
Quartet, 'Largo' in the Quintet, stand out with a singular charm,
the former for the fantasy with which a meditative motive is
discussed in different ways by the several instruments, the latter
for the beauty with which a ground bass is elaborated from its
unison opening (Ex. 24). The Purcellian flavour of this bass
should endear it to English ears. The building up of the Finale
to the Quintet by means of a recapitulation of ideas heard
earlier suggests some analogy with the method of César Franck.

Ex. 24.

Unison opening.

Repeated bars.

Undoubtedly this Quintet deserves to be considered more seriously than it has been by performers as one of the great specimens of the union of piano and string quartet.

To turn from Taneiev back to Dvořák is to begin a new day. There is a morning freshness in the air, and a boy is whistling a tune. It goes like this:

Ex. 25 a.

Will that make a sonata or be amenable to stretto in a fugue? Who knows and who cares! Is it a good tune? Not particularly, but at any rate it is a tune, and it happens to be the tune that the boy wants to whistle at the moment, and he will go on whistling it, or something like it, as long as he feels like that. Not that Dvořák was actually a boy when he wrote his String Quintet in G (with double-bass), from which this tune comes. He was in his thirty-fourth year, was married, had earned some repute in Prague as a composer both for the theatre and the concert-room, and had passed that climacteric of his career when his work had gained not only the Austrian Government grant of 400 gold florins, but, what was ultimately of more importance to him, the active interest of Brahms.[1] But this tune is one picked at random from a thousand or more illustrative of that unpremeditated quality in Dvořák's music which makes him seem a whistling boy in contrast with the conscious striving for ideals of all the Russians, nationalist and individualist alike. It is inconceivable that Dvořák, like Taneiev, could ever have tested his themes as counterpoint exercises before beginning to write on them. He may throw a weight on a figure beyond that it is able to bear. If he does, it is not because the figure is amenable to development, but simply because his mood has outlived the inspiration of the moment, and he must go on in the same vein. We have only to transcribe a few bars further to find padding which any decent composition teacher would strike out at once.

Ex. 25 b.

[1] The Quintet originally numbered Op. 18 now stands in the completed list of Dvořák's compositions as Op. 77 (see *Grove*, 3rd ed., article by O. Šourek, author of the authoritative Czech biography). A concise guide to the main facts of Dvořák's career is Karel Hoffmeister's *Antonin Dvořák*, edited and translated by Rosa Newmarch.

What was the Umělecká Besedá[1] about to award a prize to this
helpless infant? The question is answered by a perusal of the
whole Quintet. It is tautologous to the point of absurdity; vague
meanderings clinging desperately to a puerile figure often take
the place of development, and such harmonic ineptitudes as
occur in the above are not infrequent; but there is invention
here, alive and unmistakable. In view of all the popular tales of
genius ignored or spurned by the academic institutions, the contrary case of Dvořák deserves special emphasis. Here was a

---

[1] Umělecká Besedá (Society of Artists), now the principal music publishing house in Prague, with its practice rooms and other amenities affording a
central meeting place for artists, has been, and still is, the chief organization
for furthering the material interests of the Czech national music. The prize
to Dvořák for the Quintet in G was subsequent to that which he had won in
Vienna (1875).

man of over thirty whose work was still liable to exhibit every fault which would leap to the eye of an academic examiner; yet not only the local Society interested in furthering native talent but a Jury[1] in Vienna, whose members were certainly not pre-disposed towards the Czech idiom, instantly recognized that Dvořák possessed the one thing which mattered most of all.

Dvořák's creative instinct, imperfectly supported though it was at first by technical competence, prevents his work from falling into any convenient category. To the world at large he now stands as the foremost representative of his country's genius for music; in his own country he is secure of only the second place while Smetana keeps the throne. One biographer[2] finds too much foreign influence in his style to make him acceptable as a representative Czech, while another asserts that 'in the works which immediately followed the foreign recognition of his genius, Dvořák adhered closely to the rich sources of Czech folk-music; not perhaps literally to the use of the folk tunes, but to a reflection of them, just as Smetana wrote in their spirit while artistically ennobling them'.[3] Both can find justification and may even support their arguments by reference to the same works. The one may point to the suave sonority of the opening of the Sextet for strings in A as undeniably in the classical manner, while the other can instance the 'Dumka' (Elegy) and the 'Furiant', so vividly set off against the first movement of this Sextet, as examples of Dvořák's nationalism. Or again it may be said on the one side that the Quartet in D minor, Op. 34, dedicated to Brahms, has more of Brahms in it

---

[1] The grant was one awarded by the Austrian Ministry for Education to artists of talent in needy circumstances. The Jury contained besides Brahms, Eduard Hanslick, the critic, and Johann Herbeck, the conductor. Kalbeck assures us that at the time Brahms knew nothing of Dvořák's personal circumstances (Kalbeck, ii. 155).

[2] Bartoš, *Antonin Dvořák* (1914), quoted by Hoffmeister, p. xix.

[3] Šourek, article on Dvořák, *Grove's Dictionary*, 3rd ed.

than his name on the title-page, while the other side can claim that its 'Alla Polka' at any rate has come straight from the village square of Nelahozeves.[1]

The truth is that a great number of elements, among them his study of the classics and his grateful admiration towards Brahms, combined to refine and polish that sense of style in which Dvořák was naturally deficient at the start, but these influences never deflected him from his own course. He was as incapable of adopting a doctrinaire attitude towards nationalism, confining himself (as the Balakirev circle of Russians had done, or had attempted to do) to those resources for which chapter and verse could be shown in the national tradition, as he was of outgrowing the tradition which the village church and the village school, the song in the fields and the dance on the square, had implanted in his youth. Dvořák could not help being national because he was the product of his nation's most intimate life. He became international because he went out into the world and allowed all that he found to be good in it to mature into a personal experience. The conscious nationalist disporting himself on his village green refuses to know what is going on in the next village. Dvořák was eager in the discovery of new villages, from Vienna to New York; he learnt much from their manners, but his musical speech remained his own.

The large output of Dvořák's chamber music fills twenty years from 1875 to 1895. The string quartets mark the course of his experience in those years. The two first, in E, Op. 80 (originally Op. 27) and D minor, Op. 34 (1876 and 1877), display his growth in the handling of classical form. The charming Quartet in E

---

[1] A few years ago I visited Dvořák's birthplace, Nelahozeves, on a May Sunday afternoon. A spring festival was in progress; youths and girls were processing and dancing round the decorated May-tree, counterpart of the English Maypole. Their festivity was accompanied by a wind band, playing, very much out of tune, dance tunes which can only be described as crude Dvořák.

flat, Op. 51 (1879), and its later companion in C, Op. 61 (1882), show him applying the formal principles more directly to the special case of his native idiom. The Quartet in F, Op. 96 (1893), known as 'the Nigger', is, together with the String Quintet in E flat, Op. 97, and the Symphony 'From the New World', the product of his sojourn in America. How far America influenced these works may be more suitably discussed in connexion with the Symphony. Finally the Quartets, in A flat, Op. 105, and in G, Op. 106, belong to Dvořák's home-coming, when, all wanderings over and foreign customers satisfied, he indulged the desire of the artist to satisfy himself, and, giving free rein to his fancy, produced a pair of works of extraordinary lyrical beauty, simple yet exquisite in design.

He had not outgrown the quality of the whistling boy. His spirit was still young; the morning dew had not evaporated under the fierce sun of a strenuous life. To place the opening of the Quartet in G beside the extract which has been given above from the early Quintet in the same key is to realize that the impulse is the same. But a comparison will show how a lifetime of experience had given to Dvořák exactly what Hans Sachs's lesson gave to Walther's dream, the modelling of a master song.

Ex. 26.

Dvořák's music for piano solo amounts to little more than the chippings off the marble from which his symphonic works are hewn. His contribution to the duet sonata form consists of only two works, the Sonata in F and the Sonatina in G, both of only secondary importance. But the piano came to life for him in association with strings because of the wealth of tonal colour, the vivid contrasts, and the subtle blendings of diversity into unity which the association makes possible. After Brahms Dvořák is the greatest master of this era in the art of chamber music for piano and strings. Two trios and a piano quartet appeared in that prolific period, 1875–6, and they followed sundry earlier essays of the kind.

Four works, each distinct in character yet all intensely personal in style and expression, appeared at intervals between this time and his departure for America. In the Trio in F minor, Op. 65 (1884), more particularly in the lay-out for the instruments of the first movement, it is easy to detect some influence from Brahms. Indeed, not only is that duality of texture, which has been described as Brahms's special characteristic, asserted at once, but the rhythmic figures themselves bear some actual likeness to those of Brahms's piano quartets. But the likeness will be much more apparent to the eye of the score reader than to the ear of the listener, and it disappears altogether when the strenuous first Allegro is followed by a delicious 'allegro grazioso' in which the piano picks out the crisp and naïve melody against the murmuring triplets of the strings. The work is one which shows Dvořák as something more than the spontaneous maker of tunes. The long Adagio, with its rich harmonic colouring and the intimate interplay of instruments, is calculated to dispel any notion that Dvořák's more serious moods are referable to Brahms or to any one else. Nowhere is he more himself than in this mood of romantic reverie.

The famous Quintet in A, Op. 81, and the less famous Quartet in E flat, Op. 87, arrived together in the same year, 1887, and the 'Dumky' Trio, Op. 90, followed a little later almost on the eve of his departure for America.[1] It was his farewell to home, happily not his last farewell, and his farewell to this combination of instruments in which he so greatly excelled.

[1] Of a concert tour through Bohemia which Dvořák undertook before his departure Hoffmeister (p. 45) says:

'Every town in Bohemia wanted him for a farewell concert before he started on his journey. On this tour Ferdinand Lachner (violinist) and Hanš Wihan (violoncellist) accompanied the Master, and the work most frequently played was the "Dumky" Trio.'

A quintet for piano and strings has a certain advantage with performers over a piano quartet, because a string quartet is usually a permanent concert-giving organization, so that a work which employs it as a whole, together with a pianist, is likely to be more popular with the concert-givers than one which leaves the second violinist unemployed in the artists' room. With audiences this particular Quintet is more popular than its companion Quartet because of the exquisite spontaneity of its melody, by comparison with which the Quartet, for all its brightness and energy, seems a little laboured. Hoffmeister points out that in the Quartet 'the ideas are more in opposition to each other —masculine energy opposed to feminine tenderness'. Perhaps; but no analogy from the psychology of sex is needed to account for such a gem as the following from the Quintet, and the Quartet offers nothing quite so new or so inevitable as its wayward lilt.

Ex. 27.

The 'Dumka' and 'Furiant', slow movement and scherzo, of the Quintet, are among the most delightful specimens of those national types which Dvořák delighted to introduce as middle movements in his chamber works. Neither 'Dumka' nor 'Furiant' can be regarded as a musical form, indeed in the Quintet the latter is only used as a sub-title to what without it would have passed merely as an unusually piquant and brilliant example of the classical scherzo and trio. Placing this 'Dumka' with that from the String Quartet in E flat, Op. 51, and the first movement of the 'Dumky' Trio, it might be difficult for the composition teacher to find the highest common factor and declare, this is the outline of the 'Dumky' form. 'Dumka' and 'Furiant' are in fact not form but spirit; the spirit of lament and a drooping relaxation of energy on the one hand, an ecstasy induced by physical stimulus on the other. The alternation of mood is an implied condition without which each would lose its savour. It was this alternation, the living intensely in each mood in turn, that Dvořák brought to its highest artistic issue in the 'Dumky' Trio. To realize it to the full he threw over his customary structure of sonata form and trusted to his innate instinct to find musical cohesion between the opposition of moods. He could safely do so. The 'Dumky' Trio is a unique work in chamber music literature. In it Dvořák poured forth all that his country stood for in his life and his art, and he left it as a legacy to his countrymen before starting out on his mission to the gentiles.

CHAPTER V

THE ORCHESTRA

THE orchestra is pre-eminently the instrument of the nineteenth century, and the musical history of the century is largely the history of the orchestra's growth. It burgeoned under the influence of romanticism. In 1803 Beethoven used a full orchestra for his Eroica Symphony. It consisted of eight wood-wind players, five brass players, a drummer, and a small body of strings, perhaps twenty, making a total of 34. In 1899 Richard Strauss issued his *Ein Heldenleben* with the following list of orchestral requirements:

Woodwind:	1 piccolo, 3 flutes, 3 oboes, 1 English horn (also 4th oboe), 1 clarinet in E flat, 2 clarinets in B flat, bass clarinet, 3 bassoons, 1 double bassoon	16
Brass:	8 horns, 5 trumpets, 3 trombones, tenor tuba in B flat, bass tuba. . . .	18
Strings:	16 1st violins, 16 2nd violins, 12 violas, 12 violoncelli, 8 double-basses, 2 harps .	66
Percussion:	tympani, bass drum, cymbals, small military drum, tenor drum . . .	5
		105

Strauss's total of 105 players does not seem particularly extravagant to-day, but it shows in the course of a century that the heroic spirit, which impelled Beethoven to enlist the services of a third horn, has swelled the orchestra to thrice its size. So much for mere numbers. Behind the numbers we find the acquisition of new or, at any rate, 'extra' instruments, the improved construction of existing ones, and new methods of writing, which have either demanded or accepted the facilities of greater numbers. These causes of increase differ with each

section. In the woodwind it is chiefly a matter of extra instruments; *Ein Heldenleben* has nine different kinds of woodwind
instrument against the four of the 'Eroica'. The brass are
fairly divided between increased numbers and increased kinds,
but the horns and the trumpets are only the same instruments
in name, since the valve mechanism has given them their full
chromatic compass. The increase in the strings is, on the face
of it, entirely numerical, save for the harps, but the numbers
are necessitated by new methods of handling the traditional
group.

One passage in Beethoven's Ninth Symphony illustrates the
beginning of this change in the use of the strings. Throughout
that Symphony, as indeed normally throughout all the nine, the
strings (1st and 2nd violins, violas, violoncelli, and double-
basses) have acted together in the customary quintet formation.
Suddenly the words, 'Ihr stürzt nieder, Millionen', break that
formation. The violins are silent; violas and violoncelli weave
a dark-toned harmony in four or five parts for which purpose
the violas are divided.[1]

Ex. 1.

From this spring all those divisions of the strings into many
parts and their regroupings in contrasted registers, not only for
the sake of polyphony but for tone colour, which belong to the

[1] Compare with this the divided violas and violoncelli of King Mark's
Monologue in *Tristan*, Act II, and the similarly dark tone of the first
movement of Brahms's *Ein deutsches Requiem*, scored for divided violas
and violoncelli without violins.

orchestration of the romantic era. The opening of the prelude to *Lohengrin*, growing from its high-pitched chord of violins, is typical. It seems scarcely conceivable that Wagner's vision and Tennyson's were independent of one another.

> . . . and the slender sound
> As from a distance beyond distance grew
> Coming upon me—O never harp nor horn,
> Nor aught we blow with breath, or touch with hand,
> Was like that music as it came: and then
> Stream'd thro' my cell a cold and silver beam,
> And down the long beam stole the Holy Grail,
> Rose red with beatings in it, as if alive,
> Till all the white walls of my cell were dyed
> With rosy colours leaping on the wall.[1]

The technical devices first resorted to for a special descriptive end became current usage. That is the way in which the musical vocabulary, especially in the combinations of harmony and timbres, has expanded.

To-day the classification of the violins as ' Firsts ' and ' Seconds ' is merely the survival of a convention.[2] The mass of the violins is divisible into as many parts as there are desks; the violas, violoncelli, and even the double-basses are no longer merely the lower parts of the violin family; each represents a tone quality to be used either melodically or in a complete harmony of its own. In *Ein Heldenleben* the violin solo is accompanied[3] by eleven string parts (doubled by the wind), and this is no extreme

---

[1] *The Holy Grail* was published in 1869, nearly twenty years after the production of *Lohengrin*, but Tennyson, for all the music of his verse, was no musician and certainly no student of Wagner. On the quality of the orchestration of *Lohengrin* see Dannreuther's quotation from Liszt, *Oxford History of Music*, vol. vi, p. 341.

[2] Some conductors, notably Sir Henry Wood, now prefer to seat all their violinists together instead of, as formerly, firsts to left and seconds to right of the conductor, and the last desk of the second violins must be as individually competent as the first of the first violins. Elgar, indeed, at the climax of his First Symphony has written a notable passage for 'last desks only'.

[3] See full score at the number 32.

case of subdivision. The romantic composers demanded the increased numbers of strings to carry out their designs; their successors accepted the legacy and used it, sometimes as in this instance, without any commensurate addition to the scheme of colour. In any case the expansion of the string group has been primarily the composer's business.

Turning to the history of the wind, we see two impelling influences at work; on the one hand the demands of composers stimulating the instrument-makers, many of whom were themselves performers, to improve their mechanisms; on the other, the enterprise of instrument-makers and the skill of players offering to the composers resources which, in point of fact, they were more than a little slow to use.

To the first class belong the additions of keys to the woodwind instruments definitely systematized for the flute by Boehm in 1832 and applied *mutatis mutandis* to the other instruments of that class. Flutes, oboes, and bassoons were playable through practically the entire chromatic compass of the modern instruments before the invention of the Boehm action, and composers satisfied on this count, and often not very conversant with the difficulties involved, were always apt to write what they pleased without much further consideration. But certain scales were very difficult to play in, rapid chromatic passages were uncertain, and many chromatic shakes were impossible. Moreover, the holes had to be placed where the players' fingers could cover them and not in the exact positions which acoustical laws dictate. And the result of this was uncertain intonation which the player had to correct as far as possible by his manner of blowing his instrument. A composer asked that he should play accurately and in tune; the player set himself to improve his instrument and his technique, his efforts finally resulting in the Boehm action and such modifications of it as later experience has suggested.

But it is where new instruments and inventions conferring new powers upon old instruments are concerned that composers have lagged. An early instance is the case of the clarinet,[1] which remained outside the orchestra for half a century after its invention. And its history has been repeated in a dozen instances during the last century. Other members of its family—the small clarinets in D and E flat, the alto clarinet in F, which Berlioz described as 'a very beautiful instrument; one regrets not to find it in all well-constituted orchestras', the bass clarinet an octave below the ordinary one in B flat which had to wait for Wagner to receive full enfranchisement—existed long before composers felt the need of them. The cor anglais or alto oboe, used by Haydn to combine with horns and muted strings in his early Symphony in E flat, called 'The Philosopher', and patronized in chamber music or for special purposes in the theatre, by Mozart, Beethoven, Rossini, and Spontini, was long considered an 'extra instrument', and its complement, the heckelphone, or bass oboe, was still looked upon as something of a curiosity when Delius demanded it for the production of his *Dance Rhapsody* (1909).

It is less surprising that composers for the orchestra showed little anxiety to use the many forms of brass instruments which Sax and others offered. Only tentative efforts were made to give honest employment to the saxophones, virtually brass clarinets of which Adolphe Sax made a complete series, before they were forced into prostitution in the Jazz brothel.

Of considerably more interest is the slowness with which composers became reconciled to the valve and piston mechanisms added to the horns and trumpets quite early in the nineteenth century. The ultimate effect of the invention has been to revolutionize the whole of the music for all brass instruments other than trombones. Yet although the invention which per-

[1] See *The Oxford History of Music*, vol. v, pp. 44–5.

fected these instruments was made about the time of Wagner's birth (1813), he grew up using the natural horns and trumpets, and Brahms, born twenty years later, wrote his scores to the end of his life as though he contemplated performance by the natural instruments only.

One might well ask why instrument-makers took the trouble to provide perfected tools which the greatest artists showed such shyness in accepting. The reason is not far to seek. The valve instruments were not perfected in the moment of their invention, and they were coarsely blown by bad players. Instrument-makers were not primarily concerned with the development of the orchestra, and orchestral composers, having an almost inexhaustible resource in the strings, were in no hurry to have equal facilities in the other departments of their scores.

It is in the wind bands of popular music, either the town bands maintained all through central Europe which had begun with the 'Türmer' or city watchmen of medieval times, or the military bands said to have been an outcome in Germany of the Thirty Years' War (1618–48), that we meet with the real force which pushed on the cultivation of wind instruments. The wind bands, civil and military, have been a constant and devoted nurse to the orchestra. Musicians have generally despised them and always profited by them. We owe to the town musicians of Leipzig the delicate shades of instrumental colouring in J. S. Bach's 'Passions' and Cantatas, and the military exploits of both Frederick the Great and Napoleon contributed scarcely less directly to provide many of the richest colours of the modern orchestra.

Frederick the Great's organization of the Prussian bands in 1763 was undertaken to provide a definite scheme of instrumentation to supersede the heterogeneous collections of fifes, oboes, drums, in fact any available instruments, which had served previously to supply the regiments with a marching

rhythm. Oboes, clarinets, horns, and bassoons were made the
basis of the scheme, thus giving the preponderance to instruments
with a complete scale, the oboes and clarinets which could play
real tunes, the bassoons which could support them with real
basses. The imperfect horns could add a stronger body of tone,
support the tune, or supply middle harmonies of a rudimentary
kind.[1]

But the louder brass instruments of the trumpet, bugle, and
horn types were not to be kept in subjection to their weaker-
voiced companions of wood. Their penetrating sounds gave
them the advantage in the open air and their immemorial
connexion with the arts of war, their utility for the sounding
of signals, gave them prestige. 'The Trumpet's loud clangour'
was in fact bound to remain the salient characteristic of a military
band, and having regard to the imperfect state of these instruments it is evident that the greater the 'clangour' the less could
be the music of the band. The attempts to rectify the balance
were many. Both oboes and clarinets were multiplied as an
opposing melodic force, but as the oboe became better made
and better played its true character as a weak and plaintive
instrument became more evident. Single reed instruments, the
clarinets, could do better. With a purer and a stronger tone, a
greater capacity for playing both loud and soft, and a wider
compass, they were obviously more fitted to take the place in the
military band which the strings occupy in the orchestra. Their

[1]. A Saxon March preserved in the Royal Museum at Munich, and
dating from about 1720 (reprinted in J. A. Käppey's *Military Music: a
history of wind-instrument Bands*), shows that this idea of military instrumentation was no new one. Frederick the Great was merely giving it the
sanction of authority. This March in D major, with a Trio in G, is scored
for two oboes, two clarinets in D, two trumpets in D, two horns in D, two
horns in G, and two bassoons. The trumpets and horns in D are used only
in the principal March, the horns in G only in the Trio. As an instance of
the early employment of clarinets on equal terms with the oboes for
strengthening the melody, this little work is important.

numbers were increased, they were made in various sizes, small ones for high parts and large ones for low parts, and so were gradually fitted to form an effective counterpoise to the brass.

Such an increase, however, entails considerable expenditure in men and money, and obviously the only really satisfactory solution was the perfecting of the warlike brass instruments. At the end of the eighteenth and the beginning of the nineteenth centuries many experiments were put forward to this end.

The problem for all these instruments may be stated in general terms thus. Each one is a tube blown through a mouth-piece at one end and opening out into a conical bell at the other. The tone of these instruments is largely affected by the extent to which the tube is conical, and the shorter the tube the more important does the conical formation become, so that one of the chief aims of instrument-makers has been to use tubes which, as far as possible, increase in bore by regular degrees from the mouthpiece to the bell. Such a tube eight feet long produces the note CC and simultaneously the harmonic series generated by that note.

Ex. 2.[1]

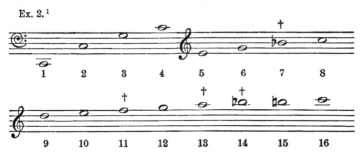

Besides their composite presence in the sound of the fundamental note, each one of these notes may be obtained separately by

---

[1] The 7th, 13th, and 14th are all flatter in actual sound than the pitch of B flat and A, the notes by which they are represented; the 11th is sharper than the true F.

using varying degrees of lip pressure, and it is by this means
that the player of a natural brass instrument obtains different
notes. He is always blowing harmonics.

Now the obvious way of filling up the blank spaces in the scale
is to provide some means by which the tube can be lengthened at
will. Additions lowering the fundamental note by tones or semitones will produce a complete new series of harmonics, giving
ultimately a consistent chromatic scale. That was early done
in the case of the trombone by fitting it with a slide. Slide
trombones were already in use at the beginning of the sixteenth
century, that is to say, before Palestrina was born, and the success of the principle is proved by the fact that the trombone of
the modern orchestra remains essentially the same as the instrument in use at that date. A slide, however, can only be applied
to instruments which contain a fairly long piece of straight cylindrical tubing. The conical bore of bugles and horns, which gives
them their special qualities of tone, makes a slide impracticable.

The trumpet with its longer length of cylindrical tube is
amenable to the slide, but the method of holding the instrument
straight up at right angles to the body makes a slide difficult
and tiring to handle, and altogether unmanageable on the march.
Such a trumpet was invented and much used by virtuoso players
in England in the latter part of the eighteenth century. Its
greatest exponent was Thomas Harper (born 1787).

Sir George Smart, visiting Munich in 1825, admired the military
band mounting guard at the Palace and wrote of it as 'about
forty strong with four trombones, but I have not yet heard
a good sounding trumpet'. On the same occasion he heard *Der
Freischütz* at the opera and remarked 'the tromboni were good
but I have not yet heard a trumpeter equal to Harper'. That
was natural, for Harper played on the slide trumpet which
instrument-makers still point to as being the perfect instrument
if only performers would surmount its difficulties of execution.

That the slide trumpet was rejected on the Continent is evidence that players and makers were not searching for the best artistic instruments but for practical military ones; in fact that the needs of wind bands and not those of the orchestra were pressing upon them most heavily.

The slide itself being inapplicable to some instruments and unpractical for others, the question arose whether its results could be obtained by other mechanism. Two methods were available and both were tried in certain instances. The first was to pierce the tubes with holes, using keys to cover the holes, a method akin to that of woodwind instruments, which has the effect of shortening the tube by cutting off from its speaking length the part below the opened hole. Applied to the bugle, the smallest and least important of brass instruments, by Weidinger in Vienna (1795), the result was the keyed bugle, an instrument of an intolerably vulgar tone. The same plan adapted to larger instruments resulted in the ophicleide, which, though having many of the disadvantages of the keyed bugle, was accepted temporarily as a practicable bass for military music and even gained a foothold in the orchestra. Another attempt in the same direction was the serpent, a descendant of the ancient cornetto (German 'Zincke'), which, though played with a mouthpiece like the brass, was made of wood covered with leather.

These experiments sufficed to show that instruments played with a mouthpiece (not a reed) lose their characteristic brilliance and nobility of tone when the note is emitted not through the bell but through a side hole. So the problem remained unsolved for horns and trumpets until, a few years later, the all-important invention of valves, the joint work of two men, Silesians, Blümel and Stölzel of Breslau, brought what was wanted.

The principle of the valve action is that by depressing a piston with the finger the wind passing from the player's mouth to the bell is diverted through an additional length of tube, which, lowering the fundamental note, produces a new series of harmonics, each of which may be sounded by the player. With three pistons (two only were used in the early instruments) the following changes can be made. The first piston lowers a whole tone, the second a semitone, the third three semitones. They can also be used in combination, the first and second together producing the same result as the third alone (a minor third); the second and third lowering four semitones (a major third); the first and third, five (a perfect fourth); all three together, six (an augmented fourth). It will be seen that when certain acoustical difficulties had been met which at first made the conglomerations of semitones not well in tune, these instruments were provided by the three pistons with a complete chromatic scale from their first harmonic upwards.

The mechanism could be easily applied to all brass instruments and was rapidly adopted for all save the trombones, which were already provided for. The result was that through the first half of the nineteenth century innumerable types made their appearance. The valves were applied, not only to the horns and trumpets of the orchestra, but to instruments of all sorts of length and all sizes of bore, from the short cornets à pistons to ponderous bass tubas. The latter became recognized as the best means of adding the complement of a profound bass to the trombones, and were adopted by Berlioz, Wagner, and Liszt in their later works, and by Brahms in his two overtures and Second Symphony, though not elsewhere in his symphonies. Wagner's bass trumpet and his quartet of tubas differing from the bass tuba both in size and in the shape of their mouthpieces, were valuable additions to the two departments of trumpet and horn tone, devised for the special requirements of sonority in *Der Ring des Nibelungen.*[1]

[1] For an account of Bruckner's adoption of Wagner's tubas as part of the symphonic orchestra see below, Chapter VI, p. 170.

The military bands soon began to suffer from the *embarras de richesses*, and as early as the year 1828 the instrumentation of both reed bands and brass bands in Germany had become so confused that a musical field-marshal was required to deal with them. This was one, Wieprecht, a civilian with a genius for organization, who obtained authority to reconstitute the bands of the Prussian Guards. His scheme for a complete brass band deserves quotation:

> 2 Cornets in E flat (3 valves each)
> 3 Keyed Bugles
> 2 Cornets in B flat (2 valves each)
> 8 Trumpets (2 valves each)
> 2 Tenor Horns—barytones
> 1 Euphonium in B flat (3 valves)
> 3 Bass Trombones (slides).

His efforts culminated ten years later in a performance of massed bands before the King of Prussia.

Meantime in France, wind bands, military and civil, had grown in importance from the time of the Revolution when open-air demonstrations and fêtes served to stimulate popular enthusiasm. The bands of Napoleon's army reached a high level of executive ability, and although the valved instruments seem to have been a little slow in gaining acceptance, when they did come, the French, with characteristic ardour, made up for lost time by giving them definite places not only in wind bands but in the orchestra itself.

The orchestra in Paris before the arrival of its champion, Hector Berlioz, was chiefly the orchestra of the opera. Such concerts as existed, the old 'Concerts Spirituels' (for which in their flourishing days Mozart and Haydn had written their famous 'Paris' Symphonies) and their successors the 'Concerts du Conservatoire', founded by Habeneck, Director of the Opera and Berlioz's arch-enemy, were not powerful enough to exercise any distinct influence upon orchestral technique. Comparatively little symphonic work was written for them. Composers made their mark in Paris through the theatre or the church, and the music of the latter was often scarcely less theatrical than was that which belonged by right to the opera-house. But the theatrical atmosphere was the very thing most calculated to encourage the free development of orchestral colouring. The needs of representation, of stage pageantry, of adjusting the musical phrase to the expression of a dramatic moment, of impressing the prevailing emotion without obscuring the voice of the singer, all tend to produce in the theatre a subtle adaptability on the part of the dramatic composer and his orchestra, which purely symphonic music does not foster to a like extent.

We have only to compare the score of *Don Giovanni* with its contemporaries, the three symphonies of 1788, to see how Mozart had appreciated the different needs of the two types. Nowhere in the symphonies do we find the sudden alternations of fortissimo with pianissimo made by the full orchestra which are so vivid a feature of the last scene, the coming of the Statue to the feast, in *Don Giovanni*. When contrasts of loud and soft are required in the symphonies, for example in the finale of the Symphony in G minor, they are got by alternating piano strings with a forte of the full orchestra. In symphonic music up to Beethoven's day the simultaneous use of many instruments as constantly means a general forte as the employment of individuals or sections of the band implies restraint of tone. A comparison of the grave-digging scene of *Fidelio* (Act II) with the Finale of the Fifth Symphony affords an instance in Beethoven similar to that found in Mozart. Most of Beethoven's extensions of orchestral technique are symphonic, but here using virtually the same large orchestra in both cases, it is in the opera that the extra instruments are ranged on the side of intimacy. In the Finale of the Symphony double bassoons and trombones are introduced chiefly for the sake of sonority. They participate in the overwhelming climax of the movement; in quiet moments they are silent. In the opera the scene begins with held chords for the woodwind, horns, and trombones pianissimo; the strings muted maintain a mysterious tremolo; the double bassoon and the double basses (without violoncelli) reiterate a figure in triplets; the whole scheme contributes to build up that sense of fearfully impending tragedy with which Leonora encounters her husband in the darkened cell. In *Don Giovanni* and *Fidelio* alike it is the menace, not the dénouement, which impels the composer to seek intimate effect from many instruments in combination, and it is in this direction especially that opera has contributed to modern orchestral technique.

Spontini,[1] spoken of by Berlioz as one of the three great masters of orchestration (Beethoven and Weber being the other two), secured his most distinctive strokes of orchestration by the opposite means to these. He would achieve forcible effect from a few instruments rather than an intimate one from many. Through whole movements, and indeed through all the big climaxes of *La Vestale* and *Olympie*, his large orchestra was employed to produce the utmost amount of sound possible. Often he wrote carelessly in such passages, doubling the parts not for the sake of a distinct colour but merely in order that additional instruments might swell the chorus of sound. On the other hand, when these fortissimo tornadoes were allowed to subside, he would produce a singularly striking effect of colour from a few individuals. In the overture to *La Vestale*, the full orchestra suddenly breaks off upon the chord of A major, the woodwind, trombones, and strings fall upon an F natural marked *fff* which dies in the space of one bar to an E marked *ppp* taken up and sustained by the horns, round which the flutes and bassoons enter and dwell softly upon a fragment of the theme. It is an exquisite moment of instrumental dovetailing,

[1] See *Oxford History of Music*, vol. v, p. 185 et seq.

a thing which can only be achieved by a great conductor who knows the genius of his instruments intimately.

Spontini's scores are more fully marked with signs of forte, piano, crescendo, and diminuendo than are any other scores of the period. His conceptions of music were too intimately bound up with the exact quality of sound required for him to leave such a matter to chance. One may, indeed, often feel that he made up his music from a basis of tone qualities, as the great symphonists made up theirs from the basis of the melodic idea. It was on this account, no doubt, that he appealed so strongly to Berlioz, whose temperament led him in the same direction, and the use of elaborate markings springs from these two, and has become more and more prevalent in modern orchestration, until it has reached an extreme point in the scores of Gustav Mahler and Edward Elgar.

Spontini was foremost among those composers who made a regular practice of writing for four horns in two pairs, each pair in a different key,[1] with the object of producing a greater range of notes than could be got from the imperfect natural instruments, were they all in one key. Obviously to multiply the instruments and place them in different keys has in the long run the same result as the use of the valves; for, as we have seen, the valves are merely changing the key of the natural instrument, but changing it more rapidly than is practicable by the use of crooks. But it was not until Berlioz gave his enterprising mind to the problem of their use that all the possibilities of their combination in various keys were thoroughly explored. An instance of his combination of them to gain full harmonies may be quoted from the early part of the 'Romeo and Juliet' Symphony, where in order to get accompanying chords in four-part harmony, he places his four horns in the keys of E, E flat, G, and F.

[1] The occasional use of the device goes back as far as Handel's *Giulio Cesare*.

Ex. 3.

The horn, indeed, offered a more engaging problem to composers at this date than the trumpet, because of its power of intimate expression in soft passages, and the virtuosity of its performers. The nature of the horns had enabled the players to find various ways of overcoming their disabilities in the matter of range. While the trumpet players were forced to restrict themselves to their open notes, the curved horns were able to make use of many notes not contained in their natural series of harmonics by means of the hand inserted in the bell of the instrument, producing closed notes. Their quality could not be equal to that of the open notes; they were always dull and muffled, but the skilful player learnt to tone open and closed notes into one another, and their contrast placed a new sound at the disposal of the composer. Even Spontini could write the following for a solo horn in ballet music (Act III) of *La Vestale* (Ex. 4). Its chromaticisms can be achieved by a skilful player using the stopped notes. Its ornaments can only be neatly executed by one possessing an extraordinarily sensitive lip. Its open and closed notes require the most careful blending. Some composers used the stopped notes merely as a makeshift; others turned them to account by placing them in a prominent part of their scores and obtaining new sounds from them.[1] Berlioz fully realized the resources offered by the closed notes and used them with consummate skill. A salient example is the beginning of the 'March to the Scaffold' in the *Symphonie Fantastique*, where both the soft A and G sharp are of necessity stopped notes.

[1] The famous passage for the fourth horn in the slow movement of Beethoven's Choral Symphony is, as Berlioz pointed out, practicable upon a natural instrument using the closed notes. But the complete scale in A flat produces a very curious effect when it is played, as it is written, upon a natural horn in E flat, entailing a mixture of open and closed notes. Whether Beethoven, who of course never heard it, merely wrote the passage relying on information which told him that it could be performed, or whether he calculated upon the unevenness of tone as one of his resources, cannot be proved with certainty now.

Ex. 4.

* Spontini here writes actual sounds for horn, using the mezzo-soprano clef.   Note the use of the sharp sign to the B♮—correct if the part is read as horn in F in the treble clef.

Such devices appealed to Berlioz's imagination and exercised his mental ingenuity; he loved to conjure with his horns in many keys, to contrast their stopped and open notes, and so to turn their disadvantages of construction into advantage for his own music. The somewhat grudging acknowledgement of the possibilities of the valve horn in his work on instrumentation is due to this; he could not willingly be robbed of the chances of exerting his skill through imperfect instruments because a perfect mechanism was offered him instead of it. Wagner in a note to the score of *Tristan* drew particular attention to his writing for the horns, and showed that though he fully accepted the possibilities offered by the valved horns he wished to preserve the use of closed notes, and from his use of the horns in *Tristan* springs the practice of differentiating between the ordinary clear sounds of the horns and the muted tone so freely used by modern composers.

In the case of the trumpets, however, Berlioz had to surrender more rapidly. The natural trumpets offered less field for his ingenuity, so he, as most of the operatic composers of Paris had done previously, supplemented them by the cornets à pistons. Attempts had been made to apply the method of stopped notes with the hand, so fruitful in the case of the horn, to its companion the trumpet; but the position of the instrument was again against it as it had been against the use of the slide.[1] Until the valve trumpet became definitely accepted, writing for that instrument remained very much what it had been in the time of Mozart. The French operatic writers constantly used two natural trumpets and two cornets, the former to employ their brilliant tone upon the striking moments which were within their range, the latter to supply melodic music both diatonic and chromatic and to fill in the deficiencies of the natural trumpet.

Rossini, indeed, in *Guillaume Tell* writes for two 'trompettes à clefs', but the music given to them is fairly tentative. Their melodies still retain the general arpeggio form which had become traditional for the natural trumpets. Halévy in *La Juive* writes for two 'trompettes à pistons' with two natural trumpets, and these valve trumpets are distinguished in Act V from the 'cornets à pistons' used more frequently. For both he writes daringly to

[1] The maker, Michael Wöggel (about 1780), had attempted to secure this possibility for the trumpet by making a bent instrument which enabled the player to bring his hand more easily to the bell. But nothing permanent came of this attempt.

the point of vulgarity; the cornets must play arpeggio figures of accompaniment such as the following:

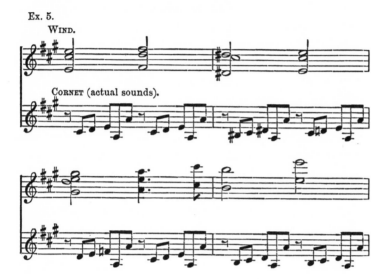

Ex. 5.

WIND.

CORNET (actual sounds).

Complete chromatic scales for both trumpets and cornets are written:

Ex. 6.

TRUMPETS IN A.

They are in fact playing on equal terms with the strings and the woodwind, and the method shows a complete change from that of Rossini nine years earlier. But the score of *La Juive* takes into account the fact that these instruments were not to be had in every theatre, and wherever the composer writes for them the parts are rather reinforcements of what is being played elsewhere than independent additions; they are in fact 'ad libitum', and not 'obbligato'.

Berlioz could not be content with such a compromise. The

very essence of his instrumental style is its exact calculation of ultimate effect; remove a single instrument, even alter the construction of one, and his most characteristic qualities leave the score. He therefore retained the natural trumpets through the bulk of his work, though in his book on instrumentation he heartily endorses the value of the new instruments. He, in common with most sensitive colourists, did not like the cornets. He warns against their lack of dignity.

The cornets never gained a foothold in the orchestra outside France, though in Paris they were accepted so much as a matter of course that César Franck found place for them in the score of his symphony, using two cornets à pistons in B flat with two valve trumpets in F. Wagner, following French precedent, used cornets in *Rienzi*; but in general both Germany and England,[1] having had cause to pride themselves on the skill of their trumpet-players, resisted the cornet's vulgar invasion.

Wagner's much lamented time of privation in Paris (1839–40) had its compensation in widening an orchestral experience which previously had been more or less limited by his own work as conductor of German operatic orchestras of inferior quality. He arrived in the autumn of 1839, was present at the first performance of Berlioz's *Romeo et Juliette* Symphony, heard also the earlier *Symphonie Fantastique, Harold in Italy,* and the *Symphonie Funèbre* first given in a great open-air performance in July 1840. Wagner has left a vivid description of the effect made on him by Berlioz's art of the orchestra. He was at once ravished by the sound of these things, yet 'repelled and even wearied by them'.[2] He felt 'almost like a little schoolboy' in

---

[1] Had the art of orchestration been more independently studied in England by composers, the skill of such players as Hyde and Harper might have had a greater effect upon the progress of this instrument in the orchestra. But there was too little orchestral enterprise in this country to make their examples effective.

[2] *My Life*, vol. i, p. 235.

the presence of Berlioz's masterly control of the massed forces of orchestra and military band in the *Symphonie Funèbre*.[1] Well might he have some searchings of heart about the effect of the six trumpets,[2] even if he could have obtained them, in his own youthful *Columbus* overture, and well might Berlioz smile over the rehearsal of Wagner's truncated score and hint that it was 'hard to succeed in Paris'.

Wagner absorbed all that the French Opera, under the influence of Meyerbeer and Halévy, and the imaginative programme symphony of Berlioz's invention, could teach him of this new world in orchestration. His ultimate style reflected neither. One may search in vain through the grotesque antics of the inhabitants of Nibelheim for any counterpart to the following from Berlioz's 'March to the Scaffold' (Ex. 7). Wagner habitually instruments the whole phrase; Berlioz here, and often elsewhere, delights in scoring across the phrase. In these six bars he passes in a rapid review every group of instruments, woodwind, brass, drums (in chords), strings both arco and pizzicato. They colour the phrase kaleidoscopically without serving to distinguish any contour of melody or progression of harmony. Where Wagner's instruments are made to share a melodic phrase between them, it is done to reinforce some specially important implication of harmony. Isolde's 'Tod

---

[1] Its prodigious score contains a military piccolo (D flat), flutes, including six in E flat, oboes, clarinets in E flat, in B flat, and bass clarinets, six horn parts, bassoon, double bassoon, four trumpet parts, two cornet parts, trombones, ophicleides, and a whole battery of percussion. Strings take a modest place as 'ad libitum' additions which for once Berlioz was able to admit, probably realizing, as he did so, that they would not be heard.

[2] The six trumpets of Wagner's *Columbus* are the natural instruments and of them he writes: '. . . dieses Instrument, welches den Deutschen so virtuosenhaft geläufig ist, in den Pariser Orchestern nur selten gut besetzt werden kann.' The mistranslation in *My Life* (vol. i, p. 236) of 'trompette' as 'cornet' entirely falsifies the remark. There were, as Wagner had cause to know only too well, plenty of cornet players to be had in Paris.

Ex. 7.

geweihtes Haupt' is an unforgettable instance, and here (Ex. 8) the progression is actually completed in the parts which began it; woodwind and brass are dovetailed into one another.

In *Tristan* certain types of colour are maintained for long
stretches. Within the span there is an infinite variation of
detail, but the details are contributory to the general type.
Painters speak of 'keys of colour', taking the simile from
musical tonality. With Wagner's orchestration the phrase can
be readopted for music in a fresh connexion. The old writers,
notably Bach, had habitually written in a certain 'key of colour',

choosing their groups of obbligato instruments and remaining
content with their scope through a whole movement or even
a whole work.[1] The acquisition of the innumerable tints of the
modern orchestra had loosened the hold of composers on this
principle. Wagner revived it, and nowhere more conspicuously
than in *Tristan*. He maintains his 'key of colour' not only
through his choice of instruments for a given scene but through
his placing of them. Trumpets may be as grave as trombones;
it depends what they are required to do. In the prelude to
Tristan the trumpets in F participate only in three bars of the
climax, and then only in their middle register. In the first scene
low trumpet notes begin to appear with Isolde's 'Hört meinen
Willen', and it is only with the pianissimo chord of the above
quotation that their contribution to the colour becomes conspicuous. The trumpet being the least amalgamable of orchestral
instruments, Wagner's ability to make it contribute to a scheme
of colour which precludes its natural brilliance of tone is the
strongest evidence of his maturity in the orchestration of *Tristan*.

Similar evidence is found, though in a less striking manner, by
tracing his handling of other instruments or groups of instruments through the several scenes of that inexhaustible score.
The dark tone of King Mark's monologue in Act II (divided
violas and violoncelli, bassoons and bass clarinet predominating)
is obvious, but note the delicate entrance of cor anglais and oboe
at the words, 'Dies wundervolle Weib'. The orchestration is
sensitive to the tender reverence underlying the words without
changing its essential character. And this sensitiveness is present
through the whole range of Wagner's orchestral tone, loud and
soft.

It is as true as any generalization can be, to say that Wagner

---

[1] Contrast for example the subdued 'key of colour' of the *St. Matthew
Passion*, flutes and oboes, with the brilliant trumpets and drums of the
Christmas Oratorio.

was the first composer to realize that fortissimo may mean as
many different things as pianissimo. An analysis of Wagner's
full orchestra chords will show that a different colour is produced
by the different distribution of the instruments over the five
octaves which represent the orchestra's normal range. The
weakness of the old symphonic orchestra, that of Beethoven's
day, was in the bass. Its fortissimo was like an old-fashioned
full organ chord supported on a rather inadequate 16-foot pedal.
The new instruments of the nineteenth century rectified that
misproportion, just as the provision of a large pedal organ of
reed and flue stops has rectified it in the modern organ-builder's
specifications. Wagner applied the resources not only to get
more tone but to get variety of tone, that is variety of emotional
implication in fortissimo. Compare, for example, the chord of
A flat in which the duet of the prologue to *Götterdämmerung*
ends, with the exclamatory chords which punctuate the 'Funeral
March'. The former is all brightness and light though the
trumpets, curiously enough, are omitted. The weight is, as it
were, pushed up. The treble woodwind, violins, and voices are
in their highest octaves; the harp arpeggio and the trombones'
figure from the 'Walkürenritt' swoop upwards; only the contra-
bass tuba and the string double-basses sustain a deep bass.
In the 'Funeral March' chords, on the other hand, the weight is
massed more in the middle octaves, and only piccolo and flutes
are left shrieking at the top, perhaps a hint of Gutrune's hysteria.
From the 'Funeral March' onward climax is piled on climax but
not until fourteen bars from the end are all the instruments
brought into requisition simultaneously. The final chord of all
with its even distribution of wind parts through the entire
compass of six octaves brings a sense of complete equipoise.
All has been expiated.

Thus in *Tristan* and *Der Ring des Nibelungen* Wagner made
his art of orchestration into an integral part of his dramatic and

emotional conceptions, and so fused colour with line (melody and harmony) that the old habit of mind, which regarded scoring as an extraneous decoration added to music which would be substantially the same without it, had to be outgrown. No longer was it possible to say, as composition teachers so frequently had said, that the best way to judge the quality of an orchestral score is to reduce it to a piano score. That may be the way to lay bare poverty of invention and inherent faults of structure which attractive orchestration tends to gloss over, especially to a not very critical ear. But when the instrumentation is realized as an essential concomitant of the form, making its own contribution to the content of the work, to ignore it may be to render obscure or even incoherent what is perfectly perspicuous in its own setting. It was Wagner more than any other who made it clear that successful orchestration depends on the capacity to think in an orchestral texture,[1] and more than that to think in the texture of the particular group of instruments in use, however large it may be. He solved for the large orchestra the problem which Brahms solved no less perfectly for small groups of instruments in chamber music, particularly, as we have seen, in the combination of piano and strings. Wagner's highest flights of orchestral imagination simply refuse to be reduced satisfactorily to a piano score despite all the skill of men like von Bülow, Klindworth, Klein Michel, and others.[2]

[1] Verdi affords a striking and simple instance of the dependence of orchestration on texture. His orchestration remained poor while his texture remained thin. The revision of a single bar in *Simon Boccanegra* quoted by Mr. Francis Toye (*Giuseppe Verdi, His Life and Works*, p. 344) shows at a glance Verdi's progress in the feeling for texture animating the revision of his orchestration.

[2] For an example compare the full score with its reduction to four-part harmony in the vocal score of the passage in Tristan's monologue (Act III, sc. i) beginning at the words 'Für diese Hitze heisses Verschmachten'. The whole passage surges forward on a bass of the 'alte ernste Weise' piped by the shepherd. Other motives mingle with this bass. The whole is a fulfilment

After him and after Berlioz any one could employ the acquisitions of the modern orchestra with effect, and it required only ingenuity to extend the range of effects by further thickening the texture, as men like Strauss and Schönberg (in the early period of the *Gurrelieder*) have done. It did not even require ingenuity, but merely assiduity, to make an orchestra sound like Wagner's, as so many of his less distinguished disciples delighted to do. For a time the peculiar glow of Wagner's orchestration was so attractive that all the second-rate composers were more than content to catch in their scores some reflection of it. His orchestra became the standard by which all others were judged. To score like Wagner was considered to be the hall-mark of good work. Any one who refused his example was written down a bad workman. Brahms refused, therefore it was said that he could not handle an orchestra, despite the fact that he had spent a full third of his life in deciding exactly what he wanted from an orchestra, disciplining his mind to evolve an orchestral texture of his own. Because he did this so thoroughly, Brahms is the most distinctive orchestrator of the generation after Wagner, although he never invented a single new 'effect'. But this statement can only be substantiated by an intensive study of his symphonies.

In the years after Wagner's death Richard Strauss (born 1864) began to make his mark as a daring orchestrator. The tone poem, 'Tondichtung', *Don Juan*, his Opus 20, first heard in Berlin in 1888, declared his emancipation from the way of the perfect classic which he had chosen in his student days. *Macbeth*, an earlier work though given the later opus number, 22, had shown him experimenting in the direction of Liszt's ideal of orchestral characterization, but it was with *Don Juan* that he

of all that has preceded it in the course of the act, and in the orchestral version it produces a wonderfully visionary effect. In the piano version it appears like only a rather crabbed piece of harmonic development.

entered into the complete heritage of both Wagner's and Berlioz's orchestras. In it he displayed something of Wagner's power of creating broad yet sharply defined themes associated with dramatic personalities, while at the same time he developed Berlioz's technique of stippling with the instruments around these representative themes. The Carnival scene in *Don Juan* set beside the Venusberg music (Paris Version) of *Tannhäuser* and the 'Nuit de Sabbat' of the *Symphonie Fantastique* reveals the double derivation of Strauss's orchestral technique. In fairly quick succession there followed *Tod und Verklärung, Till Eulenspiegels lustige Streiche, Also sprach Zarathustra, Don Quixote* (solo violoncello with orchestra), and *Ein Heldenleben*. All these not only showed his increasing power in the manipulation of the hundred-voiced orchestra, but justified abnormal musical processes of polyphonic harmony on the ground that an abnormal phase of human psychology was illustrated. The delirium of the dying man, the perverse humour of Till, the abstruse verbosity of the Zarathustrian philosophy, and the madness of Don Quixote led him along paths which ended for others, if not for himself, in that disintegration of the classical tonal system which has been pointed to as the dividing line of the centuries. His pioneership in this direction belongs to a later phase of history than that which is here discussed.

It is impossible, however, to close a chapter on the orchestra in the nineteenth century without reference to the prodigious scores of Richard Strauss's contemporary, Gustav Mahler (1860–1911). Viewed from the standpoint of orchestral technique his work in a series of nine completed symphonies is important as that of a great orchestral director who had acquired by practical experience an intimate knowledge of every timbre and combination of timbres of which a large orchestra is capable. He did with the improved resources of the end of the century what Berlioz had done with those of the middle of the century.

The first pages of his first symphony attest his meticulous care in deploying his orchestral troops. The strings holding a long sustained A (harmonic), the violoncelli and double-basses dividing each into three equal parts for the purpose, the wood-wind calling to one another 'wie ein Naturlaut', the three trumpets beginning their fanfares in the far distance, coming nearer, presently taking their places in the orchestra; all these details, with carefully inserted 'stage directions', show Mahler as an orchestral 'producer' rather than as a composer. And what is seen in this essentially simple nature-scene which begins the series of his works is characteristic of all in greater or less degree, at any rate up to the Eighth with its huge conglomeration of solo and choral voices added to the instruments, and its naïve reliance on tone-qualities, even to the use of mandolines, as contributory to the expression of a religious ecstasy.

Mahler's craftsmanship in these directions was inexhaustible, though it was sometimes expended on devices which produce no commensurate effect. In the Scherzo of the Fourth Symphony, for example, a solo violin is directed to tune up a whole tone and is then written for as a transposing instrument. At one point in the Seventh Symphony rapid chromatic scales on the string' are written to be bowed staccato but played with the same fing' on each note. Such details are virtuosity pursued for its own sa'

If the symphonies of Mahler did nothing else they should h taught composers the lesson they have been so reluctant to l that extra instruments, and the multiplication of technica' plexities in the use of them, are no evidence of extra orig' Their defect is obliviousness of that principle referred t as taught by Wagner's later works and illustrated by Strauss at his best, that of a necessary correspondence beι.. the musical texture and the instrumentation. Certain of Mahler's most carefully planned orchestral effects fall flat because they are, as it were, laid on to a too thinly woven fabric. They call for a high degree of manipulative skill on the part of the conductor and the players, but they fail to arrest the attention of the listeners without a score. In his last works Mahler certainly acquired a higher sense of the relation between texture and tone. After the Eighth Symphony came *Das Lied von der Erde* which, though called a symphony, is more in the nature of a lyrical song-cycle (alto and tenor soli) with elaborate but well-controlled orchestral commentary. The Ninth Symphony, purely instrumental, and the two movements of the unfinished Tenth return to the use of what had become the normal large-scale orchestra; both show Mahler fastening his attention more closely on thematic construction. It has been suggested that when he died in the fifty-first year of his age he was on the eve of a creative period to which the brilliant interpretative career was merely the prelude. Be that as it may, he is to be noted here as the artist whose supreme virtuosity as conductor explored and exploited to the full the resources of the orchestra at the end of the century of its richest development.

CHAPTER VI

SYMPHONY IN VIENNA

SYMPHONY is organic music. It does not depend on the use of any particular kind of musical material, or on the music being cast in any particular mould. Indeed, its organic nature makes the metaphor of cast and mould inapplicable. The one essential principle underlying it is growth. The composer's thought may start from anything, from a germ of four notes in a rhythmic pattern like Beethoven's Fifth, or from a complete 8-bar tune like the first Allegro of Haydn's 'London' Symphony in D. All that is essential to symphonic character is that the initial motive should in its inception represent to the composer's mind some issue larger than itself, and the subsequent movement (or group of movements) must reveal to the hearer what that larger issue is. If it does not do that, the initial motive will remain only a tune, a good tune possibly, one which we shall like to hear again, but still no more than itself.

The composer who has invented such a self-contained tune may set it before his hearers in any way he likes, enrich it with decorative variations, give it the relief of contrasting episodes and heighten its effect by the pleasure of recognition on its return, but the result will not be symphony, although these devices do in fact play some part in every known specimen of symphony. They are the technical means which the symphonic composer uses in the process of unfolding the larger issue of his conception, but they are equally serviceable without any such conception, in fact the composer whose ideas are of the non-fructifying tune type will be the more dependent on them for carrying on his music. He it is who casts in a mould, and even if his chosen mould should be the elaborate one known as sonata form, and the work be scored for a large orchestra, the result will still not be genuine symphony. The distinction depends on whether the technical means are used to further the principle of organic growth, or whether they are resorted to in default of that principle.

How the principle should be exhibited to the hearers depends solely on what the composer wants to say to them through his music. But in whatever way it appears it will always take the hearers, and perhaps one might say the composer himself, by surprise. Broadly speaking, the surprise may be said to be one of two kinds: it will be either that of the prophet Ezekiel in the valley of dry bones, or that of Pygmalion before his perfect statue. Both are the surprise of a new life, but the one is life from the dead, the other life bestowed on a conception of static beauty. Of the first type is the Finale to Beethoven's 'Eroica'. The dry bones of tonic and dominant are brought together, then clothed with sinews and with flesh of melody and harmony in the completed theme; they receive the breath of life in the subsequent process of development by variation. Rarely is the whole process of symphonic growth displayed *ab initio* as it is in this stupendous movement. The rhythmic life is existent in the first statement of the four-note motive of the Fifth Symphony and is felt from the beginning to be latent in the embryonic opening figures of the Ninth. Nothing of what is to come can be foreseen from the initial bars of the Finale to 'Eroica.'

All these and other examples of Beethoven, however, illustrate in varying degrees the first type, the growth of symphony from materials which in themselves are nothing, or next to nothing. Beethoven's preference for this type has resulted in a tendency to proclaim it alone to be true symphony, but to do so ignores facts. The long-drawn melody, perfect in its fully articulated features, its flowing lines and gracious poise, may, like Pygmalion's statue, come to life in symphony, and the process which brings it life may be, indeed must be, something quite different from that direct fashioning of phrases into features inevitable in the former case. The composer of such a symphony does not set out in quest of beauty; he starts with it. What next? Its life must appear in movement; the movement must declare that the gracious poise is something more than a momentary pose.

It is in this direction that Mozart's symphonic genius most appears. The consummate instance of it is the first Allegro of his Symphony in E flat (Koechel 543), a work as extreme in its way as is the Finale to Beethoven's 'Eroica' in its opposite way. The opening melody with its irregular phrase-forms, exquisitely balanced, comes as near to the ideal of complete and self-contained beauty as any twenty-eight bars of music have ever come. Any attempt at development of it along the customary lines which the analyst recognizes as belonging to symphonic form would be to dismember the statue. Mozart's procedure is singularly unconcerned with symphonic form, wholly imbued with the symphonic spirit. Not a phrase of the initial melody ever reappears except where the whole is repeated, which in point of fact happens twice, that is in the 'da capo' of the exposition and at the beginning of the recapitulation. Yet the movement is undeniably symphonic; this is no case of a tune with contrasting episodes. Everything which follows is dependent on the character of this initial vision of beauty. Many of the subsequent melodies may be shown to be expansions or enrichments of its arpeggio contours, though it is impossible to say that this or that detail is at a given moment undergoing development, as it is almost always possible to say in the case of Beethoven. Idea follows idea and all are fresh, yet none would have been just what it is without some subtle influence from that first vision. The hearer is made to hold it in mind through them all, so that when at last it returns, though it is the same in actual notes as at first, it is not the same in content. It has behind it the experience of the musical life engendered by its first statement.

Professor Tovey, in an essay on Schubert full of pregnant ideas about the aesthetic principles of sonata form, has pointed out that 'there is no surer touchstone of Schubert's, as of Mozart's, Beethoven's, and Brahms's, treatment of form than the precise way in which their recapitulations differ from their expositions',[1] and he suggests that the genius for form may be shown in the identity of the two sections as much as in their differences. Mozart's E flat Symphony displays this genius of identity. What was perfect at its first hearing remains perfect, though with a new significance, in its last. The recapitulation section differs from the exposition only in the modulation necessary to bring the second subject into the tonic key, and even that difference he seems purposely to have made as inconspicuous as possible.

Contrast Mozart's method here with that of his G minor Symphony (Koechel 550), where the more pliable subject-matter induces him to carry on the process of development right through the recapitulation. In each case the method varies with the material, and all we have the right to demand from the composer is that he should convince us that the one is the consequence of the other, that the conclusion is derived from the premisses.

We have seen Brahms developing his symphonic capacity in his handling of the small groups of instruments belonging to chamber music. The symphonic principle enters deeply into all such music, and at first sight the customary restriction of the name 'symphony' to a sonata for orchestra may appear as arbitrary as is most musical nomenclature. The Quintet op. 34 might be called a symphony for piano and string quartet.

[1] *The Heritage of Music*, vol. i, p. 102.

Nevertheless there is a difference over and above the difference of instrumentation, in itself a minor point, which makes it appropriate to keep a separate name of some sort for the orchestral work. The use of orchestra alone necessitates a different mental standpoint in the composer from that which belongs either to the group of solo players in chamber music or the collaboration of one or more solo players with the orchestra in what is commonly called 'concerto'. In writing for the orchestra the composer sets aside all that element of virtuosity, the personal eloquence of the individual performer, inherent in the concerto and attaching to some extent to the chamber music group of solo players. He is left alone with the fullest means of purely musical expression at disposal, but without the aid of that human advocacy before his public which a Joachim, a Mühlfeld, or Brahms himself, at the piano, inevitably brought to music involving solo performance.[1]

In chamber music Brahms excelled in combinations which included the piano, his own instrument, the presence of which naturally led, as has been shown, to dialogue between the piano and whatever else was chosen to go with it. In the symphony for orchestra he was thrown back solely on the germinating power of his musical thought without the rhetorical appeal of the solo performer, whether himself or another. That is why his first attempt at symphony was turned into the Piano Concerto in D minor. He could not at that stage do without the rhetorical appeal of the solo performer. It took him sixteen years filled with a wealth of varied experience before he could trust himself to evolve a purely symphonic scheme.

Brahms's chief contemporary in Vienna, Anton Bruckner

---

[1] This at least was the case before the arrival of the virtuoso conductor who now goes about the world inviting audiences to listen to *his* C minor Symphony, whether the work happens to have been composed by Beethoven or by Brahms!

(1824–96), was untroubled by any of these misgivings in undertaking the task of symphonic composition. He had, in fact, written four symphonies for orchestra, though only two had attained a public performance, before Brahms's No. 1 appeared at Carlsruhe (1876). Brahms once expressed a sense of thankfulness for having been preserved from the sin of spilling notes on to music-paper; Bruckner's life might be described as one long act of thanksgiving for the power to do so. From the time of his Second Symphony in C minor (1871–2) onwards, he was never without a large-scale work on the stocks. When he died he left eight completed symphonies, and three movements of a Ninth which surpasses all predecessors in length and elaboration.

Bruckner's First Symphony (C minor), first played under his own direction in his native town of Linz (May 6, 1868), was scored for the normal symphonic orchestra with 2 trumpets, 3 trombones (but no bass tuba), but this body was increased with nearly every work. He used three trumpets in the Third Symphony (D minor) dedicated to Wagner ' in tiefster Ehrfurcht', and subsequently the constitution of his orchestra followed Wagnerian precedent. A 'stage' band of brass (3 trumpets, 3 trombones, bass tuba, and 4 horns additional to the same instruments in the orchestra proper) was engaged to add weight to the peroration of his Fifth Symphony (B flat). In the Seventh (E major) he employed the quartet of tenor and bass tubas as devised by Wagner for *The Ring*, and in the Eighth (C minor) and Ninth (D minor) he revelled in the full panoply of the Bayreuth orchestra, with triple woodwind, 8 horns (four to interchange with the tubas), and harps.

Bruckner's known admiration for Wagner and these externals of his style labelled him a Wagnerian and brought him a certain amount both of the obloquy and the admiration which belonged to such an adherence, but while the technical influence of Wagner appears in these externals of orchestration as well as in certain idiosyncrasies of harmony, the spiritual one is chiefly discernible as an urge towards magniloquence. It cannot be said of Bruckner that there is any of that close fusion of colour with line making his orchestration an integral part of a symphonic scheme in the way that Wagner's was essential to a dramatic one. Bruckner did not gravitate towards the programme symphony which was Liszt's counterpart to the Wagnerian music-drama. He did not construct his movements on an elaborate system of leading themes reappearing through the several movements, which was César Franck's application of the leitmotive principle to symphonic form. To only one, the Fourth (E flat), did he give a title, 'Romantische', and that a term of such general significance that one wonders at it having been appropriated by one rather than by all his nine. He was indeed a romantic of the romantics, too deeply imbued with a sense of vision in the act of creation to submit it to any intellectual principle such as Franck's, or to confine it with verbal explanations in the manner of the programmists.

Bruckner, a simple soul, whose career began as a country schoolmaster and organist, used the orchestra as he had been wont to use his organ. When he found that Wagner had built a larger instrument than the one he knew, he took the country organist's pleasure in pulling out all the stops. What he played on this ever-increasing instrument, too, was like an organist's improvisation. Each symphony begins softly and each ends in a blazing fortissimo. The customary opening is a soft pedal-point of some kind, a string tremolando, a reiterated note or rhythmic figure; in the Fifth, a basso ostinato (pizzicato) replaces the pedal-point. Whatever the device may be, it seems to suggest the organist's habit of listening to the tone of his instrument before beginning to do something with it. Presently some more positive feature is added, and so the music gets under

way. Once started Bruckner gives full rein to his fertile, if not
distinguished, inventiveness. He is never at a loss for something
to do next, and he keeps just so much check on his wayward
fancy as to adhere to the old plan of a periodic recapitulation.
This is a very different thing from what has been described as
Beethoven's method of building up from nothing, or of giving
life to the dry bones. There is indeed a notable absence of bony
matter from Bruckner's structures. The first movement of the
much admired Seventh Symphony will serve as an instance.
It begins thus:

Ex. 1.

Such a theme is not readily memorized by the hearer beyond its opening arpeggio figure, even after the immediate repetition with fuller scoring which Bruckner offers. It neither impresses itself as a thing of self-evident beauty nor as a pregnant idea from which greater things may come. The sympathetic hearer, nevertheless, accepts it with reserve, tries to focus attention on it and awaits enlightenment from what follows. Immediately Bruckner passes to a quite different theme, 'ruhig', from which the crescendo over another pedal (F sharp, 20 bars) leads to the deploying of the full orchestra in a passage which can hardly be called thematic at all. This is broken off to introduce a third theme, also 'ruhig' but not referring to its predecessor.

Ex. 2.

This figure, reiterated through a number of keys, also has its crescendo to a fortissimo, from which the tone dies away once more and the exposition ends with becoming orthodoxy on a chord of B major.

The chief novelty of the desultory development of these materials which follows is that the arpeggio figure of Ex. 1 is taken downwards as well as upwards. It is for the most part quiet until the full orchestra suddenly bursts into the following loose-limbed stretto:

Ex. 3.

When this has subsided the recapitulation of the first subject occurs in full (in E major), the theme in the bass being decorated with a free inversion of itself in the treble. But one is inclined to ask why; the theme in its first statement was hardly eventful enough to command this amount of respect. The free fantasia might as well have been continued up to the coda which the solitary drum on the low E supports with its rumbling pedal through the last 50 bars or so, once more a passage of crescendo as though stops were being added until the end.

If we attempt to apply Professor Tovey's 'touchstone' to this or indeed to any one of Bruckner's sonata form movements we get no reaction at all. Neither identity nor difference in the recapitulation of his ideas appears to be of the least consequence, because the ideas have acquired little or no additional significance as a result of their preceding development. This it is which puts Bruckner right outside symphony in the sense in which the classics have defined the term for us. At the same time he cannot be said to be conspicuous as an inventor of self-contained tunes, as so many minor composers, who have mistaken themselves for symphonists, have been. Bruckner falls between the two stools of the symphonic and lyrical styles.

To say this is not to deny that he had genius of a kind. He pursued his art with a religious devotion. He had a soaring imagination which led him to project vast designs in orchestral tones which have compelled admiration; he excelled in subtle effects of harmony heightened by the instrumental colours with which he clothed them.

One instance from the slow movement of the Seventh Symphony may here be quoted to show at a glance Bruckner's high sense of the value of dynamic contrasts together with his organ-like texture. It is the bridge from the climax of the first subject section, a battering of the full orchestra, to the second subject, a tune on the strings of a naïvely classical pattern. These two points are connected by chromatically shifting harmonies sustained by horns and trumpets (as though held by the left hand) against arpeggios on violins and clarinets alternately (right-hand solo stops). The entry of the tubas offers a striking contrast; luminous colour succeeded by an opaque one (Ex. 4).

Appreciation of Bruckner was slow in coming. Three of his symphonies, the Fifth, the Sixth, and the unfinished Ninth, were not performed until several years after his death, even though in his later years, as professor of the organ and musical theory at the Conservatoire in Vienna, he was the centre of an admiring circle, and enjoyed the affectionate support of pupils in wellnigh as full a measure as did César Franck in Paris. Foreign musicians, especially English ones, have felt some surprise at his posthumous fame. Allowing something for that

Ex. 4.

extravagant insistence on nationalism which has deflected musical judgement in all countries since the beginning of the twentieth century, and remembering that 'Bruckner can only be fully understood through his own country, Upper Austria (much as Schubert can only be completely understood through his own country, Lower Austria), and through his attributes as a devout Catholic',[1] we still have to find a cause for the prevalence of his works in the concert-rooms of Europe outside Austria.

[1] Professor Alfred Einstein, *Grove's Dictionary of Music and Musicians*, 3rd ed., article 'Bruckner'. The analogy in parenthesis is not very convincing in view of the widespread appeal of Schubert's art amongst people whose geography scarcely extends to a recognition of the difference between Upper and Lower Austria.

That cause is the establishment in the last generation of virtuoso orchestras commanded by virtuoso conductors. The conductors found that they could 'make something' of Bruckner, indeed that he required them to make his music articulate. The classical symphony having life in itself allows comparatively little scope for the impress of the virtuoso conductor's personality. Bruckner's symphonies became to the virtuosi of the baton what the concertos of Vieuxtemps, Ernst, and Wieniawski had been to the virtuosi of the bow. His successor in this line of composition was himself one of the greatest of these virtuosi, Gustav Mahler (1860–1911), whose nine symphonies lie on the border-line of the two centuries.

Before returning to the classical ideal of the symphony as represented by Brahms, a further word on Mahler's artistic outlook, apart from orchestral technique, is called for. His mind was as subtle as that of Bruckner was simple. A highly sensitized creature with the keen intellect of the cultured Jew, his student days at the Vienna Conservatorium displayed an immense musical facility, which, however, produced no immediate result in composition of a lasting kind. It is significant that his first mature work, *Das Klagende Lied* (1880), was one not of symphony but of song. This appeared at the outset of his career as conductor. The interpolation of songs into the Second and Fourth Symphonies and the separate examples, *Des Knaben Wunderhorn*, *Lieder eines fahrenden Gesellen* and settings of poems by Rückert, show his gift for lyrical writing, and an almost pathetic desire to attain simplicity through struggle. There is a curious juxtaposition of extreme sophistication and extreme naïvety in his larger works. The naïvety is uppermost in his First Symphony in D (1888), the opening of which has been already described. There is a charming humour in the variations (third movement) on a nursery song, *Frère Jacques*. The childlike side of Mahler is his most engaging quality. Here and in the Fourth Symphony in G major it carries an occasional reminder of the manner of Humperdinck.

It is with the Second Symphony that the inner struggle begins, and thenceforward Mahler was increasingly obsessed with the desire to stamp his work with an autobiographical character. His conversion to Catholicism imminent at this time was an event of deep spiritual significance to himself. The opening movement of the Second Symphony (C minor) is planned on a grand scale and proceeds from a theme of turbulent energy in which his admirers find the influence of Beethoven's type of construction and thought. But the analogy with Beethoven cannot be maintained very far. Mahler's mind is much nearer to that of Liszt in which 'poetic content' counted for more than purely musical thinking. The symphonic design appears rather haphazard; it is broken in on by the setting for contralto voice of 'Urlicht' (*Des Knaben Wunderhorn*), in itself a beautiful treatment of words chosen to declare the trend of his religious experience.

Der liebe Gott wird mir ein Lichtchen geben,
Wird leuchten mir bis in das ewig selig Leben!

Again choral voices co-operate in the finale with a hymn 'Aufersteh'n'. Not only in his choice of words but in the whole style and shape of this work, the stress laid on representative themes, the employment of a distant orchestra of brass and percussion in addition to the elaborate paraphernalia of what had become his normal orchestra, Mahler shows himself to be following out a psychological programme perspicuous to himself, but not easily apprehended by any one else.

The same is the case with the Third Symphony (D minor). After an enormous amount of orchestral bombast in Part I, Part II begins with a pretty minuet tune in the eighteenth-century manner. Again, after two movements in which the composer seems to have become absorbed in the task of over-scoring pleasant dance-rhythms, an alto voice begins solemnly

to declaim Nietzsche's 'O Mensch! gib Acht' (*Zarathustra*), and
is followed by another number from *Des Knaben Wunderhorn*
sung by a female choir while a boys' choir imitates the sound of
bells to the syllables 'Bimm, bamm'. Incongruity could scarcely
go further. Mahler loses all sense of symphonic unity in his determination to pursue in a single work every impulse of his many-
sided nature. He recovers his balance and his sense of humour
in the Fourth Symphony (G major), which, scored for a comparatively small orchestra without the heavier brass instruments,
is a picture of childhood. Here the genial themes of the three
orchestral movements lead naturally to the song 'Wir geniessen
die himmlischen Freuden' (*Des Knaben Wunderhorn*) of the finale,
directed to be sung with childlike expression, but without parody.

For ten years (1897–1907) Mahler was conductor, then artistic
director, of the Vienna Opera. It was then that he had the
fullest opportunity for the exercise of his great interpretative
gifts in the production of opera. That he should have found
time for the completion of four such enormous scores as the
Symphonies numbered V to VIII during that busy period is
evidence of his abnormal mental activity. The first three of this
series (V to VII) are purely orchestral; the Eighth is the setting
in two extended movements of the Latin hymn 'Veni Creator
Spiritus' and the last scene of Goethe's *Faust*.

The Fifth Symphony (it cannot well be described by key
since it begins in C sharp minor and ends in D) is, like the Third,
divided into two parts. Part I contains a 'Trauermarsch' and
a 'Stürmisch' movement, 'Mit grösster Vehemenz'. There is to
be a long pause between the parts. Part II contains a Scherzo
in graceful 'Ländler' rhythm, a sentimental Adagietto, and a
Rondo-Finale. The scheme has more the character of an over-
grown suite form than of symphony. In that it contrasts with
the Sixth Symphony, which returns to the traditional four-
movement shape (Allegro, Scherzo, Andante, and Finale) and the

consistent development round a single key (A minor) as the tonal centre. The orchestra of the Sixth is very large even for Mahler, containing eight horns, six trumpets, four trombones, and a whole battery of percussion, but here more than anywhere else he seems to be addressing himself to the problem of making the classical pattern fulfil the purposes of his magniloquent self-expression. It is certainly more consistent, if less attractive, than its companion the Seventh Symphony (beginning in B minor and ending in C), which is relieved from ponderousness by two movements called 'Nachtmusik' carrying the imaginative suggestions of the title, in their picturesque scoring.

It is only after the study of these prodigious scores that one can perceive the growth in concentration and clarity of design which is claimed for the Ninth Symphony. Between them and it came Mahler's period of strenuous conducting work in America as well as the choral Eighth Symphony and the song-symphony called *Das Lied von der Erde*. There can be no doubt of the intense personal feeling which infuses the four movements of the Ninth. They consist of an elaborate first movement in which the instruments combine in an intimate colloquy about themes of more definite significance than those of the earlier orchestral symphonies; a second movement of the 'Ländler' type, vigorous and at times boisterous; a 'Rondo Burleske' which recalls the 'Stürmisch' movement of the Fifth Symphony; and a final Adagio which is the most spontaneous of Mahler's slow movements. This Adagio with its pianissimo ending marked 'ersterbend' has given rise to much sentimental writing about Mahler's consciousness of his approaching end, yet the two completed movements of the Tenth Symphony show him launching out into another great project with unabated vigour.

All this later phase of Mahler's art belongs chronologically to the first decade of the twentieth century, though technically it appears as a late phase of that post-romantic symphonic

revival which is our concern here. Indeed, though a quarter of
a century has passed since his death, the musical value of his
immense output is still disputed. To what extent these symphonies hold a presage of a new art is not to be discussed here,
and this brief record of them necessarily emphasizes their *fin
de siècle* characteristics.

At this point it will be well to return to Brahms and to that
classical ideal of symphonic growth which the great C minor
symphony reasserted before the world in 1876. A comparison
between the first pair of Brahms's symphonies (Op. 68 in C
minor and Op. 73 in D major) and the pair of string quartets
(Op. 51, No. 1 in C minor, No. 2 in A minor) has already been
drawn. The first of each was the product of much thinking; the
second came with something like the spontaneity habitual to
Schubert. The scores bear evidence of these contrasted processes.

The slow introduction of the C minor lays the most solid
foundations. It takes a ruminating survey 'un poco sostenuto'
of all the melodic material which is to spring into a more vigorous
life in the Allegro. Its opening harmonic progression, first heard
against the thud of the drum, haunts the subsequent movements
after its significance has been fully exposed in the development
of the first.   Compare the following quotations:

Ex. 5.

Opening of first movement.

The introduction to the Finale thus links all its dramatically stirring events with the sombre mood from which the symphony takes its beginning. These identities have something of the consciousness of the cross reference. The Second Symphony does not refer back. Identity between movements only appears in the tendency of the themes to revert to the bend down and up again of the semitone first murmured by the basses. One questions whether its recurrence in the Finale is devised at all; it is like the seed growing secretly till it becomes a great tree so that the birds of the air lodge in its branches. (Ex. 6.)

The slow movement 'Adagio non troppo' is the only one in the D major Symphony in which Brahms relapses even momentarily into that ruminating mood which is the basis of the whole of the C minor Symphony. Its double theme (Ex. 7) may be compared with that of Example 5.

Ex. 6.
Second Symphony.

Ex. 7.

But apart from this detail, two symphonies by one man, both following broadly the traditions of sonata form, could scarcely have less in common than have the C minor and the D major of Brahms. In that before all else we can measure the gulf which lies between Bruckner and Brahms. The one constantly starts again to run an habitual course; the other begins a new life with each work.

These different characters entail different handlings of the symphonic form. In the first movement of the C minor Symphony the contrast between first and second subject sections hardly exists. The latter is merely represented by a momentary lull in the energy, a plaintive phrase on the oboe, and a haunting call vanishing into the distance with the horn's low E flat, from which point the violas return to the charge and renew the strenuous mood (in E flat minor) of the principal theme. All that is essential to the main character of the movement is comprised in the strong-featured first subject adumbrated originally in slow time, then transformed by the quick. On the other hand, the second subject of the D major's first Allegro is expanded by a whole chain of melodies beginning with the folk-like tune on the violoncelli and continued by stronger rhythms which sweep aside the suavity of the folk tune and develop a purely instrumental texture.

Again, if we compare the recapitulations of these two movements we find that the first is by far the more regular. In it all the ideas of the first statement are passed in review to lead to a coda which culminates in the restoration of the 'poco sostenuto'. In the Second Symphony all that relates to the gentle first subject is condensed on its reappearance into a few bars, so that the more vital material of the second subject section may be reached the sooner. Ultimately the movement comes to rest in a coda of quiet charm 'in tempo, sempre tranquillo' introduced by one of the most eloquent passages ever written for a single horn.[1] (Ex. 8.)

Each one of the four symphonies of Brahms takes a different emotional course. The First triumphs over the spirit of heaviness; the Second lives in light; the Third begins on the flood-tide of energy but the tide ebbs; the Fourth sums up a lifetime of experience in musical thinking. The first three are synoptic in their portrayal of the rising and falling tides of feeling. The last stands apart from them; in it Brahms appears increasingly absorbed in tracing out a design for its own sake. In the synoptic symphonies the expression of feeling dictates the design, a different one in each case; in the Fourth the design controls the feeling and this new outlook issues in the tremendous chaconne-like pattern of its Finale.

The slow movements of the first three are all, broadly speaking, in a lyrical song form (principal theme with episodes and coda) like that which Brahms favoured in his last group of piano pieces (Opp. 116–119) though more richly developed, especially that of the Second Symphony. The slow movement of the Fourth, unlike its predecessors, resembles the concise and balanced type of Mozart's modified sonata form[2] and displays that concentration on subtleties of design which marks the Fourth Symphony apart from its fellows. Again in the first three symphonies the movements which replace the Scherzo are all of the allegretto type, though that of the Second alternates the allegretto with true scherzo episodes, whose one beat in a bar is equivalent to

---

[1] This passage may be cited as one which shows Brahms at his happiest in handling the orchestral instruments as though they were a chamber music group. The suggestion is heightened by the curious fact that in the printed score the directions 'un poco stringendo' and 'ritard' are written into the horn and first violin parts only, as though the first violin were a leader responsible for combining the ensemble of the string group with the solo horn.

[2] Compare the slow movement of Mozart's Symphony in E flat (Koechel 543).

Ex. 8.

in tempo ma più tranquillo.

the crotchet of the oboe's initial tune. The Fourth Symphony has
an 'Allegro giocoso' as far removed from the gracious allegretto
measures of the others as it is from the conventional triple time
scherzo. Brahms here lets himself out to play before settling
down to his last and greatest formal problem, the chaconne-like
Finale.

Of the four finales only that of the Second Symphony follows
what may be called a normal course. But here we must leave
the plan of viewing the symphonies in a cross-section of their
several movements and, taking each in order, consider the finales
in relation to what has led up to them.

Once the organic growth of the symphonic idea through all
its movements is fully grasped, the Finale will naturally become
the most important, because the most revealing part of all.
The eighteenth-century symphonists never completely grasped
that fact. Even Mozart sometimes and Haydn very frequently
show themselves still under the influence of the suite form, the
ruling principle of which was the best wine first and when men
have well drunk then that which is, if not worse, at any rate

lighter.[1] Beethoven struck the decisive blow for symphonic unity when he made the heroic idea culminate in the amazing originality of the Finale to the 'Eroica' Symphony. After that, and the six others with which Beethoven followed it, every composer knew that his responsibility in writing symphony was cumulative. The knowledge accounts for all the laboured attempts to create climax which have defaced so many promising works by Beethoven's successors in the last century. It also contributed to, if it did not account for, such contrasting manifestations as the miracle of Schubert's C major, and the remarkable eloquence of Tchaikovsky's 'Pathetic'. Besides such strokes of genius as these one finds all sorts of technical devices consciously adopted by thoughtful composers from Schumann[2] to César Franck in pursuit of the maxim, ὁρᾶν τελός.

Brahms faces each problem as it arises, and each symphony finds its own solution in its Finale. Mention has already been made of the way in which the introduction to the Finale of the First Symphony forms a link with what has gone before. It does much more than that. The theme ultimately to emerge in C minor hovers over the characteristic chord progression recalled from the first movement (see Ex. 5). It is temporarily superseded by other factors in the situation, by the struggling stringendos of the pizzicato strings, by the emergence of that theme of greeting[3] on the horns which first turns decisively to the major key (Ex. 9), and by that solemn response of the trombones (asserting themselves now for the first time) and

[1] The type is exhibited at its highest by Bach's Overtures for orchestra. See *Oxford History of Music*, vol. iii, p. 164.

[2] See what Dannreuther says of Schumann's finales, more especially that of the Symphony in D minor. *Oxford History of Music*, vol. vi, p. 94 et seq.

[3] The quotation with words is from a note of Brahms to Clara Schumann dated Sept. 12th, 1868, eight years before the symphony appeared. See *Letters of Clara Schumann and Johannes Brahms*, vol. i, p. 231. English edition published by Ed. Arnold. The rhythm in the symphonic version is slightly different.

Ex. 9.

Hoch   auf'm   Berg,   tief   im   Tal,

grüss'   ich   dich   viel   tau - send   mal!

bassoons (Ex. 10), which comes almost as a rebuke to the optimism of the horn's glad note.

Ex. 10.

These are all principal characters in the drama of the Finale. When the strings take off their mutes to plunge into the broad C major tune of the Allegro they are banished, but only for the moment. Each one returns to exert its essential influence on the action later. Moreover, they prevent the C major tune from dominating the score in such a way as to pose itself as the climax of the symphony. In that Brahms's originality most appears, and because of his originality in handling the complex situation, the obvious gibe about the tune's likeness to that of Beethoven's Ninth[1] missed its mark. Brahms's symphonic thought passed through the C major tune and on beyond it.

---

[1] It is worth while to recall here that when Hans von Bülow unwisely called Brahms's C minor 'the tenth symphony' he did not mean to suggest that it was the successor to Beethoven's Ninth, but rather that it was the tenth in a series of masterpieces of which he regarded Mozart's C major (the 'Jupiter'), not Beethoven's, as the first. See a paper dated from Sydenham, Nov. 4th, 1877, published in *Ausgewählte Schriften*, p. 369.

After its repetition at the beginning of the development section it never appears again in full, though it generates a great part of the music of the coda. In place of recapitulation Brahms passes straight from the horn theme (Ex. 9) to the second subject group, and the 'più allegro', where again the return of the C major theme is expected, rides forward boldly to the A major chord of the trombone theme (Ex. 10). Thus Brahms shows himself master of his material right up to the end.

The 'Allegro con spirito' which brings the more lyrical Second Symphony to its exhilarating conclusion is not based on the interplay of what may be called thematic personalities to the same extent. In its forthright statements of melodic ideas flowing naturally from one another the composer shows his hand at once. He is keeping nothing back with which to create an unexpected climax. The structure is composed of the three orthodox sections of a sonata form movement (exposition, development, and recapitulation) each clearly differentiated from the others, and each beginning with the first motive in D major, sotto voce.[1] From this same opening each section weaves the material afresh into new designs of cumulative interest. The long passage 'tranquillo' and later 'sempre più tranquillo' which leads back from the tonal climax of the middle section to the beginning of the third is beautifully designed to prepare the way for the highest flight of all in the coda. Apply Professor Tovey's 'touchstone' here and the power of Brahms's moulding is instantly realized.

Chronologically Brahms's four symphonies divide into pairs. An interval of six years separated the first performance of the Second Symphony (December 30th, 1877) from that of the Third (December 2nd, 1883). Both Second and Third were produced by

---

[1] In his symphonic finales Brahms never used the double bar followed by repetition of the exposition. In the first movements of the first three symphonies he preserved that convention of the classical form, but abandoned it in the Fourth.

the Vienna Philharmonic Society under Hans Richter, and the
Fourth at Meiningen (October 25th, 1885) followed the Third
closely. But it has already been suggested that the first three
may be regarded as synoptic in their relation between form
and expression, while the Fourth stands apart. It must be
remembered also that the interval between the Second and
Third Symphonies was filled by Brahms with a quantity of other
work in its essence symphonic. The Violin Concerto produced
by Joachim at the Leipzig Gewandhaus (January 1st, 1879),
where the D minor Piano Concerto had been hissed twenty years
before, is related by more than its key to the Second Symphony.
The two overtures, the *Tragic* and the *Academic Festival*,
followed in 1880, the one a mood picture in a single movement,
the other the only instance in which for a special purpose Brahms
moulded existing melodies[1] into a symphonic design. The year
1881 saw the production on November 22nd of the Pianoforte
Concerto in B flat, which begins with a tale of chivalry told by
the horn and the piano, includes unexpectedly an 'Allegro
appassionato' with the ring of bells in the middle of it, and
throughout musters all Brahms's early virtuosity of the keyboard to assist the orchestra in the display of exuberant impulse.
Brahms himself played the solo part in this concerto all over
Central Europe in the months following its first appearance at
Stuttgart.[2] It was the climax of his personal success as interpreter of his own music which had been begun with the early
sonatas for the piano. It was also the climax of the heroic period
in his composition.

The Third Symphony announces the end of that period. It
begins exultantly where the Concerto left off, but from the first

[1] For the students' songs in the *Akademische Fest-Ouvertüre* see Erk's
Deutscher Liederschatz, Band I, as follows: 'Wir hatten gebauet ein
stattliches Haus' (199), 'Weihelied' (169) two bars only, 'Fuchslied' (197),
'Gaudeamus igitur' (180).

[2] See May, vol. ii, p. 194.

the minor mode of its 'motto' theme grinds against the leaping
major arpeggio of its principal subject.[1]

Ex. 11.

Here is a return to something of that conflict through which the
First Symphony fought its way, but the issue is contrary. The
shadows close in around the later movements, and the light
gradually goes out from the Finale. There is here, too, something
of that treatment of themes as dramatic personalities which was
traceable in the First Symphony. The 'motto' exerts its influence
throughout save in the interlude of the ' Poco allegretto '; another
important episode is carried on from the slow movement into
the Finale, becoming more heavy-spirited in the later version
(Exs. 12 and 12 a), and it is with an etherealized recollection of
the opening theme, originally so full-blooded, that the coda
sinks to silence.

This will be the appropriate place to note in parenthesis a
technical mannerism of Brahms's orchestration. In ending a
movement softly, and all four movements of the Third Symphony

<hr />

[1] There was a time when serious musicians shook their heads over the
'false relation' (A♮, A♭) of this opening and doubted its legitimacy. Now
that modern music has rendered us insensitive to such things the significance
of the passage is apt to be overlooked.

Ex. 12.

Ex. 12a.

are so ended, he made the whole orchestra join in the final chord.
Moreover he was a little careless about the distribution of the
instruments over the whole compass of the chord, and almost
invariably allowed the major third to be too prominent for
satisfactory effect in pianissimo. Often Brahms's full orchestral
chords, loud as well as soft, are less resonant than those of more
instinctive orchestrators using the same instruments, Wagner
for example, because in Brahms the instruments are placed
according to the melodic or contrapuntal requirements of the
moment rather than for the sake of their contributions to tonal
balance. But in these chordal endings no melodic or contrapuntal interest is involved, and a little rearrangement, more
particularly in the wind parts, would have eliminated the
'wobbly' effect with which conductors have to contend in order
to round off Brahms's soft endings in their proper mood of
serenity.

No famous symphony since Haydn's 'Farewell', and that was
a jest, had ended in the diminuendo as Brahms ended the
Third Symphony. It is curious how little this seems to have
been noticed as an innovation. This symphony was an immediate
success. Richter is reported to have spoken of it as 'Brahms's
"Eroica"'; Joachim, to whose care Brahms confided it after its
first hearing, imagined for its Finale an association with the
story of Hero and Leander. In the horn and violoncello tune
he saw Leander joyously breasting the waves of the Hellespont.
But that seems to hint at tragedy which the character of the

coda denies. When the stress and turmoil have subsided, a
passage, 'un poco sostenuto', in the major key, anything but
tragic, uniting the theme of the finale with the 'motto', and
drawing them into a mood of pensive recollection, arrives as
the conclusion of the whole matter (Ex. 13).

In view of this conclusion one cannot concur in the statement
that 'nothing of the quiescent autumn mood which we have
observed in the master's chamber music of this period is to be
traced in either of his symphonies'.[1] It is here surely that that
mood takes possession.

It was still on him when he began the Fourth Symphony.
The quiet symmetry of the opening theme in E minor is something quite different from the impulse behind the initial ideas of
any works of his heroic period. The first 18 bars display the
pattern at leisure. When the cadence is reached Brahms begins
calmly to elaborate it almost as though the movement were to

Ex. 13.

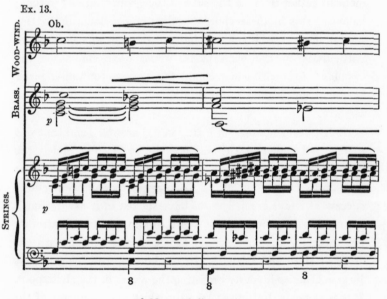

[1] May, vol. ii, p. 208.

be one of variations. He rouses himself from the quiescent mood with a certain sense of effort. Clara Schumann perceived this at once when Brahms according to his habit sent her the piano score of the Fourth Symphony before it was made public. She wrote with her customary enthusiasm, but added,

> 'If I might be allowed to mention something I don't altogether like, I would point to the second motive of the first movement, which seems to me too independent and not welded on to what precedes it, whereas in your works one thing usually evolves so wonderfully out of the other. It is as if you suddenly repented of having been so amiable.'[1]

The motive in question is

Ex: 14.

which comes sharply on the woodwind and horn. Its presence is to be justified later, in fact the reconciliation of widely divergent

---

[1] Letter, Dec. 15th, 1885. See *Letters of Clara Schumann and Johannes Brahms* (Eng. trans. Litzmann), vol. ii, p. 103.

rhythmic elements in the texture is the chief source of the fascination of this inexhaustible movement. It is the 'unamiable' motive which creates the problem. Its solution is found mainly in the passage (from letter H to L of the full score) which leads into the amplified recapitulation of the opening theme. Only a fuller quotation than it is convenient here to make could illustrate the way in which this motive is subdued by the double influence both of the principal theme and of that mysterious arpeggio figure over a sustained bass note to which originally it offered an uncompromising opposition. Had Brahms made answer to Clara Schumann's complaint, and that was a thing he rarely did even to her, it must have been one of con-currence with the criticism as far as it went, accompanied by a gentle reminder that the critic must not halt at the first appear-ance of a symphonic idea. True, he might have said, it is not amiable nor welded on to anything which precedes it, but you will find the welding in what follows.

There is a delicate problem in tonality underlying the lyricism of the 'Andante moderato'. The horns in C announce the opposi-tion and reconciliation between the scales of C and E, the latter being the main key of the movement. The harmonization of the reposeful E major tune with recurrent D natural and C natural carries the problem forward, and the coda led by the horns in C with the phrase which began the movement finds the solution in an exquisite and wholly unexpected cadence (Ex. 15 a and b). Between these extremes is unfolded a design, comparable, as has been suggested, to Mozart's designs in modified sonata form,

Ex. 15 (a).

Wood-wind.

Horns.

but entirely individual in its content. Observe how a sharply pointed subsidiary theme, interjected at first, 'unamiably' perhaps, by the woodwind, is mollified into the suave second subject played by the violoncelli.

Ex. 16.

The 'Allegro giocoso' sweeps out of its course all the subtleties, rhythmic and tonal, which have prevailed through the first two movements of the symphony. Its boisterous mood, the wilful cross-phrasing, breaking the squareness of a rhythm made up of two- and four-bar phrases to an extent unusual in Brahms, the fullness of the orchestration which does not despise the tinkle of the frivolous triangle, all combine to make it the most carefree of Brahms's third movements in the symphonies. One point of form deserves particular attention, the adroit avoidance of the expected Trio traditionally belonging to the Scherzo proper. The woodwind toying with the principal theme (key D flat) seem to be approaching such a Trio, and the horns introducing a new theme, 'poco meno presto', in the same key actually begin it, but the matter goes no further. The new theme is rudely interrupted after a few bars by the full orchestra's insistence on a return to the prevailing rhythm. It bursts in (Tempo I) with what was originally the tenth bar of the principal subject; the horn's engaging middle theme is voted out of order, and gets no second hearing (Ex. 17).

Looked at from the point of view of key relationship the 'Allegro giocoso' is the triumphant assertion of C major which had as it were insinuated itself into the previous movement. Three drums—Brahms had never previously used three in his sym-

Ex. 17.

phonies—reinforce the assertion, hammering with aggressive
emphasis their tonic, dominant, and subdominant through all
which follows the return to the Tempo I.

So positive a third movement, one which has none of the
character of interlude belonging to the allegretto movements of
the earlier symphonies, called for something exceptional in the
way of Finale, if the scheme was to attain symphonic balance.
The gravity of the initial movement as well as the sovereignty
of E minor had to be restored, but the return to the opening

mood and key would in weaker hands have produced a sense of anticlimax. Brahms met the situation with an altogether unprecedented solution of its problem. His 'Allegro energico e passionato' has been referred to above with intention as 'chaconne-like'. It has often been described indifferently as 'chaconne, passacaglia, or ground',[1] but the terms are not synonymous and Brahms did not claim any one of them for this movement. Both the classical dance forms, passacaglia and chaconne, were triple time movements developed in varying degrees of freedom over a ground bass. Bach's Passacaglia for organ and his Chaconne for violin exhibit the types at their highest point of technical development.[2] In the one the chosen melody is present in one part or another through all the variations; in the other the variations refer to the melodic contours and preserve the general harmonic scheme, but no part of the theme, melody or bass, is constantly present.

Brahms's handling of this eight-bar theme is nearer to the method of Bach's Chaconne than to that of his Passacaglia, but some at least of his variations cannot accurately be described as being on a 'ground' at all. The theme, started with emphasis by the wind (more especially by the three trombones which now appear in this symphony for the first time), is not given out as a ground bass but as a melody supported on plain harmonies. It may assist analysis of the wealth of ideas springing from it to view it first in the skeleton form of a melody with figured bass (Ex. 18).

It is the upper part which is presently to become the 'ground'. It passes to the bass from bar 32 onwards, and remains there through eight repetitions, that is to the end of the first group

---

[1] See Fuller-Maitland's *Brahms*, p. 154, and compare Kalbeck, iii, p. 478.

[2] Harvey Grace (*Organ Works of Bach*, p. 90) claims that 'as Bach sometimes places the subject at the top his work [the Organ Passacaglia] is a combination of the passacaglia and the chaconne'.

Ex. 18.

(bar 96). The second group in 3–2 time, consisting of four repetitions, is begun with an exquisite flute arabesque over a pedal E, which can be considered to be a highly ornate version of the melody of Example 18. In the three other repetitions of this group, all in E major, the actual contours of the melody are less directly traceable, but in the solemn passage of the trombones its major version is used as a bass.

The third group, returning to E minor and 3–4 time, opens with an unmistakable recapitulation of Example 18, both melody and harmony. In the next seven repetitions, the melody is given once in the bass, once in an inner part, and five times with increasingly free variation in the treble. Then follow two further repetitions both of which are recapitulatory. The first of them repeats melody and harmony of Example 18 in exclamatory figures (fortissimo and marcato); the second reintroduces a theme which was first heard on oboe and clarinet near the beginning (bar 17), and now returns in triumph on the full orchestra.

A fourth group (Letter I in the full score) then begins softly
with the melody still in the treble (first horn and violin) and
contains five repetitions in which the newly generated melodies
unite in dwelling on the chromatic A sharp B progression of the
original. They culminate in four bars of preparation for the
torrential coda 'più allegro', which develops further those
chromatic harmonies suggested by that same progression. The
course of that development may be made clear by the following
skeleton of the harmonic scheme, which also shows how in the
coda Brahms at last breaks loose from the eight-bar shape of
his theme.

Ex. 19.

Finally, at the summit of energy, the theme becomes contracted into a terse coda figure,

Ex. 20.

which brings the movement to an end in an abrupt E minor cadence.

From this summary analysis it will be obvious that Brahms has here set himself to work within certain strict limitations, both rhythmic and tonal. The eight-bar repetition resulting from the shape of the theme is never departed from until the four-bar preparation of the coda, and the whole movement is bound to the note E as tonic. There is no modulation of key, only change of mode (minor, major, minor). This to some of

Brahms's contemporaries seemed wilful asceticism, repellent like a self-mutilation. All the wealth of modern technique, its exuberant freedom of rhythm, its kaleidoscopic changes of key, was at his disposal, but he chose to leave it on one side, to return to an archaic form long since outgrown. Why?

A letter which Brahms had written to Clara Schumann[1] many years before he reached the Fourth Symphony throws some light on his own point of view. He was then sending her his own arrangement of Bach's Chaconne for the pianist's left hand.

'The Chaconne is in my opinion one of the most wonderful and most incomprehensible pieces of music. Using the technique adapted to a small instrument, the man writes a whole world of the deepest thoughts and most powerful feelings. If I could picture myself writing, or even conceiving such a piece, I am certain that the extreme excitement and emotional tension would have driven me mad. If one has no supremely great violinist at hand the most exquisite of joys is probably to let the Chaconne ring in one's mind. But the piece certainly inspires one to occupy oneself with it somehow. One does not always want to hear music actually played, and in any case Joachim is not always there so one tries it otherwise. But whether I try it with an orchestra or piano the pleasure is always spoilt for me. There is only one way in which I can secure undiluted joy from the piece, though on a small and only approximate scale, and that is when I play it with the left hand alone.'

Something of this joy in achievement in face of difficulties passed into his composition of the Finale to the Fourth Symphony. He allowed himself the large orchestra, for that the symphony demanded, but he would wring out from a matter-of-fact formula his own world of deep thoughts and powerful feelings. It should be the more eloquent for its battle with the self-imposed limitations. Hence his title 'Allegro energico e passionato'. Not contrast only but contrast in unity was the thing to be expressed, and it led him to a supreme exercise of

[1] *Letters of Clara Schumann and Johannes Brahms* (English translation), vol. ii, p. 16, dated June 1877.

that faculty for bringing new out of old, which is so constantly illustrated in his handling of the variations form.

But it must be noted that these variations are unlike any of the earlier sets which appear in the course of Brahms's piano and chamber music. These latter, following the contours of their longer themes, may generally be described as groups of miniatures. The very labels, Var. I, Var. II, &c., separate each from each. Here the invention of new melody clothing the bare bones of the theme keeps the music sweeping forward, while the group arrangement indicated in the analysis given above corresponds roughly to the main divisions of a sonata form movement (exposition, development, recapitulation, and coda). The more one studies it the more irresistible appears its cumulative power, and the more is the Finale felt to be the natural consequence of the preceding movements. This, however, is something which cannot be established by argument, for there is no thematic link between the several movements of the Fourth Symphony like those which have been pointed out as traceable in the three earlier symphonies. Only the broad key relationship, E.C.E.,[1] asserts their outward unity. Their inner unity can only be described as a sense of equipoise rudely disturbed by conflicting experiences and triumphantly restored at the last. Because of it one is tempted to think of this work as the highest example during the period under discussion of that principle of organic growth which is the essential factor in symphony. Of Brahms's four symphonies, each one a masterpiece of its own kind, the Fourth is most fit to stand beside the 'Jupiter' and the 'Eroica'.

[1] It may be compared with the F-D flat relationship of the piano sonata Op. 5 noted in Chapter II.

CHAPTER VII

THE SYMPHONY ABROAD

A CERTAIN element of unreality pervades both the French and Russian works of the late nineteenth century which carry the title 'symphony'. In many specimens we feel that their composers were not so much impelled to write symphonies as determined to prove that they could outgrow the symphonic poem and kindred forms of illustrative music. We must bear in mind the conditions of the two countries, some of them already described in relation to chamber music, in which such works came to birth. Further, Liszt in the middle of the century formed the chief connecting link between the extreme west and the extreme east of European music. His influence was paramount in the independent development of orchestral music, particularly in the direction of the symphonic poem, a term of his own invention.[1] Both countries had native exemplars of the type of which the term formed a general and convenient description. The *Symphonie Fantastique* of Berlioz and the *Kamarinskaja* of Glinka are the starting-points of each. A common aim and a personal friendship between Berlioz and Glinka helped to cement a Franco-Russian *entente* from the days of Berlioz's visit to Russia, or even before it.[2]

But Liszt did more than supply a name for what already existed. His own symphonic poems were a stimulus to the exercise of an unfettered musical imagination in the handling of the orchestra. It is easy to imagine how they appealed to men actuated by such ideals as those which Rimsky-Korsakov described as belonging to the 'Balakirev circle',[3] men impatient of the past and anxious to 'break new ground forward'.

[1] See *Oxford History of Music*, vol. vi, p. 149.
[2] See Berlioz's article on Glinka, *Journal des Débats*, 1845.
[3] See *supra*, Chapter IV, p. 112.

The strength of Liszt's influence on the French composers who flourished after the Franco-Prussian War is less easily accounted for, but it is undeniably present in the works of all the leaders with the possible exception of Gabriel Fauré. Saint-Saëns avowed it openly. D'Indy, in his determination to establish the reputation of his master, César Franck, as the latest if not the last of the great classics, rather deprecated the influence of Liszt, but it is patent to eye and ear in Franck's scores, *Les Æolides, Le Chasseur Maudit, Les Djinns,*[1] and even the *Variations Symphoniques.* Franck's fondness for the sub-title 'poème symphonique' applied to vocal and instrumental works impartially is merely an external indication of a deeper indebtedness traceable both in the general attitude towards 'programme' and sometimes in actual features of style. In d'Indy's own works such as the two mountain symphonies, *Jour d'été à la montagne* and *Symphonie sur un thème montagnard,* and the *Wallenstein* trilogy, a series of three symphonic poems, the same influence is clearly discernible.

It may seem a little surprising that these French composers, who came to the fore largely on a wave of national feeling, should have appealed so little by word or deed to the example of their countryman, Berlioz. The Russians indeed acclaimed him more than the French. The 'Balakirev circle' certainly showed no reluctance to learn the art of orchestration from him. Balakirev, Borodin, and Rimsky-Korsakov himself most of all, profited by Berlioz's wizardry with an orchestra. But he seems almost a stranger in his own home. He founded no 'school' there, and the group of composers who began to make their

[1] In the strictest sense of the word *Les Djinns* for piano and orchestra is a symphonic poem. Not only is it based aesthetically on Victor Hugo's poem (No. 18 in *Les Orientales*) but the structure of the verse, the lines short at first, expanding in the middle, and gradually contracting again towards the end, is actually reproduced in Franck's musical phraseology.

mark in the years just after his death owed little to him. He was not French enough. His obliviousness of the limitations of good form was repugnant to some of them. Liszt's urbane cosmopolitanism and that quality of virtuosity which passed from his early career as pianist into his later one as composer, that air of always knowing how to do things big or little, made him a more congenial tutor to artists who aspired to success in the most cultured capital of Europe.

Saint-Saëns began his symphonic career too early to profit at the outset by Liszt's example in composition. He was a boy of 18 when he wrote his First Symphony (in E flat) and got it both performed and published. This was in 1853, the very year of the 'new paths' in Germany from which our period started. He followed it up with two more symphonies which did not get the same amount of publicity, but one in A minor (known subsequently as the Second) fared better. It was published twenty years later, and the composer considered it sufficiently representative of himself to conduct a performance of it twenty years later again, when he came to London to be fêted by the Philharmonic Society.[1] It is a polished piece of work with a fugal first movement, evidence of Saint-Saëns's close study of traditional methods and of his ability to adapt them to his purpose.

The First Piano Concerto and two violin concertos are more or less contemporary with the Symphony in A minor (1859), after which there was a distinct break in composition of this kind. For a few years Saint-Saëns undertook teaching at the École

[1] On June 23rd, 1898, Saint-Saëns 'appeared in a triple role as organ-soloist, conductor, and composer. He played an organ solo "Fantasie in Db" (dedicated to H.M. Queen Elizabeth of Rumania), he conducted his Ballade "La Fiancée du Timbalier" (sung by Madame Blanche Marchesi) and his Symphony in A minor'.—*History of the Philharmonic Society of London*, by Myles B. Foster, p. 457. How much the symphony was touched up in the twenty years between composition and publication it is impossible to say.

Niedermeyer, where Fauré and Messager were among his pupils. He turned also to theatrical composition and it was not until 1868 that the Second Piano Concerto, the now well-known one in G minor, opened a new period of orchestral music. There followed the group of symphonic poems for orchestra beginning in the fateful year 1871 with *Le Rouet d'Omphale*. This with two others, *Phaéton* and *La Jeunesse d'Hercule*, are pictures from classic mythology. *Danse macabre*, third in order of composition, is the only one based on an actual poem[1] in the manner promulgated by Liszt.

In the mythological pieces Saint-Saëns stands back from his subject as it were. He does not pretend to any deeper interest in them than as images which can give direction to his musical ideas. The hero spinning among the women, Phaeton rashly braving the sunbeams, Hercules spurning pleasure for virtue, suggest to him a musical plan for each which he follows out with dexterity. An orchestra of normal size colours the pictures appropriately, and while the hearer's pleasure in the result may be enhanced by knowledge of the subjects, there is nothing in Saint-Saëns which will seem obscure to those who listen to his 'poems' without a preliminary glance at the programme. Saint-Saëns in fact uses his subjects merely to stimulate a mood and help him to the evolution of a form. What the personality of the performer does for him in the concertos, whether those for his own instrument, the piano, or the Violin Concerto in B minor, or the Violoncello Concerto in A minor, the picture does for him in writing for orchestra alone. He followed Liszt again in his general conception of concerto form, linking the several move-

---

[1] Some verses by Jean Lahor which begin:

> Zig et zig, la mort en cadence
> Frappant une tombe avec son talon,
> La mort à minuit joue un air de danse
> Zig et zig et zag, sur son violon.

See *Saint-Saëns*, by Arthur Hervey, p. 89.

ments adroitly, but not adhering pedantically to Liszt's principle of thematic metamorphosis. Without some element either of personal virtuosity or of picturesque suggestion to guide him he could not be quite at his ease. He could not compass a purely symphonic design. He essayed it again nevertheless and on a larger scale than before in the Symphony for orchestra with organ in C minor which he wrote for the London Philharmonic in 1886 and dedicated to Liszt.[1] There has been no doubt of the success of this symphony before the public both of London and Paris, but as compared with the concertos and the symphonic poems it is laboured and lacking in distinction.

It is to be noted that it appeared just at the time when three other French composers made their single ventures in the composition of a symphony. Fauré's Symphony in D minor had been produced in Paris at the Châtelet (March 15th, 1885), Edouard Lalo's Symphony in G minor first appeared at a Lamoureux concert (February 13th, 1887), and César Franck was even then at work on his Symphony in D, though it did not get a public hearing till February 17th, 1889. Of these Fauré's received no more than a respectful hearing and was allowed to remain unpublished; Lalo's had a *succès d'estime*; Franck's was ultimately, though not till some years after his death, to attain a popularity, at any rate in England, which would rival that of his Slavonic contemporaries, Tchaikovsky and Dvořák.

Edouard Lalo (1823–92), though born and educated at Lille, was of Spanish extraction. The fact is not necessary in order to account for that lilt of rhythm, the dance of his melody, which has carried his *Symphonie Espagnole* round the world. The Latins of Northern France are in some sense cut off from

---

[1] It was played at the Philharmonic Society's concert in St. James's Hall on May 19th, Saint-Saëns conducting. Liszt died at Bayreuth on July 31st. His last visit to England had been paid just before the production of Saint-Saëns's Symphony and had lasted from April 3rd to 22nd. See *Grove's Dictionary*, 3rd ed., vol. iii, p. 210.

their natural heritage. They turn south to warm themselves in the sun. Their composers have no need to claim Spanish blood in order to feel in their veins the pulse of the Spanish dance, to revel in the radiance of Spanish colour and the languor of Spanish nights. Bizet, Chabrier, Debussy, and Ravel have in turn willingly succumbed to these influences, so much so that they may almost be said to have taught Spanish composers what Spanish music is.

Lalo had the singular fortune to meet with a Franco-Spanish interpreter. Pablo Sarasate had received his musical education under Alard at the Paris Conservatoire and was at the height of his fame as a virtuoso of the violin when he produced Lalo's Violin Concerto in F at the Concert National in Paris in 1874. It was immediately successful, but the more frankly melodious *Symphonie Espagnole* in five movements, combining the characteristics of symphony, concerto, and suite, immediately superseded it in popular esteem when it appeared in the following year. It is on the *Symphonie Espagnole*, as played by Sarasate and innumerable other violinists since, that Lalo's world-wide reputation as a symphonist rests, and no attempt to praise the orchestral Symphony in G minor, produced a dozen years later, as a work of more serious aim, can shake that position. Lalo, like Saint-Saëns, needed the stimulus of the virtuoso's personality to bring his genius to full life. Left alone with an orchestra, his construction became more conscious, although he never fell into that pomposity, baleful legacy from Liszt, which descended on Saint-Saëns in planning the Symphony in C minor. If Lalo as symphonist must be regarded as a composer of the second class, he is at least free from the taint of the second-rate. He was a little unfortunate in the G minor Symphony in lighting on a motto theme which, changing minor for major, was almost identical with that of Brahms's Second Piano Concerto written a few years earlier.

LALO. Symphony in G minor.

Ex. 1.

This permeates the whole symphony, appearing in several altered forms, and ultimately emerges in triumph near the end of the finale.

Ex. 2.

The textual likeness is mere coincidence, and in the 'eighties, when Brahms's concerto was still more or less German property, it was not likely to strike the ears of audiences at the Lamoureux concerts in Paris. To-day the likeness is less easily ignored. Its character is essentially 'Brahmsian', and to hear it is to remember with what titanic power Brahms handles themes of its type. The remembrance dwarfs Lalo's comparatively tentative effort. The symphony is in four movements. The short opening Andante leads into an 'Allegro non troppo' on a theme of more sharply pointed rhythm; a charming Vivace (Scherzo) in E major is followed by a less distinctive Adagio in B flat, and the Finale based on a rhythmic version of the motto theme carries the movement forward energetically till it culminates in the broader version quoted above (Ex. 2). Among many touches of Lalo's gracious humour, a quality which the *Symphonie Espagnole* more consistently displays, is the opening of the Scherzo, where the first chords suggest that the movement is to be in the conventional key of B flat and the tripping tune poised on a D sharp shifts the tonality whimsically into E major.

It is not necessary to recapitulate here those characteristics of César Franck's style in instrumental composition which were fully described in the discussion of his chamber music. The Symphony in D minor affords a full exposition of them. Nor is it possible to discuss in detail the several 'poèmes symphoniques' which were the precursors of the full-length symphony. In Franck's case the production of a symphony seems the inevitable climax of his personal development, while in the cases of most of his French contemporaries and several of his pupils one is left with a lurking suspicion that they essayed it because the symphony was regarded as the hall-mark of complete attainment.

D'Indy grows lyrical about the wonders of Franck's symphony, describing with the aid of Guy Ropartz's phrase, 'le motif de la croyance', its spiritual programme of constant ascent towards pure joy and the living light. The 'theme of faith' is so constantly quoted in concert programmes that it is well to remind ourselves that it is part of the interpretation discovered in the music by disciples and not of a design avowed by the master. Franck is in intention at any rate writing pure symphony, that is, resting his faith on the capacity of his musical ideas to grow and fructify from the first thematic germ muttered by the basses

Ex. 3.

to the triumphant coda of the Finale. It is a symphony of ascents, which, after all, is the most usual scheme of design, the one to which Bruckner constantly worked. Its quality is to be judged by what is put into the scheme. Franck's thematic invention is far more decisive than Bruckner's, and the personal character of his melodies leaves his French contemporaries as far behind as that of Brahms leaves the Germans. His delight in the subtleties of harmony, particularly the high value which he sets on semitonic progressions, is as amply illustrated in the symphony as in the chamber music, and the method of accumulating ideas, so that those of the earlier movements get their fulfilment in association with those of the Finale, is pursued even more consistently here than elsewhere.

Franck uses a larger orchestra than Brahms ever thought necessary for the symphony, though not so large a one as Bruckner and the other post-Wagnerians pressed into service. The use of the cor anglais, to which the beautiful melody of the slow movement is assigned, was considered an innovation, and therefore blameworthy, when the symphony made its first appearance. To the ordinary clarinets he adds a bass clarinet chiefly for the sake of greater warmth in the colouring of the woodwind bass, and although his four horns and two trumpets are the chromatic instruments of modern usage, he preserves the old habit of the French theatrical orchestra of employing with them two cornets à pistons. For these he has no very distinctive use beyond increasing the brass chorus. They may be regarded merely as a stop which his organ happened to possess, and it has often been pointed out that Franck's orchestration, like Bruckner's, bears a good many traces of the organist's 'registration'. There is never any doubt, however, that both of them get the sound they want from the orchestra.

It is on the rhythmic side that Franck's construction is weak. The greater part of the symphony is an aggregation of four- and two-bar phrases which rarely expand into anything else. However skilfully they are contrasted by internal varieties of rhythm, or dovetailed into one another with 'overlaps', the monotony of their shape is inescapable. The better one gets to know the work the more this fundamental weakness forces itself on the ear.

Strip it of its decoration, of the glow of its instrumental colouring and the element of surprise entailed in its ingenious passage to and fro from one key to another, and one becomes aware of the absence of any real movement through many a long length of its melody.

The first subject section of the Finale affords a salient illustration. The following melodic outline is handled with every conceivable variety which pitch, modulation, and dynamics can provide, but not until the fifty-fifth bar is there the smallest suggestion of any extension of the initial rhythm, and then it is only a matter of six bars in which the arpeggio is treated with a slight quickening of the pulse by cross-phrasing (Ex. 4).

Bruckner's rhythmic weakness is looseness; Franck's is tightness; but rhythmic weakness of whatever sort is a thing fatal to

Ex. 4.

the spontaneous growth of the symphonic organism. Franck's Symphony is a noble work surely, perhaps the most noble attempt ever made to compensate by secondary interests for a deficiency in the primal one of symphonic design.

Franck's followers in the decade after his death laboured to till the field of the French symphony. Two meritorious examples are Ernest Chausson's Symphony in B flat, produced by the Société Nationale of which he was secretary (April 18th, 1891), and Paul Dukas's Symphony in C, the score of which bears the dates 1895–1896.

Chausson's symphony shows unmistakable signs of discipleship. The unison motive of its opening slow movement is clearly destined from the first for an 'apotheosis' of some kind, and sure enough it comes near the end of the Finale and is just of the kind that was dear to Franck's heart, the theme broadened out on the violins and accompanied by a rhythmic arpeggio in the bass, which had begun the third movement 'animé'.

VII   Q

Ex. 5. (a) Opening.   CHAUSSON. Symphony in B♭.

(b) Finale (string parts only).

Note, however, that Chausson's is not a grandiose ending, and that although all the instruments join in the last bars it is beneath a piano chord that the opening motive is last heard, solemnly murmured by a few bass instruments (double bassoon, horn with violoncello, and double bass soli). Between the first and last hearings of that motive Chausson's three movements (there is no scherzo) contain much that is more original in thought and conspicuously beautiful in the manner of its expression. Indeed the 'Allegro vivo' to which the slow introduction leads is the vigorous handling of a broad melody which has little in common with Franck.

Ex. 6.

The energy of this movement increases up to the end in a duple-time presto, which allows the feeling that the first Allegro has included in itself the element of scherzo. Chausson gets the effect of hurrying to a tumultuous close by the use of this theme in two forms at once.

Ex. 7.

(Extreme parts only.)

The slow movement depends on a more subtle sense of orchestral tone colour than Franck possessed, though it was certainly courting an obvious comment to write such a tune as the following for cor anglais:

Ex. 8.

Très expressif.

A few bars from this movement, in which the chief theme (horn and trumpet) is decorated by woodwind and supported by strings, will illustrate the advance of Chausson's scoring on that of his master (Ex. 9).

The harmonic structure is of a kind which seems ultimately to derive from Wagner, especially *Tristan*, and the emotional effect of the accented appoggiatura (see violoncello, viola, and 3rd trombone in bar 2 of the example) is one which Tchaikovsky was finally to exhaust in the 'Pathetic' Symphony. The decorative method of using the woodwind round the main structure is a favourite one of most of the French and Russian orchestrators of the period, particularly Saint-Saëns and Tchaikovsky. It is prominent also in the slow movement of Dukas's Symphony.

Paul Dukas (b. 1865) is an eclectic. Educated at the Paris Conservatoire in the 'eighties, he was not directly a pupil of Franck but of Dubois and Guiraud. The growing importance of Franck and his school exercised a formative influence on him, and having first made some mark with a concert overture, *Polyeucte* (praised for its faithfulness to the spirit of Corneille's tragedy), which Lamoureux produced in 1892, he settled down to the composition of this large-scale symphony from which he rigorously excluded all considerations other than those inherent in the fulfilment of the musical design. He called it simply *Symphonie en trois parties*: I, 'Allegro non troppo vivace, ma

très chanté.

con fuoco '; II, 'Andante espressivo e sostenuto '; III, 'Allegro spiritoso '.

The first starts without preamble of any sort; a chord of C major on the full orchestra, a tremolo on the strings, and the following theme given out by the strings with an air of business-like purpose in its presentation (Ex. 10).

It is not in itself a very eventful theme; its value will depend entirely on what grows from its subsequent treatment. The movement shows a determination to employ its possibilities of rhythm and of harmony consistently. The composer's command of form of the classical type is beyond question, and with the exception of certain episodes relating to a calmer second subject

Ex. 10.

V'CELLO and C.B.

(A minor) the whole of the extensive first movement is expanded
from the germs of these six bars. Unlike Franck and his pupils
Dukas allows each movement to grow spontaneously out of its
own thematic material. In that respect the Symphony is a
definite reaction from the 'cyclic' method extolled by d'Indy
as Franck's contribution to the evolution of symphonic form.
While it is remarkable for its harmonic enterprise and its rich
orchestral colouring, qualities which mark it decisively as a
work of the last decade of the century, it takes its stand on the
classical method; it places comparatively little reliance on
momentary expressiveness or even on the individual character
of themes, perhaps too little on what after all are the initial
attractions to the normal listener. The whole is a powerful piece
of musical thought, and if it were not considered an insult to
mention the name of Brahms in connexion with any work of
Gallic extraction, it might be said that Dukas alone of the late
nineteenth-century symphonists comes within measurable distance of what Brahms had achieved some twenty years earlier.

Dukas's Symphony may be taken as the high-water mark in
French symphonic music which had begun its rise with the fall
of the Empire in the Franco-Prussian war. In the year after
its production (1897) the Société Nationale brought out a more

modest work by Dukas, and one destined to bring him a fame far beyond that of the more recondite symphony. This was the scherzo, *L'Apprenti Sorcier*, a brilliant piece of descriptive writing, in which the principle of symphonic development was humorously used to picture the witch's cauldron boiling over and the havoc wrought by a magic which had got out of control. Perhaps there was a parable in that. Had Dukas discovered that after all he was the sorcerer's apprentice rather than the sorcerer himself? At any rate he went no further in purely symphonic composition. Debussy had arrived on the scene; the faun had begun his afternoon reverie. The Parisian mind was already more than a little wearied by the attempt to wrest the substance of music out of German hands. Debussy had found an attractive substitute for the more substantial form in the shadows and symbols of Mallarmé. Most of his countrymen followed him to steep themselves in the new impressionism, leaving d'Indy at the Schola Cantorum to find the proof of Franck's principles in theory rather than in practice. Meanwhile, another Belgian, not a musician but a poet and dramatist, Maurice Maeterlinck, influenced the direction in which both Debussy and Dukas were to move. His *Pelléas et Mélisande*, set to music by the former, ruled the line, as has been said, between the two centuries. His *Ariane et Barbe-Bleue*, undertaken as a subject for the latter's art, enabled Dukas to cross the line and take a place as one of the progenitors of the art of the new century.

The progress of the symphony in Russia rested on a wider basis of native genius than its counterpart in France. Tchaikovsky and Borodin approached the symphony from opposite points of view, but between them they established a recognizably Russian type. Tchaikovsky's early association with the Rubinstein brothers, Anton and Nicolas, gave him a cosmopolitan outlook. His music was from the first aimed at those audiences of Europe who, dazzled by the virtuosity of Anton Rubinstein, Liszt's only rival at the piano, had accepted the 'Ocean' Symphony as a great work of art. Tchaikovsky, too, would be a citizen of the world. If he picked up some folksongs of 'Little Russia' as themes for his Second Symphony it was not with the purpose of creating a local type, but because those particular tunes had for him a personality which he wanted to embody in his own music, just as had the characters of Hamlet, of Romeo and Juliet, of Paolo and Francesca, which he embodied in his most brilliant symphonic poems. The expression of personality in terms unmistakable to all hearers was the goal of his art, whether the work were called symphony or symphonic poem, overture or suite. In the symphonic poems, the overture '1812', and the like, he showed himself a stronger musical dramatist with an orchestra than he appeared to be when actually writing for the stage. In the six symphonies he dramatized his own emotions. This no doubt is broadly true of all symphonic composers; it is Tchaikovsky's consciousness of the necessity for doing so as an impulse towards composition, which makes it specially true of him. The programme for the Fourth Symphony, which he described to Madame von Meck,[1] shows his attitude conclusively. He did not intend it for publication. In the moment of putting it into words he realized its inadequacy. 'There lies the peculiarity of instrumental music,' he wrote; 'we cannot analyse it.' He was aware that his words had none of the dramatic eloquence which was the beginning and end of the music. By so much did he approach nearer to the symphonic ideal than the objective programmist could do. It was because in the last three symphonies that process of dramatizing personal emotions had become the all-absorbing passion of Tchaikovsky's life that

[1] The whole is set forth in *Life and Letters* of P. I. Tchaikovsky; the matter is well summarized by Mrs. Newmarch in her notes on the Fourth Symphony, *Concert-goer's Library*, vol. iv.

these symphonies took the world by storm and offended the
fastidious. The critic who wrote of the 'Pathetic' Symphony
that it 'is a veritable Castle of Otranto with no real depth of
mood anywhere in it'[1] was wrong, but there was plenty of
excuse for his error, in which he was by no means alone. The
long pedal-point leading to the return of the second subject
in the first movement, the trombones dropping their glutinous
tears at stated intervals into the persistent lament of the
descending melody, seems calculated to deceive the very elect.
And it was the elect that it did deceive.

Ex. 11.

---

[1] George Bernard Shaw. See *Music in London*, 1890–4, vol. iii, p. 169.

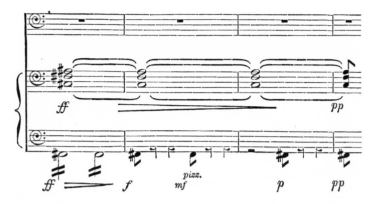

They thought that such blatancy could not be sincere, but it was. The crowds who flocked to hear the 'Pathetic' Symphony in the 'nineties, and who still flock to it now that it is forty years old, were and are untroubled by the theatrical mechanism. They could respond at once to the real depth of mood which lies behind the blatant assertions, which inspires the freshness of the melody in 5–4 time, impels the reckless march of the 'Allegro molto vivace', and enables the final diminuendo to justify all Tchaikovsky's displays of dolorous pedal-points.

Tchaikovsky awakened Western Europe to the existence of Russian music, carrying his own works to Vienna, Paris, Berlin, and London. Western Europe not unnaturally responded by hailing him as the typical representative of his country, and was not so far wrong in doing so, although Tchaikovsky had definitely held aloof from the National movement, and from those circles which Rimsky-Korsakov has described for us. National movements in art, and especially in music, are apt to be so much more national than the nation itself that the inhabitants of the country which gives them birth have considerable difficulty in recognizing them as native. In order to pursue his mission of revealing the soul of his country the national artist has to begin by viewing his subject from outside. He analyses appreciatively those qualities of the national temperament which the native generally takes for granted as the commonplaces of life. The English tourist landing for the first time at Boulogne sees in the uniforms of the gendarmes evidence of the Latin flair for the picturesque; the Frenchman visiting London regards the policeman on point duty as the epitome of British phlegm. Neither sees any parable in his own guardians of the law. Just so the conscious nationalist looks at his own country with the eyes of a foreigner. While he is still persuading his own people to see themselves in the mirror of his art, his unconscious colleague, who believes himself to be thoroughly cosmopolitan in his outlook, has proclaimed his country's characteristics to the whole world.

That was very much the case of Tchaikovsky and Borodin. The latter had been dead nine years when his Symphony in B minor made its first appearance in England[1] and was presented to an audience thoroughly familiar with Tchaikovsky's methods and all that they stood for, but knowing little or nothing of any other modern Russian music. Something in common between them could be immediately realized, a vividness, not merely in the instrumentation of clear bright colours[2] but in the maintenance of a simple rhythmic line in the melody, the love of pressing a point home by reiteration, and the refusal ever to cloud the main issues by the development of subsidiary episodes. But Borodin's melody appears at once more primitive and more refined than Tchaikovsky's, primitive in the use of shapes suggested by folksong and peasant dance, refined by the careful selection of apposite details.

[1] Philharmonic Society, Feb. 27th, 1896. The concert was conducted by Sir Alexander Mackenzie.

[2] The score published by Bessel is described as 'édition revue par N. Rimsky-Korsakov and A. Glazounov'. So much of Borodin's work has been subject to that editorship that it is impossible to say how far vividness of orchestration is a characteristic of Borodin's art.

Entirely free from that morbid strain which goes with Tchaikovsky's determination to be self-revealing, Borodin exhibits an intellectual control of his material which is essential to true symphony. The cynical generalization that the Russian, in art as in politics, is a realist who sees things as they are and proceeds to make them a good deal worse, may be applicable to Tchaikovsky but is not true of Borodin. In this symphony, which is closely contemporary with Tchaikovsky's Fourth, he regards the elements of his country's music as clear-sightedly as Tchaikovsky regards his personal emotions. He proceeds to make them a great deal better by an instinct for musical shapeliness which idealizes the material without destroying its virility. Compare Borodin's treatment of a pedal-point (Ex. 13) with Tchaikovsky's quoted above. The much earlier E flat Symphony of Borodin shows many of the same traits of style but it has been left unjustly in the background, perhaps because of the popularity of the B minor. The exquisite sparkle of the Scherzo and the romantic colouring of the Andante in the

VII

Ex. 13. BORODIN. Symphony in B minor.

B minor give the work a special place in the affections of concert-goers, but the corresponding movements of the E flat might well share something of that place.[1]

Rimsky-Korsakov's attitude towards the symphony was peculiar. His first important essay in composition was a symphony which he wrote while still serving in the Navy, and its date is earlier than those of Borodin or Tchaikovsky which have been discussed. A later work (Op. 32 in C minor) also bore the title of symphony without description or qualification. Rimsky-Korsakov's devotion to principles of musical structure and the determination which he showed to acquire technical accomplishment seemed to dispose him to take a classical view of the symphonic form, but his genius lay all in the direction of descriptive programme music. His Second Symphony was the now famous 'Antar', later described as 'Oriental Suite'; the symphonic poem, 'Sadko', was its close contemporary, and these with the symphonic suite 'Scheherezade' are his most characteristic

[1] It must be remembered that the orchestration of both Borodin's symphonies as we have them has been revised by Rimsky-Korsakov and Glazounov.

works for the orchestra. He revised and re-orchestrated his
own works with as much critical zeal as he bestowed on the
unfinished works of his contemporaries. He was unflagging in
pursuit of his ideal of technical perfection, but while in other
composers that ideal has frequently had the effect of leading
towards absolute music, often losing its way in formality and
emotional aloofness, in Rimsky-Korsakov's case it was used to
quicken the pictorial sense, to heighten the orchestral colouring
and clarify the connexion between his musical expression and
the literary or poetic idea which inspired it. There is in fact
little of that spontaneous growth of musical ideas which has
been described as the essence of symphony. The themes are
laid out in most subtly devised patterns in accordance with the
requirements of the pictorial situation of the moment, and all
the resources of a musically creative mind are requisitioned to
contribute to an audible pageantry. Rimsky-Korsakov is the
musical embodiment of the *Thousand and One Nights*.

Other Russian composers of the period who essayed the
symphony were Mily Balakirev (1836–1910), prime mover among
the nationalist group, whose success however was greater in the
picturesque overtures on Russian, Czech, and Spanish themes,
and the symphonic poem *Tamara*; Serge Taneiev, whose severe
classicism in chamber music has been discussed in an earlier
chapter, and Basil Kalinnikov (1866–1901), whose interesting
and vigorous Symphony in G minor, owing much to the example
of Borodin, was played through the capitals of Europe during
the time that the Russian symphonists were in vogue.[1] Balakirev contemplated and wrote parts of three symphonies
during his long career, though only two, in C major and D
major, were ultimately completed, at dates (1898 and 1908)

[1] Kalinnikov's symphony was introduced to London by Serge Kusse-
vitsky on May 26th, 1908. That it was well received was proved by the
fact that it was given at the Bristol Festival in the same year and at the
Promenade Concerts at Queen's Hall in the following year.

after the works of his compatriots, on whom he had exerted so strong an influence, had made their several appearances.

But none of the Russians after Tchaikovsky devoted themselves to the symphony with anything like the assiduity of Alexander Glazounov. His brilliant youth and his subsequent declension have already been discussed, but it must be recalled here that his First Symphony was produced at Weimar under the auspices of Liszt as early as 1884, and that seven others followed it in rapid succession. It has been suggested that Glazounov's development away from the ideals of illustrative music of the Balakirev group can be traced in the dedications of his works.[1] His earliest works pay homage to the nationalist composers of his own country. The Second Symphony (F sharp minor) is dedicated very naturally to Liszt, the Third (D major) to Tchaikovsky, the Fourth (E flat) to Anton Rubinstein, the Fifth (B flat) to Taneiev, and the Sixth (C minor) to his colleague, Felix Blumenfeld. But this probably means no more than the composer's catholic-minded desire to pay honour wherever honour was due, and after the dedication to Liszt that which has the most obvious appropriateness is the name of Glazounov's patron and publisher, M. P. Belaiev, on the score of the Seventh Symphony (F major). The Eighth (E flat) bears no dedication.

The series is autobiographical in the sense that in it can be traced Glazounov's development from a boyhood in which initiative and initiation are almost evenly balanced to a maturity in which there is complete command of every technical resource, a power of moulding forms on a larger scale than Borodin's, a power of thinking in musical terms without the incentive of external suggestions of any kind, and a superiority to the vulgarizing influence of sensationalism. In the later symphonies, indeed, Glazounov attained a fine balance of thought and expression which at once endeared them to the more reflecting kind

[1] Montagu Nathan, *History of Russian Music*, p. 247.

of musical mind; in England, for example, to such a man as Stanford who performed them at the Royal College of Music, produced the Eighth Symphony at the Leeds Festival, and secured for the composer the degree of Doctor of Music *honoris causa* in the University of Cambridge.

Glazounov made his first appearance in England when he conducted the Fourth Symphony at a Philharmonic concert. In the decade between this and the appearance of the Eighth his work gained the esteem of all discriminating musicians, but never the affections of a wide public in this country. This may indicate a limitation which at first is a little difficult to account for. Glazounov does not, like Bruckner, traverse the same course in each symphony. His initial themes differ widely in character. Being an instinctive orchestral composer, he has no temptation to dally with the organ-loft crescendos of Bruckner and of Franck.

Yet if we examine a few of these initial themes and their treatments and compare them with Tchaikovsky and Borodin we find that they have not the dramatic power of either of these masters with whom the initial theme is invariably an arresting gesture of some sort. In the Fifth Symphony Glazounov intends to arrest by emphasis, in the Sixth by reserve. The Seventh opens in a mood of pastoral quietude, the Eighth with gusto (the theme of the Eighth here quoted is set against a background of rustling strings) (Ex. 14).

But none of them is quite conclusive; of none does one say at once, 'that is a Glazounov tune'. Rather one says: this is the sort of tune which is found everywhere in the generation which followed immediately on Brahms and Wagner. The ideas are generic rather than individual, and those quoted from Nos. V, VI, and VIII seem almost interchangeable. No amount of skilful musicianship can atone for the lack of the essential impulse behind the themes and their relation to one another in

Ex. 14. (a)

GLAZOUNOV. Symphony V.

Moderato maestoso.

(b)

simile.

Symphony VI.

Adagio.

p dolce.

pp misterioso.

Symphony VII.
Allegro moderato.

Symphony VIII.
Allegro moderato.

the growth of a symphonic design, and while it is possible to go through the scores of Glazounov and discover every other merit in them, in the end the conclusion is apt to be that the whole elaborate structure has not quite justified itself.

This, however, is true principally of his first movements. The greatest of Glazounov's merits is that he warms to his work, that the slow movements and scherzos (the latter in original rhythms and unhampered by the classical tradition of 3–4 time) present piquant contrasts, and the finales have a brilliance of their own and a directness of style which differentiates them

clearly from the opening allegros. None of the greater Russians
made a fetish of thematic continuity through the several movements of their symphonies, although Tchaikovsky allowed his
motto themes in the Fourth and Fifth Symphonies to strike
across his later movements for a dramatic purpose. Glazounov
goes forward and attains his climaxes in finales by the novelty
of his ideas, not by any process of recapitulation.

The Sixth Symphony (op. 58 in C minor), dated St. Petersburg
1896, is generally considered to be the high-water mark of
Glazounov's symphonic creations, and a closer examination of it
here may serve to illustrate his qualities. Its ' Adagio misterioso ',
beginning with the fugato quoted from above, leads to an
' Allegro passionato ' in which the same theme in a flowing
duple time[1] takes the lead, and is developed with exuberant
energy. A second theme, ' più tranquillo ', is the chief point of
contrast,

Ex. 15.

_____

[1] It is written as 2–2, but the movement in triplet quavers gives it more
the character of 12–8.

but, as in Brahms's C minor, the second subject remains in an ancillary position, and it is from the arpeggio of the first that the main interests of the movement unfold themselves.

The first Allegro is followed by a 'Tema con variazioni' and an Intermezzo, and as the seven variations are of sharply contrasted characters and some bear such titles as 'Scherzerino', 'Fugato', 'Notturno', and the last of them is labelled 'Finale', the centre of the work takes on rather more of the character of an orchestral suite of short connected pieces than of symphony proper. It is in these variations that Glazounov's skill as an orchestrator appears at its best. Each one growing out of the simple

Ex. 16.

theme[1] has a distinctive character and a delicate colouring of
its own, and until the 'Finale' the lighter instruments, strings,
woodwinds, and horns, are the chief speakers. In the course of
the 'Notturno' the dropping fourth of the theme develops into
a new figure on the woodwind,

Ex. 17.

adding a ring as of distant bells which insinuates itself into the
'Finale' to the set of variations, and also pervades the dainty
'Intermezzo' (3–8 time) which follows the variations.

After so much digression a last movement of a very positive
character is needed to balance with the first and to leave a final
impression of symphonic energy. This Glazounov achieves in a
movement in C major based on the following tune, in which the
stamp of feet marking the syncopated rhythm of the dance is
almost audible in the orchestration:

Ex. 18.

[1] Suggestive of that gentle type of Russian folksong which attracted
Tchaikovsky when he wrote the slow movement of his Quartet in D. See
Chapter IV, p. 98.

Nothing can be urged against this theme on the score of deficient personality. Its cross accents are hurled to and fro; its shape is changed in a number of ways, notably,

Ex. 19.

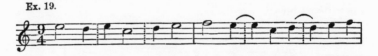

and with vigorous counterpoints set against it the whole movement sweeps along irresistibly to a climax until the ringing bell theme (Ex. 17) with chromatic harmonies peals out on the full orchestra, proving that, after all, the imaginative fancies of the variations were not altogether digressions from the main progress of the symphony. The movement is immensely effective at a first hearing. The more closely it is studied, the higher must be the estimate of the composer's power of handling the cumulative forces of the symphonic form.

It has already been suggested that the question of national idiom becomes a complex one in the case of the Czech composer, Antonin Dvořák, and in the discussion of his chamber music above some further elaboration of the point was promised in connexion with his symphonies.

There has been so much confusion about the dating and numbering of Dvořák's symphonies that it will be well first to recapitulate the plain facts. There are in existence nine symphonies by Dvořák, of which four were composed before the grant of the Austrian Ministry for Education (1875) brought him to the notice of Brahms and introduced him to the world at large. These are:

No. 1. Symphony in C minor, discovered amongst Dvořák's MSS. as late as 1923.

No. 2. Symphony in B flat, of about the same date (1865), still unpublished.

No. 3. Symphony in E flat.

No. 4. Symphony in D minor.

Numbers 3 and 4 were withheld from publication by Dvořák although No. 3 had been publicly produced in Prague under Smetana's direction. They were both published after his death by Breitkopf and Härtel. All these early works have been much acclaimed by that posthumous criticism which invariably scrutinizes every remaining production of an acknowledged master. But Dvořák's own carelessness for their survival shows that he did not regard them as the product of his maturity.

The series of five symphonies by which Dvořák represented himself to the world is as follows:

No. 5 (called No. 3) in F, originally op. 24, now op. 76. 1875.

No. 6 (called No. 1) in D major, op. 60. 1880.

No. 7 (called No. 2) in D minor, op. 70. 1884–5.

No. 8 (called No. 4) in G major, op. 88. 1889.

No. 9 ('From the New World') in E minor, op. 95. 1893.

The disordered numbering is due to the fact that it was not until after 1887, when Dvořák dedicated the F major Symphony to Hans von Bülow, that Breitkopf and Härtel undertook its publication, and von Bülow then very properly took on himself the task of making it known. Meantime the D major and the D minor had gone forth as numbers 1 and 2.

The D major was dedicated to Hans Richter, who already had done much to propagate the knowledge of Dvořák's work, and in this dedication, like that to von Bülow, the composer showed a lively sense of favours to come. Dvořák himself conducted it together with his patriotic *Husitska* (Hussite) overture and the second of the *Three Slavonic Rhapsodies* at a concert of the Philharmonic Society (London) on March 19th, 1884. This was the period of his great success before the English public. He paid two visits to England in that year, returning in the autumn to conduct the *Stabat Mater* in Worcester Cathedral and the D major Symphony at the secular concert of the Three Choirs Festival. For the next few years England was ready both to sing the choral music of Dvořák and to listen to the D major Symphony as often as Richter and others chose to play it. In 1885 the Philharmonic Society produced the D minor Symphony as 'composed for this concert (March 26th) and conducted by the composer', and the next time that Dvořák chose to write a symphony, Op. 88 in G, not only did the Philharmonic give its first performance (April 24th, 1890) but the English firm of Novello secured the publication of the score.

Thus Dvořák's symphonies won the heart of the British public at a time when those of Brahms were still considered difficult of comprehension and the very name of Tchaikovsky was generally unknown. His English fame stimulated American ambition. What England patronized the United States determined to possess. The 'National Conservatory of Music of America'[1] wanted a director and American music wanted the quality of nationalism. What more simple than to acquire the man who was everywhere spoken of as leader of a national music in Europe, plant him in New York, and require him to produce music redolent of the soil of America! Dvořák accepted the directorship in 1892 and held it till 1895. He took both the teaching and the commission to create an American music quite seriously, and the first and most important outcome of the com-

---

[1] The National Conservatory was founded by Mrs. J. M. Thurber with a charter from the State of New York in 1885. For an account of its activities see the American Supplement (1920) to *Grove's Dictionary*, edited by Waldo Selden Pratt.

mission was the Symphony in E minor, 'From the New World', produced by Anton Seidl before the Philharmonic Society of New York on December 16th, 1893.

The 'New World' Symphony, as it was soon popularly called, became an immediate favourite with the public on both sides of the Atlantic and in London proved to be the only one by Dvořák which was not swept under by the rising tide of Russianism. In America it became the subject of a controversy which still echoes in the programme notes supplied to audiences of orchestral concerts. Did the title mean that the music was really and truly the outcome of the New World, or was Dvořák still a Czech at heart recollecting his country's attributes in exile? It required only a little common sense to set this controversy at rest even before the arguments of the disputants had been stated. A year's sojourn in New York was hardly likely to convert the Czech peasant into the '100 per cent. American', and those who wanted to find recollections of his country's music could have no difficulty in doing so. It is worth noting that the scene in his opera, *The Jacobin*, most intimately bound up with his childhood's life at Nelahozeves, that in the schoolhouse where the old schoolmaster conducts a singing class, is full of small musical details which instantly recall the manner of the 'New World' Symphony.[1] It is equally certain, however, that Dvořák in America set himself to assimilate what was presented to him

[1] Compare with the slow movement and Scherzo of the symphony the accompaniment to Terinka's song—

(a)

&c.

and the rhythmic use throughout the scene of an augmented triad—

(b)

as the possible source of an American idiom, the negro melodies which were sung to him by Mr. Henry T. Burleigh,[1] a negro singer of cultivation, then a student of the National Conservatory. He was keenly attracted by these naïve and simple ditties, especially by those features of them which contrasted with the classical key system, and by their peculiarities of rhythm, more particularly the suggestions of syncopation, which at that time had not become sophisticated as they have been since. He would sometimes stop the singer to inquire particularly of such a point as the use of the flat seventh in the scale, whether that was the way that the negro slaves sang it. His interest is clearly reflected in the Symphony in such a point as

Ex. 20.

as well as in the principal theme of the Finale. A particular favourite with him was *Swing low, sweet chariot*, of which the tune is

Ex. 21.

Swing low, sweet cha - ri - ot,   Com-ing for to car-ry me   home,

Swing low, sweet cha - ri - ot,   Com-ing for to car-ry me   home.

[1] Henry T. Burleigh has since become well known to Europeans as the arranger of a large number of 'Negro Spirituals'. I had the pleasure of meeting him in New York in 1923, when he sang to me some of the songs which had so charmed Dvořák thirty years before. His soft tenor voice and the plaintive humour of his rendering cannot fail to make their appeal to any sensitive listener. What is written here of the 'New World' Symphony is based on my conversations with Mr. Burleigh and on correspondence with him and with Mr. H. E. Krehbiel. A large part of a letter the latter wrote to me at an earlier date will be found incorporated by Mrs. Newmarch in the English edition of Hoffmeister's *Dvořák*.

Its outline is unmistakable in the second subject of the first movement, and it has been pointed out as conclusive evidence that Dvořák did actually quote at least one specimen of negro melody in the 'New World' Symphony. But even here it must be observed that the characteristic syncopation of the song is absent from the melody of the symphony, which after the first phrase continues quite differently.

Dvořák had never made a practice of quoting his traditional native melodies in his symphonic works. His own genius was essentially melodic and he held the creation of melody to be the first business of a composer. Even the *Three Slavonic Rhapsodies* for orchestra (Op. 45), although ostensibly national in intention in a way that the symphonies made no claim to be, are without quotations of the kind. As Šourek has said, they enshrine the 'Volksgeist' not the 'Volkslied', and, written in 1878, they may be regarded as a prelude to Dvořák's richest symphonic period. In the four symphonies produced in Europe, so far from stressing local idiom, he had reached out beyond it, designing apparently to assimilate his native speech to the usages of classical style to prove that his own melodic invention, coloured though it necessarily was by national traditions, was capable of attaining universality of expression.

This is what he wished to do with the slave songs of the American negroes, to absorb the essence of their style and allow it to influence his own melodic creations just as far as it could do so spontaneously without conscious quotation. The phrase from *Swing low, sweet chariot* is no more than a sign of incomplete absorption. In point of fact others of the negro songs follow something of the same curve, for example *Wai my brudder*:

Ex. 22.

&c.

Krehbiel wrote of the Largo of the 'New World' Symphony,
'It is the musical publication of a mood which came over him
[Dvořák] when he was reading the story of Hiawatha's wooing.
He was fond of Longfellow's poem and even thought of it for
an opera subject.' Here is an American source of inspiration
far removed from the negro, yet in the principal theme of the
Largo on the cor anglais the influence of such 'Spirituals' as the
two following is as evident as anywhere else in the symphony:

Ex. 23. (a)

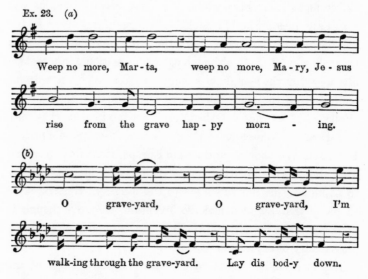

Weep no more, Mar-ta, weep no more, Ma-ry, Je-sus

rise from the grave hap-py morn - ing.

(b)

O grave-yard, O grave-yard, I'm

walk-ing through the grave-yard. Lay dis bod-y down.

The reference above to *The Jacobin* has suggested that the
rising third was characteristic of Dvořák's melody long before
he went to America, and to this may be added the further suggestion that the strong appeal of the negro songs, and perhaps
also of the Indian folk-tale, to Dvořák, was that he found something akin to himself and his own people in it. Undoubtedly the
sophistication of the life he was required to lead in New York
was antipathetic to him, and he seized greedily on everything
he could find there which was in tune with the rural simplicity
of his upbringing. The 'New World' Symphony bears no trace

of the white civilization of America. When Krehbiel, pointing
to a passage near the end of the Finale, suggested that the
viola's accompaniment to the Largo melody was 'curiously like
Yankee Doodle', Dvořák replied, 'Why, that is the principal
theme in diminution', which it undoubtedly is.[1]

Ex. 24.

The resemblance to *Yankee Doodle* will hardly strike the
European ear, and certainly the symphony as a whole has no
affinity with those phases of transatlantic life which the European
thinks of as 'Yankee Doodleism'. What would Dvořák have
thought of the modern exploitation of the negro in American
music? He was spared the experience of it. His was a romantic

[1] See letter mentioned above, Hoffmeister, p. 78. Compare the example
24 with O. G. Sonneck's description of 'Yankee Doodle' in *Grove's Dictionary*,
3rd ed., vol. v, p. 766.

interest happily able to ignore the fact that the realistic imitation of negro habits by the white man must lead to the degradation of both.

Dvořák's artistic creed was a simple one. He believed in melody as the prime source of the artist's individuality. He knew his own melody to be stamped with the characteristics of his country's traditional melody, and whether he composed for England or for America he remained true to himself. He refused no enrichment of experience, but he desired to assimilate each experience and make it part of himself. In this desire he may not always have succeeded as thoroughly as he did in the case of the negro elements incorporated in the 'New World' Symphony. He was sometimes too ready to accept influences, as he was to listen to the advice of others, but in the main his impressionableness, combined as it was with an unshakable individuality, was a gain to him.

The undeniable influence of Brahms on Dvořák's symphonies further demands a little consideration. It was in fact just the influence which Dvořák needed to consolidate his work in its early stages. It was exerted very little if at all on the musical material, that is the melody, but was powerful in its effect on his construction, in which, as we have seen, Dvořák was demonstrably deficient at the outset of his career. This must be emphasized, because it has become a commonplace of criticism to detect the influence of Brahms whenever Dvořák falls into a reflective mood, and when in fact he is often most himself. The 'deep shadows' of the Symphony in D minor are attributed to Brahms, while the 'cheerful tone' of the one in D major is held to be characteristic of Dvořák and of Dvořák only. This is misleading.

Take the opening of Dvořák's Symphony in D, remembering that Brahms's Symphony No. 2 in the same key had appeared a couple of years before it, and, though the idea is all Dvořák's

own, it will be seen that the constructional plan is very close to
that of Brahms even to the point of an identity in the harmonic
sequence (Ex. 25).

An episode in a more pointed rhythm, 'un poco più animato',
follows the quotation and leads to the reassertion of the opening
phrase by the full orchestra. Look further on after the double
bar to the way in which Dvořák approaches his development
of this idea, and the impression must be confirmed that not
merely Brahms's general method of structure but the example of

the Second Symphony in particular is acting as his unconscious guide.

The Symphony in G, because of its freedom from precedent of any kind, may be said to be the crown of Dvořák's work. It fascinates from first to last by the spontaneity of its melody and the sense it produces that those melodies, sometimes sharply contrasted to the point of incongruity, could only have been handled as Dvořák handles them. From the very outset the dark shadows and the cheerful tone vie with one another, and neither Brahms nor any one else can advise about the future of such diverse elements as the following:

Ex. 26.

It is impossible to show the originality of Dvořák's development of these ideas without more liberal transcriptions from the
score than are possible here, but one further extract must be
given to show how the denouement is prepared and reached by
the re-entry of the theme on the trumpets at the beginning of
the recapitulation. As the instrumentation is essential to its
character the score is given in full. Even in this moment of
highest excitement Dvořák's scoring is very light. There is
absolutely none of that overbearing insistence on mere tone
which Tchaikovsky, Glazounov, and indeed all the representatives
of the big nations take delight in. It should be noticed particularly how the horns in bars 9 and 10 reinforce the woodwind with
their chords on the weak quaver, and how when the trumpets
in C sail in with the tune, the trombone accompaniment is
lightened to allow the tune to be salient. While the whole of
the score is marked *ff* at that moment the trumpets, which are
the singing parts, are to be content with a forte (Ex. 27).

It is only fitting that a chapter in which the symphony has
been pursued from Paris to Moscow and from Prague to New
York should include some mention of what was accomplished in
England by native composers during the period which it covers.
Our composers were exceedingly active and their orchestral
works more readily came to a public hearing than did their
chamber music. Some of them were produced at the orchestral
concerts which Hans Richter conducted at St. James's Hall
from 1881 onward. There were two institutions in London
which were ready to afford them opportunity, the Philharmonic
Society and the Crystal Palace Orchestral concerts. The Philharmonic was a society of musicians which aimed at producing
whatever was likely to be of interest to its members, amongst
whom were many composers. The Crystal Palace concerts were
the result of Sir George Grove's evangelistic zeal during the
years of his secretaryship. August Manns was engaged to form

a band and to conduct there Saturday afternoon concerts in order to popularize the best in orchestral music wherever it was to be found.[1] Grove, devoted as he was to the classics of the symphony, was ready to encourage any attempt made by his younger contemporaries to emulate the glories of the classics. Both institutions suffered from the tendency to insist overmuch on the classic traditions of the symphony, and the many English composers whose works they brought forward were undoubtedly hampered by their sense of duty towards classicism. They were perhaps too anxious to excel in what was constantly pointed to as the highest form of orchestral music, and there was even a

Ex. 27.

Ex. 27 *cont.*

Ex. 27 *cont.*

Ex. 27 *cont.*

Ex. 27 *cont.*

Ex. 27 *cont.*

curious tendency to regard success in slighter forms of composition as a little derogatory to the composer's reputation.
This misprision even haunted Arthur Sullivan when, having
proved his skill in every form of composition, including the
symphony,[1] he discovered in light opera the form of art ideally
suited to his genius.

Frederic Cowen (born 1852) had a melodic talent and a skill
in handling the orchestra which was happily proved in suites,
overtures, and pieces with such fancy titles as *The Language of
Flowers*, *In Fairyland*, and *The Butterfly's Ball*. Between the
years 1869, when his First Symphony in C minor was given at
St. James's Hall, and 1897, when Richter produced one in E,
called 'Idyllic', he wrote six symphonies. No. 3 in C minor, called
'Scandinavian', came nearest to achieving permanence. First
produced in 1880, it was frequently given in London (three times
at the Crystal Palace) and even gained some acceptance abroad.
Most of his works were duly honoured by the Philharmonic as
they appeared, went the round of English concert societies, and
then disappeared. No. 4 in B flat minor, called 'The Welsh',
produced at the Philharmonic in 1884, had that much vogue.
This was the period of Dvořák's success in England when the
idea that the symphony should reflect some local colour was in the
ascendant. That idea is found in the titles of Stanford's 'Irish'
Symphony (Richter, 1887) and Parry's 'English' Symphony
(Philharmonic, 1889). The programmes of the Philharmonic in
1889, one of the many seasons during which Cowen was the
Society's conductor, illustrate rather remarkably the progress
of the native symphonists, since at three consecutive concerts
in May and June were heard three such symphonies, each
conducted by its composer. They were Cowen's No. 5 in F,

[1] Sullivan's Symphony in E, called the 'Irish', was first given at the Crystal
Palace in 1866. A concerto for violoncello and orchestra was produced
there by Piatti in the same year. This was also the period of his overture
In Memoriam, which attained a far wider popularity.

Parry's No. 3 in C (the 'English'), and Frederic Cliffe's No. 1 in C minor.

The right of Stanford's and Parry's symphonies to their respective national titles is unquestionable, but they earn the right in different ways. Stanford was a devoted student of the folksong which all the world had recognized from the time of Moore's *Irish Melodies* onward to be a type of very distinctive beauty. He steeped himself in its modes and rhythms, arranging for voice and piano with delicate skill innumerable traditional melodies.[1] His original songs, the opera *Shamus O'Brien*, and the rhapsodies for orchestra on Irish folksongs attest the strength of the influence on his personal style. The 'Irish' Symphony is part and parcel of that devotion. Parry was scarcely aware of the existence of English folksong when he wrote the 'English' Symphony, though it was to be found not far from his Gloucestershire home, and indeed might have been discovered had he looked for it among the humbler tenants on his family estate at Highnam. But a young English squire, educated at Eton and Oxford, was in the 'eighties not much in the way of discovering what the farm labourers sang on Saturday nights. Nor did he feel any need to seek inspiration at such a source. 'Love of country, of freedom, of action and heartiness' were the qualities[2] which he conceived to be the heritage of the Englishman, and therefore of English music, and it was these qualities which he wished specially to embody in the 'English' Symphony.

[1] See *Songs of Old Ireland*, words by A. P. Graves, music arranged by C. V. Stanford, 1882. *Irish Songs and Ballads*, by the same, 1893.

[2] Parry's book *The Evolution of the Art of Music*, 1893, contains a valuable chapter on 'Folk-music' which quotes one English tune, *The Carman's Whistle*, and makes some generalizations on rather insufficient evidence about the characteristics of English folk-music. The phrase quoted above is his sum of them. *English Country Songs*, by Miss L. E. Broadwood and Mr. J. A. Fuller-Maitland, published in the same year, was the pioneer publication of that revival in English folksong of which Mr. Cecil Sharp was to be the protagonist in the next generation.

Parry produced four symphonies within the decade of the
'eighties; No. 1 in G (Birmingham Festival, 1882), No. 2 in F,
called the 'Cambridge', written for the Cambridge University
Musical Society conducted by Stanford (1883), No. 3 in C, the
'English', and No. 4 in E minor (Richter, 1889). The 'Cambridge'
Symphony had as its background the undergraduate life of the
University, but the Fourth Symphony appeared without any
descriptive title or suggestion of programme. Twenty-one years
later, however, Parry re-wrote No. 4 in E minor for a concert of
the Philharmonic Society (1910), and issued it with descriptive
titles to its four movements which showed the symphony to be
in line with that subjective attitude of mind which dominated
his later years. It was now given the general title 'Finding the
Way', and its four movements bore the mottoes, 'Looking for
it' (first Allegro), 'Thinking of it' (slow movement), 'Playing on
it' (Scherzo), and 'Girt for it' (Finale). Similar in design was the
'Symphonic Fantasia', 1912, actually a symphony in four linked
movements, bearing as sub-titles the words, 1. 'Stress', 2. 'Love',
3. 'Play', 4. 'Now'.

But this aspect of Parry's art is best considered in connexion
with vocal music in which his thought runs clearer. He was
never quite at ease with the orchestra, and though the symphonies from first to last are examples of that striking combination of great physical energy with an introspective mind, which
made the fascination of his personality, no one of them completely convinces the most sympathetic listeners that in it the
way has been found.

Parry's symphonies then belong to two periods of his career,
the first four to that time when he played a leading part in what
has been called 'the English renaissance'; the revised No. 4 and
the 'Symphonic Fantasia' to the years of his age when he had
become rather isolated from the main current of events, and was
on the whole well content to be so. The isolated figures in

musical history frequently become more approachable when the current which swept past them has spent its strength, and a revival of interest in the more recondite aspects of Parry's art may yet be found in the future.

Some revival is no less due to the greater works of Stanford, but it is harder to say where revival should begin, because his list of works, with opus numbers running up to near 200, contains every conceivable form and combination, amongst which there is a considerable portion still remaining in manuscript. The 'Irish' Symphony (No. 3) was followed in 1889 by another in F, which got its first performance in Berlin. Stanford at this time kept in close touch with both Joachim and von Bülow and was able to secure for his work a measure of reciprocity which was not, however, a very large one considering the extent of his labours for modern German music in England. Three other symphonies followed at intervals. No. 5 in D, *L'Allegro ed il Penseroso* (1895), is a musical reverie on Milton's poems containing a peculiarly intimate slow movement. No. 6 in E flat, 'In Memoriam G. F. Watts' (1906), is a finely conceived work in an elegiac manner. No. 7 in D minor (1912), written for the centenary celebrations of the Philharmonic Society, has some conscious restraint of style in its three short movements, as though the composer were a little anxious to reprove the exuberance of the age by a return to something like those proportions which belonged to the symphony when the Philharmonic was founded. Stanford was essentially a stylist, and it was the suspicion of a consciously adopted manner for the occasion, here and elsewhere, which limited the appreciation of his genuinely lyrical inspiration and his unfailingly apt workmanship.

Were we to draw the line strictly at the turn of the century not only would the later phases of the work of Parry, Stanford, and their contemporaries be excluded, but the name of Edward

Elgar (1857–1934) would not even be mentioned here. It was only in the last years of the century that Elgar's name became widely known as a composer whose writing for the orchestra had a vivid quality hitherto unknown in English music. The performance by Hans Richter of *Variations on an Original Theme for Orchestra* (Op. 36) at St. James's Hall in 1899 was the decisive announcement of Elgar's arrival on the scene. The word 'Enigma' at the head of the score, the dedication 'to my friends pictured within', and the initials of those friends appended to the several variations, aroused curiosity, but the music itself did more; it revealed the hand of a master. From that day forward everything that Elgar might have to say with an orchestra was a matter of immediate public concern. He was in no hurry, however, to venture on the dangerous ground of the full-length symphonic form. He was fully occupied in the next few years with the series of oratorios produced at three triennial Birmingham festivals, and with sundry minor, but by no means unimportant, orchestral works.

Elgar was well on in his fifty-second year when Richter produced at Manchester on December 3rd, 1908, his Symphony, No. 1 in A flat. It is doubtful whether any purely orchestral symphony ever fired the enthusiasm of the general public so immediately. Given a few days later in London, it was repeated on every available occasion and sometimes in the most unlikely surroundings. Enterprising commercialists of the universal-provisioner type were even known to engage an orchestra and to advertise performances of Elgar's Symphony as an attraction to their palm courts and lounges. It went abroad to European capitals and was speedily produced in America. Nothing like the impression it created had been known in England since the furore over Tchaikovsky's 'Pathetic' a dozen years before, and about it hung none of the morbid suggestion of personal tragedy which had whetted the appetite for Tchaikovsky. It was laid out on grandiose lines the like of which a country still ignorant of Bruckner and Mahler had never known, and its tone is one of exaltation. Elgar's favourite direction, 'nobilmente', proclaims the emotional mood of this and almost every subsequent work of his on a larger scale. The leading theme of the Symphony in A flat might be labelled 'the splendour of achievement', a counterpart to Franck's 'motif de la croyance'. Structurally Elgar has a good deal in common with both Bruckner and Franck; he shares in some of their weaknesses. But his melody is broader and richer than Franck's and infinitely stronger as an expression of personality than Bruckner's. Moreover, his treatment of the orchestra is entirely free from those suggestions from the organ-loft which hang round the two earlier masters.

The Symphony in A flat was quickly followed by the Violin Concerto in B minor, a work of symphonic dimensions written for and first played by Kreisler (1910), by a Second Symphony in E flat designed to be a 'loyal tribute' to King Edward VII and dedicated to his memory (1911), and the symphonic poem, 'Falstaff', based on scenes from Shakespeare's Henry IV (Leeds, 1913). These, with the slighter Violoncello Concerto in E minor which appeared after the war, represent the bulk of Elgar's symphonic work.[1]

The Second Symphony is emotionally contrasted with the First. While its first movement is described as 'Allegro vivace e nobilmente' the exuberant vivacity of the principal theme mitigates the consciousness of nobility. It bears the motto from Shelley,

> Rarely, rarely comest thou,
> Spirit of delight,

and as in Brahms's Third Symphony, the 'Spirit of delight' fades

[1] A Third Symphony was projected and had been announced for production by the British Broadcasting Corporation, but when the composer died on Feb. 23, 1934, it was stated that the score was in too fragmentary a condition to give any certain indication of his design.

from the Finale in a wistful diminuendo which combines the principal themes of both the first and last movements.

The ending of this symphony may be, probably is, influenced by the memorial character of the work hinted at in the dedication. There is more in this than the conventional 'loyal tribute'. Not only had King Edward VII honoured Elgar with such appreciation as Royalty can confer, but Elgar was in effect the musical laureate of the short Edwardian era in English history. His music closely fitted the tone and the temper of the time between the South African war which clouded the end of Queen Victoria's reign and the greater disaster of 1914, a time when the restraints of Victorian manners were relaxed, while the wealth of Victorian society had not been dissipated. A pleasure-loving King headed a brilliant society. His dangerous illness at the beginning of his reign focused the devotion of his subjects. Liberal hopes of a new era of prosperity were entertained. No one foresaw the days of darkness. Did Elgar prophesy them in the last pages of his Symphony in E flat? Possibly, but he was of his time. The *Pomp and Circumstance* marches and the 'Cockaigne' overture mirrored its more obvious characteristics; in the opulent symphonies he probed deeper to the heart of things, and they remain its most abiding monument in art.

CHAPTER VIII

OPERA AND DRAMA

THE name of Wagner has hovered menacingly over these pages.
Even in discussing the symphony it is with difficulty that we
avoid the simple classification of composers as pre-Wagnerian
and post-Wagnerian, because after the magic of Wagner's
orchestration had worked itself out in *Tristan*, composers for
the orchestra in whatever form had at their disposal, if they
chose to use it, a new instrument, one almost as different from
the orchestra of the classical symphony as was Chopin's piano
from the harpsichord of Bach. Wagner became from that date
(1865) a force to be obeyed or resisted, but impossible to ignore,
and it may even be argued that his influence was as powerful
on those who refused to succumb to him as on those who hastened
to signify their allegiance. The whole musical world in the latter
part of the nineteenth century was commonly estimated as
Wagnerian and anti-Wagnerian, an estimate which necessarily
ignored the case of the contemporary composer, Brahms for
example, who was so profoundly conscious of Wagner's original
genius that if he copied him in anything it was in the unswerving
determination to be himself. It took some twenty years after
the death of Wagner for the musical world to recover its balance
sufficiently to think apart from him, and that brings us to the
time which marks the end of our period.[1]

We now return to the beginning of it, to that moment in the

---

[1] Twentieth-century music including the 'back to Bach' and the 'forward
with Schönberg' shibboleths may be summed up as a turning away from
Wagner in one direction or another. Mr. Cecil Gray has told us that
'Wagner . . . means, and always has meant, precisely nothing to Sibelius'.
That, rather than the fact that the first of his symphonies was composed
in 1899, is the reason why Sibelius has not been discussed in the preceding
chapter. Sibelius belongs entirely to the twentieth century.

autumn of 1853 when Wagner, having visited Paris with Liszt and grasped for the first time the melody of Beethoven's String Quartet in C sharp minor, discovered that he must either 'explode or compose'. For five and a half years he had written no music. They had been years of exile alike from his country and his art, but in them his mind towards his art had been clarified by the bulk of his literary work, including *Die Kunst und die Revolution* (1849), *Das Kunstwerk der Zukunft* (1850), *Oper und Drama* and *Eine Mitteilung an meine Freunde* (1851). He had sketched out a drama, *Wieland der Schmiedt*, and, most important of all, he had, as we have seen, completed the poem of *Der Ring des Nibelungen*. It was with the reading of the *Ring* to Liszt and his admiring circle that the desire to transmute the epic into music came on Wagner with overwhelming force.

We have not here to unravel the tangled skein of Wagner's personal life. That process may be said now to be all but completed by the publication of many volumes of correspondence and the sleuth-like industry of innumerable biographers, both German and English. The point to be realized and held fast is that behind the amazing contradictions of behaviour, the opposing forces of character which made him loved or loathed as a man, Wagner was completely subject to one immutable law, which was for him morality, religion, and life itself. That law was the accomplishment of what came to be known by the title of his most famous literary essay, 'The art-work of the future'.

In such essays he had thought out the problems which his earlier operas had raised. His plan was clear enough. Nevertheless in designing the tetralogy he had set himself a task which seemed impossible of fulfilment, for it must be remembered that the task was something far more than merely composing the inevitable and right music to a four days' drama. That in itself was manageable, given a few years of quiet life in which to concentrate on it. *Das Rheingold* was completely scored six months after he had begun it, and the whole of the music to *Die Walküre* was sketched by the end of the year (1854). At this pace the *Ring* might have been finished and a fair copy made in the composer's faultless script in no more years than it takes days to perform.

When he set out on it this was more or less what Wagner expected to do, but he knew that even so the task would be only just begun. He had to convert the world. He would not have much difficulty about converting the world to his music. Already it was sought after, whatever the professional musicians and the critics might say against it. But there was nowhere in Europe an opera-house which could produce the *Ring* adequately even if it would. He would have to create a new race of artists having altogether different ideas of interpretation from those of the best opera singers of that day, and a new public which would come, not because his music was richer in attractions than that of his contemporaries, but because they understood, needed, and lived by the recreative life of the musical drama. The *Ring* itself was to be merely the prelude to the art-work of the future. It would begin the world's conversion. Further, perhaps nobler, expositions of the principle, some designs for which were already seething in his brain, would follow it up and complete the conversion. Other artists, some day, perhaps in a not too near future, would continue his achievement. Meantime, an exile from home, poor and in debt, without settled means of livelihood, with a wife who could not understand it all, and friends who could not see that the end was worth the sacrifice of themselves, their wives and families, their goods and chattels, he must struggle on single-handed, simply because he was Wagner, the one man who knew what the world would lose if the great work were not accomplished in what remained of his life. He was already forty when he returned to Zürich to compose as an alternative to explosion, and to restudy his Wotan in the light of Schopenhauer's philosophy.

The time-table, if there was one, was not to be carried out. Through 1854 all went well. The only distractions were a summer 'cure' at Seelisberg, the comings and goings of his wife Minna (the goings coinciding with the deepening of friendship between Wagner and Mathilde Wesendonck), and a sketch for the dramatic treatment of the Tristan legend which Karl Ritter placed before him. In ruminating over his own very different ideas about the treatment of this subject Wagner tells us that he considered an episode in which Parsifal on his wanderings should visit the death-bed of Tristan.[1]

But Tristan and Parsifal were not distractions from the composition of the *Ring*. At this stage they merely illustrate for us Wagner's capacity for envisaging his work as a whole from the moment that he addressed himself to it seriously. Even the irksome visit to London to conduct concerts of the Philharmonic Society in the spring of 1855 did not deflect him. Back in Zürich at the end of June, he started on the fair copy of *Die Walküre*, and though the thought of *Tristan* became more insistent and he weighed against it the possibility of another drama, *Die Sieger*, the full score of *Die Walküre* was completed by March 1856. He allowed himself some breathing space before, at the end of the summer, he plunged into *Siegfried*, and this too was well forward when in the spring of 1857 he took up his residence at the desired 'Asyl' on the Wesendonck property.

It was there that he began the second act of *Siegfried*; it was there also that the spring sunshine of a Good Friday morning brought him back to thoughts of *Parsifal*. It is entirely charac-

[1] *My Life*, p. 617.

teristic of Wagner that these thoughts set him to work on *Siegfried* with a will. Every experience was fuel to the flame of the artist, and he recklessly sought emotional experiences more dangerous than the sunshine on Good Friday, that the flame might burn the more brightly. This is the explanation of the affair with Frau Wesendonck which the year's residence at the 'Asyl' brought to a crisis. In September Hans von Bülow and his wife Cosima visited the 'Asyl'. Hans at the piano interpreted the rough drafts of two acts of *Siegfried* 'with consummate skill'; Cosima when pressed for an opinion 'began to cry'.[1] In September, too, the poem of *Tristan* was completed and carried to Mathilde Wesendonck. Love was confessed between them. Wagner wrote of it, 'On this day, at this house I was born again. Then my former life ended; my after life began. In that exquisite moment I was alone with myself.'[2] The pronoun is indicative. Any other lover would have written, 'I was alone with you'. To Wagner every experience, the love of woman, the philosophy of Schopenhauer, a ray of sunshine on a Good Friday morning, alike, was something to be absorbed into himself. In the end it left him alone with a self to be reborn in his art. But though the revealing words might escape him in a moment like this, so little did he understand himself in the normal relations of life that it was not to be expected that anyone else could. How his accumulation of experiences wrecked the life of the 'Asyl', sent him out on a second exile more painful than the first, and threw him into conditions of outward life which came near to destroying the inner life of the artist, is all matter of common knowledge.

The immediate effect of the 'rebirth' was that Wagner was

[1] *My Life*, p. 669. It is evident that for reasons which are obvious Wagner in writing this passage of his autobiography is anxious to stress as delicately as possible the personal sympathy between himself and Cosima and to make little of the relations between himself and Frau Wesendonck.

[2] Kapp, *The Women in Wagner's Life*, English ed., p. 121.

thrown out of his stride, could make no further progress with the *Ring*, while his ardour blazed up to accomplish *Tristan und Isolde*. Through all the turmoil of his uprooting he never flagged in this intent, and, moreover, even in the white heat of creation he could realize that *Tristan* might have practical advantages over the larger scheme as an introduction of his musical drama to the world. Its few characters, the concentration of dramatic interest on love and destiny, the simplicity of its stage-craft, made it possible for him to commend it to impresarios as a practicable theatre piece. It did, in fact, through von Bülow's performances in Münich in 1865, begin the work of the world's conversion.

The score of *Tristan* was virtually finished in August 1859, and it was in the interval between its completion and production that Wagner's fortunes sank to their lowest ebb, and even the tenacity of his artistic purpose weakened. Through all that time, until the arrival at Stuttgart on May 3rd, 1864, of the King of Bavaria's secretary with the royal summons to Münich, he was parrying the buffets of ill fortune of every kind. The most public of them was in the scandalous reception of his revised *Tannhäuser* in Paris (1861), but that was so obviously scandalous that he could meet it with becoming dignity. More injurious to himself were the endless shifts for money, the attempts he made to surround himself with material comforts, the pitiable appeals to the affections of friends, the cravings to enjoy the companionship of women. That *Die Meistersinger*, begun in 1861, was not finished until October 1867, after Wagner had retired to Triebschen with Cosima, is a measure of how these distractions slowed down the progress of his art. The marvel is that there is no evidence of their disintegrating influence in *Die Meistersinger* itself. Through it all Wagner guarded the flame, but even he doubted whether it could ever be fanned to the height demanded for the consuming of Walhalla.

The *Siegfried Idyll*[1] marks the end of Wagner's storms and stresses; in a sense it closes his personal story, at any rate as a factor in his art, which is the aspect from which alone it concerns us here. Cosima's justification was that she saved him from a world which was becoming too much for him. By herself making the sacrifice which he had demanded from all who approached him, a sacrifice[2] which involved herself, her husband von Bülow, and to a certain extent their children, she saved Wagner from extinction and secured the completion of his work for posterity. She gave him inward peace and outward comfort. She bore him a son. Henceforward she stood between him and the world and attracted to herself all its buffetings. The creation of the Bayreuth theatre was far more her work than Wagner's. She fulfilled his dream, and her crowning glory was that she allowed him the belief that the fulfilment was all his own.

The composition of the *Siegfried Idyll* was supposed to be the first-fruits of a new symphonic era in Wagner's artistic career, but it led nowhere. It celebrated her achievement, and subsequently all that her achievement could do for him was to give him the conditions in which the projects of his unsatisfied early manhood, the *Ring* and *Parsifal*, could be worked out to their conclusions.

---

[1] The inscription on the autograph is:

Triebschener Idyll
mit Fidi-Vogelgesang und Orange-Sonnenaufgang
a l s
Symphonischer Geburtstagsgrüss
Seiner Cosima
dagebracht
von
Ihrem Richard
1870.

'Fidi' was the parents' early pet name for their son, Siegfried.

[2] The reality of Cosima's personal sacrifice is proved by the diary which she kept subsequently, and which is freely quoted from in Du Moulin-Eckart's *Cosima Wagner*. (See English ed., chap. vii.)

If we turn to the opening of the third act of *Siegfried* we realize at once the resilience with which Wagner addressed himself again to his long-abandoned score. That prelude is the return to his principal subject, the force behind all nature, the wisdom which directs and foresees, which moved the waters of the Rhine on their appointed course (cf. the prelude to *Das Rheingold*) and which can subdue the gods themselves to its law. See it in Erda's first rebuke to Wotan (*Rheingold*, Scene IV):

Ex. 1.

Tag däm-mert den Göt - tern.

Wagner had just reached the point of this inevitable return, as he had planned it in his drama, when he laid the *Ring* aside for *Tristan* in 1857. Had affairs at the 'Asyl' gone differently, had they been more like what he has described in his autobiography, a party of friends rejoicing together in the gradual unfolding of a high artistic project, would he have gone straight on from the story of the young Siegfried into this return to the foundations? Wagner was probably as near to the truth as he could be when he wrote:

'For the time being we had sounded a sort of funeral peal over the *Nibelungen* by playing so much of it and it was now completely laid aside. The consequence was that when later on we took it out of its folio for similar gatherings, it wore a lack-lustre look, and grew even fainter as if to remind us of the past. At the beginning of October, however, I at once began to compose *Tristan* . . .'

Neither the tears of Cosima nor the enchantment of Mathilde account completely for this 'lack-lustre look' in what hitherto had been the core of his being. He was up against a dead wall. He could not go on because he was not yet grown up to the stature of his theme. Ten years of bitter life experience were needed, ten years in which the fire of his *Tristan* should burn itself out, and give place to the altruism of his Hans Sachs; ten years in which brain and hand should mature together, before he could tackle the awakening of the all-wise Erda by the god grown old but still potent in his acknowledged impotence. The spear-brandishing Wotan of *Das Rheingold*, the wounded and angered Wotan of *Die Walküre*, and the cynical Wanderer who throws his warnings and his taunts to Mime, Alberich, and Fafner in the earlier acts of *Siegfried*, must all contribute their shares to this last sight of him before he willingly submits his spear to the superior force of Siegfried's sword. All this and more is to be found in the prelude to Act III based on the primitive motive from *Das Rheingold*, across which the spear theme strikes.

Technically Wagner displays here a grip on harmonic resources which had been maturing through the years of his own wanderings. See, for example, in the course of the prelude the combination of the sequence in Example 1 above with the chords of the Wanderer's motive.

Ex. 2.

Such progressions are developed with titanic vigour until the whole structure collapses in the chromatic chords of Erda's eternal sleep.

Here then we find the Wagner of the *Ring*, 'born again', and the rebirth leaves him alone with himself, and able to create. The experience lasted to enable him to complete his design in the overwhelming peroration of *Götterdämmerung*. It is his last explosive outburst of composition. In *Parsifal* there is none of that sense of a stored-up energy which must be released. When he settled to it he was no longer alone with himself. Then, possibly for the first time since *Rienzi*, he found himself composing for a public, the worshippers at the Bayreuth shrine. Great though its incidental beauties are, *Parsifal* fails of that character of new-born inspiration which sustains its predecessors.

When Wagner laid the foundations of the *Ring* on principles which he had declared in *Das Kunstwerk der Zukunft*, the fellowship of all the artists in his 'Tanz- Ton- und Ticht-Kunst', a radical change in his musical technique of the theatre became inevitable. Henceforward the first business of the voices must be to declaim the poetry, and that led him in beginning *Das Rheingold* to a rigid application of the old principle, 'for every syllable a note'.[1] Though he was ready to modify this for expressive purposes on occasion (see 'O gebt uns das Reine zurück' in the last appeal of the Rhinemaidens to Wotan), it remained his normal standard in setting words to music. Verbal repetition for the sake of a musical phrase was ruled out with stern logic, and, except in the case of the Rhinemaidens who are dramatically one personality and speak with one voice, he set his face in *Das Rheingold* against anything in the nature of vocal ensemble. It is a drama of conversation in which each participant takes his turn, and each disputant waits to reply until the speaker of the moment pauses for breath. As the characters must always be talking to each other there are no soliloquies, and Wotan, a character to whom soliloquy is essential, since it is his inmost thoughts and not his actions which matter, must always be given some one, Fricka or Loge, at whom to talk.

This displays Wagner's failure to distinguish at the outset of his enterprise between the principles of the spoken and of the musical drama. The conversations of *Das Rheingold* move heavily because words are slowed down to the pace of musical declamation without the two compensations which the musical dramatist has at his disposal, ensemble and soliloquy. In his understanding

[1] This was the principle formulated by Archbishop Cranmer in a letter to King Henry VIII (1545) for the singing of the Liturgy in English. See Burney, *General History of Music*, vol. ii, p. 577.

of this distinction between the sung and the spoken drama Mozart as a musical dramatist was infinitely superior to Wagner at this stage. In readopting the methods of Mozart in *Die Meistersinger* Wagner showed his capacity for growth, but the whole of the *Ring* and *Tristan* suffer from this limitation, though not so severely as does *Das Rheingold*.

Wagner's rigorous exclusion of soliloquy breaks down in the opening of *Die Walküre*, where both Siegmund and Sieglinde must be alone with their thoughts. One would have thought that the love of the twinborn pair would produce some relaxation into ensemble singing at the climax of the act. But no, he is adamant. Brother and sister sing prolonged solos to each other; they listen politely each to each, and the man has the last word. It required the incandescent love of Tristan and Isolde to obliterate the conversational restriction in united song.

These restraints, due to a false analogy with the spoken drama, were compensated for, as far as it was possible to do so, by two factors, the suppleness of the vocal line of each single voice and the expressive power of Wagner's polychromatic orchestra. One of the more ignorant contemporary criticisms of the new music-drama was that it was all recitative and orchestration. *Das Rheingold* gives some excuse for the criticism. Through the greater part of it the melodic web is woven by the orchestra while the vocal declamation based on verbal rhythms is set in to the resultant harmony. Even here, however, a comparison of Wotan's first and last greetings to Walhalla ('Vollendet das ewige Werk', and 'Abendlich strahlt die Sonne') illustrates Wagner's fusing of the declamatory phrases into lyrical song as the emotion becomes more personal.

In *Die Walküre* the voice regains its immemorial position as the melodic leader with Siegmund's 'Lenzlied', and henceforward, aria, that is vocal music having a melodic shape of its own, and recitative, the melodic shape of which is verbal, are merged into one. Brünnhilde's appeal to Wotan (*Die Walküre,* Act III, sc. 3) will illustrate this fusion:

Ex. 3.

It is with such melody as this that those analysts who see the whole texture of the *Ring* as a network of leitmotives, each one to be ticketed with an appropriate name, get into difficulties. One quotes it in his catalogue as 'Rechtfertigungsmelodie', another is at pains to show it as a minor version of what he labels 'Walsungenliebe', the theme which dominates the orchestra in that culminating moment of the 'Abschied', where Wotan prophesies Brünnhilde's ultimate union with Siegfried. The relationship is undeniable, but it occurs here both as recitative and as aria, and not at all as the quotation of a leitmotive.

It is in such things as this that Wagner defeats all attempts at thematic classification, and justifies his claim to have based his musical style on the symphonic method of Beethoven. Here is that spontaneous growth of ideas, which has been described as the essence of symphony, appearing equally as the essence of musical drama.

Wagner's leitmotive system was the part of his technique which was immediately exploited by his interpreters. The amateur visiting Bayreuth for the first time in its earlier days went armed with a little book of extracts, and he was assured that to recognize each theme wherever it occurs and to apply to it a proper name of some sort was the first duty of the Wagnerian neophyte. This was merely doing on a grand scale what the programme annotator does when he quotes the first and second subjects of a Beethoven symphony and adds that the rest of the movement may be left to speak for itself.

Looking at the *Ring* as a symphony on a colossal scale, *Das Rheingold* may be called the exposition, and it is natural that there the thematic material should appear in the form of direct statement, definition of contrasted characters, persons, and objects being the first necessity. *Die Walküre* and the first two acts of *Siegfried* representing dramatically the human story depending from the cosmography of *Das Rheingold*, are musically a vast development section, involving incidentally the elements of both slow movement and scherzo. It has already been suggested that the third act of *Siegfried* begins a process of recapitulation, and, as in the cases of Beethoven's greater symphonies, recapitulation and coda involves the most expansive development of the whole design.

The listener must become conversant with the thematic material at the outset, and the outline in which it is presented in *Das Rheingold* gives him every opportunity of doing so. But he must exercise his power of symphonic listening more acutely as the drama progresses, and bring himself to a state of comprehension far beyond the mere recognition of identities. The habit of attaching a verbal label to each thematic germ is likely to prove a deterrent to his progress, and as such it is to be deprecated. In the prelude to *Siegfried*, Act III, for example, it is not the recognition of the 'Spear' or of the Wanderer's harmonies which matters, but the tone picture of the impending cataclysm that the confluence of ideas presents.

Debussy's taunt[1] that the leitmotive system suggests a world of harmless lunatics who present their visiting-cards and shout their names in song, irritably refuses to take account of this process of development. It must be allowed that in some passages the themes recur too mechanically at the bidding of the text; for example when *Siegfried* runs to the spring and cuts a reed with his sword, and the sword theme leaps up in the orchestra. It matters nothing how he cuts the reed; for the moment he is merely using his sword in lieu of a pocket-knife. It is because, properly speaking, the sword theme represents not just a sharp tool, but the power of the young hero to win his way by cutting through all obstacles, material and spiritual, that this use of it seems derogatory to its dignity. Richard Strauss is credited with having declared that he would make the language of music so concrete a thing that he could say 'knife and fork' in it. That probably was a dinner-table extravagance,

---

[1] Article in *Gil Blas*, after listening to the *Ring* at Covent Garden in 1903.

but if it represents anything of Strauss's aim it shows him to be diametrically opposed to Wagner. The latter might, as in this instance, drop into using his musical ideas as though they were nouns substantive in a sentence, but his aim was to use them in the orchestra as 'the loam ("Boden") of endless, universal Feeling, from which the individual feeling of the separate actor draws power to shoot aloft to fullest height of growth'.[1]

Wagner's selection of material to this end is best appreciated by considering not only what he chooses but what he discards.[2] To read through almost any scene in the 'development sections' of the *Ring* with the main motives in mind, is to discover that Wagner left certain of them severely alone in countless places where the text would justify allusion to them. The forest scene (*Siegfried*, Act II, sc. 2) provides an instance. The hero with his newly forged sword enters, led to the battle with the dragon by one dwarf while the other scuttles out of sight behind the rocks and tree-trunks. But the sword theme and all the distinctive heroic themes are absent. Only occasional suggestions from the forging songs of the previous act protest against the small-minded dwarfish rhythms of Mime's music and contrast with the dark rustling of the overhanging forest leaves. The latter (not a leitmotive at all in the sense of a short self-contained figure of marked character, but rather a figure of accompaniment comparable to that in the slow movement of Beethoven's 'Pastoral' Symphony) diffuses its mysterious influence through Siegfried's later reflections and provides a unifying principle of the many strands of thought. The appearance of the sword theme when he rouses himself to cut the reed is the first suggestion of the

[1] *Das Kunstwerk der Zukunft*, translation by William Ashton Ellis, vol. i, p. 190.

[2] Wagner's method of distributing his themes and developing them in groups through the several scenes is well analysed and put into a tabulated form by Mr. A. E. F. Dickinson in *The Musical Design of the Ring* (The Musical Pilgrim Series, Oxford University Press).

restless energy which had been the most prevalent characteristic of young Siegfried throughout the first act. It may not be quite happily chosen; it might have been reserved still further until the moment when Siegfried draws his sword to real purpose as he rushes on the dragon, but at any rate Wagner's reticence in its use is proved in all the long scene which leads to this point. It and its companion heroic themes cannot be said to have pursued Siegfried in the manner suggested by Debussy's lunatic with a visiting-card. An important aspect of his character, and a long musical scene in which he is the central figure, have been developed virtually without any of the musical motives associated with his personality. By such means as this the motives are built up into larger contours; the several scenes form contrasts in symphonic designs, and the cumulative effect of scene following scene is produced.

The matter of key distribution is closely bound up with this larger thematic development just as in the symphony, and the relations of key also bear their part in delineating the emotions of the characters on the stage. The finale to *Siegfried* will illustrate this, and a close examination of one passage, Brünnhilde's reconciliation to her womanhood, will give an insight into Wagner's handling both of thematic development and of harmonic structures to clarify his stage situations. Brünnhilde has awakened to find Siegfried beside her. His reverent fear of the maid has been succeeded by ardent passion for the woman. She has repulsed his embrace with the words:

> Kein Gott nahte mir je!
> Der Jungfrau neigten scheu sich die Helden
> Heilig schied sie aus Walhall.

The light of her god-protected world dies; she finds herself in a strange world dark with human violence and passion. Only gradually a new light dawns, the light of a love which transcends physical passion. It is that light which she hails, as on her

first waking she had hailed the sun itself, in the following
passage:

Ex. 4.

Looking at it with the cold eye of the analyst, one perceives
that it has a close correspondence with the melody quoted above
(**Ex. 3**) from *Die Walküre*. Its chromatic bass stands as it were
half-way between that minor melody and the major one, called
'Walsungenliebe'. The bass clarinet which introduced the 'War es
so schämlich', completes the exposure of her 'Angst'. Moreover,
harmonically this is a bridge passage tending to throw the mind
forward to a resolution of its chromatics in the key of **E** major.
This is achieved in a new song melody; eight bars on the
orchestra (the same which form the principal melody of the

Siegfried Idyll) which rock the conflict of emotions to rest and have the character of an old-fashioned ritornello introducing an aria. What follows is in fact aria pure and simple, even capable of analysis into a ternary form, with E as the principal key. Nothing less definite could suffice to signalize Brünnhilde's acceptance of her womanhood and her joy in Siegfried's manhood.

If we analyse the subsequent key system of the finale, we find that after this halting-point the modulations are chiefly through flat keys until the final coda-duet celebrates their union ('Lachend erwachst du') in C major.

The aria, 'Ewig war ich', presents several minor difficulties. Its detachment from the warp and woof of leitmotives is a little disconcerting at this late stage of the drama's development. Wagner may be accused of going back on himself, of reverting to opera. Yet even apart from its musical beauty dramatic justification can be found in the unique moment, never to be recreated, but which is to be lived once and for all.

Its internal difficulties are two and concern the setting of the words and the key. For once we find vocal melody which has quite evidently been born independently of the words set to it (they are actually ill-fitting), and, after the careful preparation of E major, the voice begins, rather to the damage of the theme, in E minor. If we did not know that the third act of *Siegfried* was composed before the *Siegfried Idyll* we might imagine the aria to be an adaptation from the *Idyll*.[1] The most natural explanation seems to be that Wagner had long associated this musical idea with the dramatic moment of complete concord between Brünnhilde and Siegfried; he may even have found it in the course of that search for peace of mind and body which had been so feverishly yet so fruitlessly pursued during the long years between the 'Asyl' and Triebschen. He had probably dwelt

[1] It is conceivable that both are adaptations from some other work planned by Wagner, but there is no evidence of that.

on it in thought quite apart from the text of the drama. It had to arrive in the moment of his hero's content, since it represented to him the fulfilment of his own. Hence the words are fitted as best they may be to the self-existing music. The minor mode seems to be used for the opening stanza because Brünnhilde is still half looking back, still conscious of her 'Angst', and she is not wholly at peace with herself and her lover until the 'tranquillamente' of the return of the melody to the words, 'Ewig licht lachst du'.

These examples show Wagner's attitude towards his technical material becoming less doctrinaire as his work neared its accomplishment. The last one belongs to that part of it which was composed in the light of the practical experience which *Tristan* and *Die Meistersinger* had brought to him. Without that experience *Götterdämmerung* could scarcely have been saved from the glaring inconsistencies of the story, planned originally as *Siegfrieds Tod* before the whole tetralogy was conceived.

As a dramatic story *Götterdämmerung* is the worst part of the *Ring*. The mechanical magic of the Ring itself and the Tarnhelm, happily inoperative while those talismans remained in Fafner's lair, are disastrous to any human consistency of action, and the equally mechanical use of 'potions' which enable the Gibichungs to play havoc with Siegfried's memory come near to making the plot as unintelligible as that of *Die Zauberflöte*. Siegfried knows that Brünnhilde knows that he, disguised as Gunther, has forcibly robbed her of the ring. Yet he never thinks of passing it over to Gunther along with Brünnhilde herself, and conveniently remembers when accused that he took it from Fafner's 'Neidhöhle'. When the Rhinemaidens ask for it, he tells them that his wife would scold him if he parted with it. So the greater part of the second and third acts become much ado about nothing, and as far as Siegfried and his personal story are concerned we merely await with anxiety the second 'potion' and the hero's death on Hagen's spear.

The first act with its change of scene to and fro between the Walküre's rock and the hall of the Gibichungs is clumsily devised. The second act with its chorus of vassals to greet the arrival of Gunther and his bride, the trio vowing vengeance, and the bridal procession of Siegfried and Gutrune is couched in the old romantic-opera manner of *Lohengrin*. Through all this paraphernalia Wagner, the musician of infinite resource, hacks his way, his eyes turned to that final scene in which Brünnhilde shall redeem all by her transfigured womanhood. His ultimate triumph is made the more splendid by its emergence from the turgid rigmarole of a badly constructed drama.

It is the grand scale of the music which converts this last section of *Der Ring des Nibelungen* from *Siegfrieds Tod* into *Götterdämmerung*. Not the personal fortunes and misfortunes of the hero, but the 'Twilight of the Gods' is its chief theme, and this is made evident at the outset in the epic severity of the scene of the three Norns. Here the music carries us back to the prelude of *Das Rheingold*, the prophecies of Erda (see Ex. 1) and the last colloquy between her and Wotan. The rope they weave is the golden rope of Wagner's music, and in it all the strands are subtly blended till at last Nothung's keen blade cuts through the polyphony, and the ejaculations of Siegfried's horn lead to the fulfilment of the curse.

Ex. 5.

Zu lo-cker das Seil, mir langt es nicht.

Soll ich nach Nor-den nei - gen das En - de,

straf - fer sei es ge - streckt! Es riss!

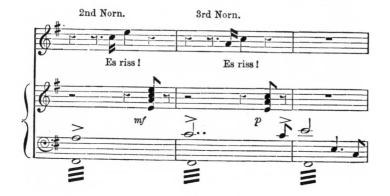

2nd Norn.

Es riss!

3rd Norn.

Es riss!

All that follows must be held in relation to this, and the episodes which most serve to do so are Waltraute's mission to Brünnhilde (Act I, sc. 3), Alberich's counsel to Hagen (Act II, sc. 1) and the Rhinemaidens' prophecy of impending ill to Siegfried. After the heroic themes have been finally recapitulated in the 'Trauermarsch', after Gunther has fallen on Hagen's sword, Brünnhilde's epilogue 'Schweigt eures Jammers jauchzender Schwall!' is begun, not with any of the musical themes which relate to the hero, but with that of the world's wisdom (see Ex. 1) which has been described as Wagner's principal subject. To this theme Brünnhilde, as she hurls the brand on the pyre, proclaims the end of godhood.

In the might of this peroration, the puny ring itself, forged by Alberich, sinks into insignificance. Hagen's exclamation 'Zurück vom Ring!' is scarcely audible, and even in theatres where the complicated stage-craft is sufficiently well managed to enable the spectator to see all that is supposed to occur in regard to it between Hagen and the Rhinemaidens, little attention can be spared to the action while the flame of Wagner's orchestra is enveloping the towers of Walhalla. Was it, one asks, a part of Wagner's intention from the first that the vaunted world power of the ring should be always chimerical, a dream of gods and men destroyed with every attempt to wield it effectively? That, at any rate, is what he makes of it.

VII   X

Wagner's spiritual advance between his planning of *Der Ring des Nibelungen* and *Tristan und Isolde* may be measured by his handling of the idea of magic. The 'potions' of *Götterdämmerung* have been described as mechanical. That of *Tristan* is psychological. In *Parsifal* he groped his way towards realization of the sacramental magic. In *Tristan* the searcher for definite verbal meanings to attach to leading themes is met at once with a problem. Is the yearning chromatic progression which is clearly the principal subject of the whole drama to be labelled 'magic' or 'love'?

Ex. 6.
(a) Prelude.　　　　　　　　　　　　　　　　　　　Tristan.

(b)　　　　　ISOLDE.

O　　zah　-　-　me

Kunst　　　　der　Zau　-　-　be-rin,

(c)

Mir er - ko - ren, mir ver -

- lo - ren, hehr und heil, . . .

kühn und feig! Tod . . . ge - weih-tes

Its appearance at the beginning of the prelude is so fraught with human feeling that if it is magic it is certainly not the magic of a wonder-working potion. Yet it reappears in the score in a concise, almost a trite, form (Ex. 6 *b*) when Isolde recalls the Sorceress's art. Again the sight of Tristan at the helm makes her murmur her 'Mir erkoren' to its rising melody (Ex. 6 *c*). The answer is that the magic of *Tristan* is the magic of love, life-giving yet deadly, potent yet unmanning, working its spell on the lovers long before Brangäne mixes the draught in which they discover one another. There is all the difference in the world between this compelling moment and its trivial counter-part in *Götterdämmerung*, when Siegfried's eye lights on the expectant Gutrune. Isolde knows, even if Tristan does not, how little their fate has been affected by Brangäne's trick. She pours scorn on Brangäne's self-reproaches (Act II, sc. 1), while again this theme is borne onward in great waves of orchestration.

> Dein Werk? O thör'ge Magd!
> Frau Minne kenntest du nicht?

It was in facing death together that the two realized that their love always had been, and always must be, their life. In the light of that realization the draught shared between them becomes the focal point of their drama, and its power has nothing to do with any hocus-pocus of the medicine chest.

Not only this but all the musical material of *Tristan* is treated by Wagner as within the action of the lovers' mentality. The themes do not delineate characters and objects at all; they are never used as so many musical nouns substantive. This accounts for the amazing continuity of texture, a continuity so complete that every aspect of the lovers' absorbing passion into which the music enters can be traced back to that chromatic progression of harmony in the first bars of the prelude. All this world, the real world of their night as opposed to the garish seeming of day, is contained in it, and flows from it. See the harmonic structure of the throbbing chords which support the melody of the great love duet ('O sink' hernieder'). The shouts of the sailors, the hunting horns of King Mark, the rude incursion of Melot, and even the bluff devotion of Kurwenal are all 'Taggespenster', unrealities interrupting or delaying with their diatonic musical forms the ever unfolding possibilities of this eternal chromaticism.

It is little wonder that such a theme conceived in such terms and carried through a four-hour drama with such undeviating single-mindedness brought down the censure of 'healthy-minded' people on the 'Tod-geweihtes Haupt' of its composer. The personal revelations and Wagner's enforced departure from Munich at the time of *Tristan's* first production there under von Bülow's direction were all calculated to prevent his contemporaries from regarding it dispassionately as a work of art. Even those who did so could find plenty of justification for their repugnance by pointing to the enervating influence of its eroticism translated into terms of perpetual convolutions of chromatic harmony. Yet gradually the conviction grew that *Tristan* is a unique masterpiece, perhaps the unique masterpiece of the musical drama. In it Wagner fulfilled all that was genuine in his theory of the union of the arts and carried it out with a spontaneous lyrical fervour to which no other theme but the magic of love could stir him. It raised him to a height which no other composer for the theatre has reached before or since. It is the height of symphonic music unchecked by that need for manipulating an elaborate paraphernalia of the theatre which hampered him in carrying out the design of *Der Ring des Nibelungen*.

Between the completion of *Tristan* and the beginning of the music to *Die Meistersinger* had come the revision of *Tannhäuser* for the disastrous production in Paris. He finished the re-writing of the Venusberg scene by the end of 1860, recasting it in the light of the new technique evolved through his experience of the *Ring* and *Tristan*. Comparison of the old and the new *Tannhäuser* shows how completely the experience had changed the composer, and how true was the contention of his literary works that there is a real line of demarcation between the romantic opera and the musical drama. The new Venusberg scene is no mere matter of intensification, of heightened orchestration and elaborate ballet; it asserts a wholly different scale of values. Venus herself is cast in the larger than life-size model of the deities of the *Ring*. The discrepancy in style cannot be bridged over, and it is possible to argue that Wagner ought either to have re-written the whole or left *Tannhäuser* in its original form. Yet the new version has this dramatic justification that it explains the later action. Tannhäuser is not merely a man in whom the carnal and the spiritual are at war; he has dwelt among immortals and henceforward mortal life on the highest plane has for him the taint of insipidity.

After the refashioning of *Tannhäuser* Wagner naturally reverted to his old wish to write a counterpart in comedy to the 'Minnesänger' contests of song. He approached *Die Meistersinger* from a more objective standpoint than that which had brought him to his recent works. He refers to the influence of Titian's famous Assumption of the Virgin seen in Venice[1] as the incentive to composition; it impelled him to *Die Meistersinger* just as

[1] *My Life*, vol. ii, p. 802.

Beethoven's String Quartet in C sharp minor heard in Paris had sent him back to the *Ring*. He began straight away on the overture and composed the greater part of it in the train between Venice and Vienna.

The overture to *Die Meistersinger* is a vivid picture of the Guild, its masters and apprentices, its civic dignity and ceremonies. The innocent fantasies of the young Walther are intermingled; the lovers are caught in the meshes of the Guild's network of interests. A famous passage of counterpoint (note the distinctions of expression) weaves the several strands together.

Ex. 7.   *p aber sehr ausdrucksvoll.*

There is no hint, however, in the overture, of Hans Sachs, and in the drama itself he makes his appearance last of the masters

but quite unobtrusively, giving the company his 'Gott grüss' euch'
while Pogner and Beckmesser are attempting in their several
ways to put the young Walther in his place. No orchestral leitmotive distinguishes the man who is the real hero of the comedy
and Wagner's own mouthpiece. The character of Sachs only
begins to emerge when the other masters have begun to show
their muddle-headedness.

Arrived in Vienna, Wagner in conference with Cornelius applied
himself to collecting the materials with which to fill the canvas
of his picture of the old life of Nürnberg. He obtained from the
Imperial library the loan of Wagenseil's *Buch von der Meistersinger holdseligen Kunst*, 1697.[1] From this and other literary
sources he not only obtained the technical knowledge of the
poetic and musical odes and manners of the guild worked in
with such skill to the parts of David and Kothner, but he
steeped himself in that sense of devotion to art through obser-
vance of its formularies which makes the picture of the masters,
exclusive of Beckmesser, a sympathetic and kindly one.

It is this more than anything else which shows the distance
Wagner had travelled along the road of human experience. One
cannot recognize in *Die Meistersinger* the intolerant revolutionary
of the Dresden riots; it is swept clean out of him along with the
egocentricity which made *Tristan* inevitable. In the struggle
between the masters and Walther he can discern the rightness
of the reactionaries and the wrongness of the idealist, and yet
remain heart and soul with the latter. And it is this mellowness
of temper in Wagner which makes the character of Sachs
possible. He could plan it in words years before, but he could
not have composed it a moment earlier.

The most entrancing quality in *Die Meistersinger* is this
gradual emergence of the character of Sachs. Wagner does not

----

[1] See *Wagner and Wagenseil*, by Herbert Thompson, Oxford University
Press, 1927.

set the stage for him as he does for all the other outstanding
figures. Throughout the first act Sachs has no music of his own.
Through those addresses in which he speaks for the freedom of
the maiden's choice and upholds the instinct of the 'Volk' it is the
masters' music which accompanies him on the orchestra. He is
merely the most enlightened member of the group. When at last
the masters have dispersed and the apprentices have run off with
the furniture of the song-school, leaving Sachs alone in the empty
church, it is a phrase from the trial song sung by Walther,

> Es schwillt und schallt,
> es tönt der Wald
> von holder Stimmen Gemenge;

which haunts him, and tells us what are his thoughts.

Ex. 8.

Wagner is no longer shy of soliloquies, and 'Wie duftet doch
der Flieder' (Act II) and 'Wahn! Wahn!' (Act III) are what most
enlighten us as to the deeper qualities of Sachs's character. It is
the rough shoemaker who enters to what may be called his
'trade theme' at the beginning of the second act, and it is that
theme which contests for supremacy through the course of the
subsequent soliloquy. See how subtly Wagner fuses them
together.

Ex. 9.

Und doch,   's will halt nicht gehn

After all it appears that Sachs's trade and his dreams of art
are one and the same thing. Again, when, to Beckmesser's
dismay, he is rousing the echoes of the town with his cobbler's
ballad, a new theme is heard in the wind instruments blending
with the verse 'O Eva hör' mein' Klageruf', a theme which later
will take possession of the prelude to the third act as that in
which are summed up all Sachs's longings, aspirations, and
renunciation of personal desires.

By such means are the strands of character skilfully inter-
woven into a completely articulated design. It is the unself-
consciousness of Sachs which endears him to us above all
Wagner's ostensible heroes. Indeed so spontaneously is he
pictured that the conscious reference to *Tristan und Isolde* at
the moment of his self-abnegation seems to be Wagner's one

false stroke in regard to Sachs. In other ways, too, the quotation from *Tristan* is a shock. It comes as an incursion from a different emotional world. The magic-love theme seems entirely foreign to the virginal simplicity of the love music of Eva and Walther.

The geniality of manner which enabled Wagner to carry his comedy safely through all the sermons on principles of criticism, musical appreciation, and song construction, even to the final laudation of 'heilige deutsche Kunst', is not extended to the villain of the piece, the ridiculous and insufferable Beckmesser. The fun which he tried to extract from the drubbing of Beckmesser is overdone, brutal, and clumsy. We know the cause of this; the character was conceived as a retaliation on his critical enemy, Hanslick, and it mars the whole work. The conception of Beckmesser alone prevents *Die Meistersinger* from attaining that unity of purpose and balance of design which is the consummate achievement of *Tristan*. Apart from that blemish *Die Meistersinger* is remarkable as evidence of Wagner's power to project himself into a world beyond himself. On *Tristan* he concentrated a burning personal experience; in *Die Meistersinger* he escaped from the experiences of his storm-tossed daily life.

The object of dwelling on these samples of the musical-dramatic art of Wagner has been to give some hint, it can scarcely be more within the limits of a single chapter, of that increase of suppleness which he acquired in bending his theories to practice. The further he went the more purely musical did his designs become. The quintet in *Die Meistersinger* throws theory to the winds and rehabilitates the operatic conceptions of *Don Giovanni* and *Fidelio*. After this none could say that Wagner ruled out from his music-drama any musical expression which had belonged to opera. His reform was seen to be merely a determination to preserve a right relationship of parts to the whole, and the more closely we study the later parts of the *Ring*,

Tristan, and *Die Meistersinger* the more convinced we become of
the rightness of Wagner's handling in the vast majority of cases.
He began with the idea of music fertilized by poetic drama; he
arrived at poetic drama created through music.

Parsifal is not in the same category with these. Do what we
will to receive with reverence its lofty thought expressed in the
ritual dignity of the Grail scenes, to enter sympathetically into
the intensity of Amfortas's agony and the healing consolation
of the Good Friday music, yet there remains the sense of an
unrealized vision. Wagner seems ill at ease in handling the
subject. His construction has returned to the consciousness of
his earlier style. He is not impelled forward by that creative urge
which is the all-pervading element in *Tristan* and *Die Meistersinger* and carries *Götterdämmerung* through to its triumphant
issue.

Sainthood was unknown to him;[1] it is equally unknown to those
who sneer at Parsifal as a stained-glass window figure. To them
it may be unknown because they do not believe in it. Wagner
believed in it intensely. Almost he persuaded himself to be a
Christian, but not quite. He grasped at it, but his grasp failed,
he fell back on old terms of expression, old type figures of good
and evil like those of the medieval morality plays.

So his technique both of words and music reverts to some of
the artificial methods which had belonged to *Das Rheingold*.
The young Esquires of the Grail are present in the first scene
solely that Gurnemanz may tell to them what the audience must
be made to know. Contrast Gurnemanz's narration with the
way in which past history is revealed through Isolde's passionate
outbursts in the first act of *Tristan*. While Gurnemanz is seated
under the tree the drama waits and the music labours till the
story is brought to a halting conclusion with the harmonized

[1] 'There has been hardly any successful male saint in fiction' (Charles
Gore).

version of 'durch Mitleid wissend'. Isolde's memories are themselves drama from which music flows.

Again, Parsifal enters accompanied by his heroic theme, though
he is but a stray youth who does not even know his own name.
There is nothing like the gradual unfolding of a character that we
have seen in the case of Sachs. Indeed the leitmotives of *Parsifal*
are throughout used much more as labels than they are anywhere
in Wagner since *Das Rheingold*. The Holy Spear, a melody
broken by a downward turn but rising up straight and clear
after its shame has been purged by Parsifal; the Grail, typified
in the 'Dresden Amen', and its attendant sacramental themes;
the characters of Amfortas, Kundry, Klingsor, all epitomized
in short motives repeated rather than developed in the texture,
are all no more than rather tentative symbols.

To contrast Kundry with the Brünnhilde of *Götterdämmerung*
is to realize that in drawing her, Wagner is back at the medieval
conception of Woman, the frail creature of flesh, temptress of
mankind, a creature to be redeemed by superior virtue and to
find her salvation in submission and silence. In the last act
she appears only as the penitent and not only is she vocally
silent, but her experience contributes nothing to the orchestral
texture. At the moment of her baptism, Parsifal's words are
accompanied by the theme of sacramental faith, and only a
stage direction in the text tells us that she bows her head and
weeps bitterly; nothing of her emotion passes into the music.
By thus much less than the others can *Parsifal* be regarded as
poetic drama created through music.

It contains magnificent passages of music 'fertilized' by the
poetic idea. The two orchestral 'Verwandlungen' leading into
the temple of the Grail (Acts I and III) with their strongly
contrasted tones of exaltation and of mourning, render the
scenic change otiose and superfluous. Here Wagner's orchestra
says all that needs to be said and modern audiences are fain to

shut their eyes to the clumsy stage devices of the Bayreuth theatre while they fill their ears with the searching tones of Wagner's orchestration.

The prelude to Act III, picture of Parsifal's wanderings, 'Der Irrnis und der Leiden Pfade kam ich', is one of the most original of Wagner's graphic ideas. Its virtual obliteration of the key system has already been pointed to as prophetic of that new orientation of the musical material which belongs to the twentieth century. The thrust to and fro of the melodic intervals (perfect 5th, diminished and augmented 5th, diminished octave) deserves analysis from a purely technical point of view. A few bars of the score are quoted below for that purpose. But over and above the technique there is the sense of 'thirsting in a land of sand and thorns' which is not only descriptive of Parsifal's state, but the very condition of the soul from which the vision of the Grail brings rescue and relief. In this passage is summed up the travail of the artist's life.

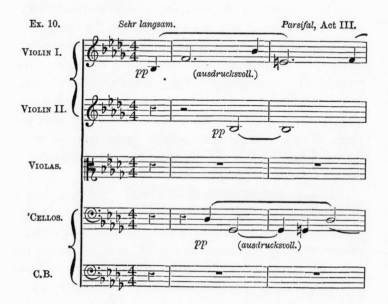

Ex. 10.   *Sehr langsam.*   *Parsifal*, Act III.

CHAPTER IX

AFTER WAGNER

It is the fashion of the unhistorical mind to assert that the antagonism to the Wagnerian music-drama was engineered by stupid and obscurantist publicists and fanned by personal antipathies. It would be idle to deny that there was a strong admixture of both these elements in contemporary criticism, but it is a distortion of the facts to pretend that the two together account for it. Wagner was a stumbling-block to some of the best musical minds of his time and he gave ample excuse for mis-understanding to the second-best minds. Brahms was among Wagner's admirers and was willing to show his admiration as occasion offered. He would not allow his friends, anti-Wagnerites to a man (and woman), to abuse Wagner in his presence. When the preparations, copying parts, &c., for the concerts of Wagnerian selections in Vienna were going forward in December 1862, Brahms joined the party and worked away at a selection from *Die Meistersinger* then unfinished, though, as Wagner says with a hint of scorn, he 'was often hardly noticed at our gatherings'.[1]

Composers more directly interested in opera watched Wagner's progress with apprehension and something like dismay, and it would be quite unfair to put their misgivings down to a personal jealousy. Tchaikovsky, after seeing all the music dramas (he was at the first Bayreuth of 1876), wrote his complete rejection of the Wagnerian theory as a basis for 'the art-work of the future' in a letter to his friend Mme von Meck.[2] If the opera of the future must proceed on these lines, then he reflected that at least it was open to composers to refrain from writing operas.

[1] *My Life*, p. 847.
[2] See *Life and Letters of P. I. Tchaikovsky.* Letter to Mme von Meck, Dec. 31st, 1882.

But he did not refrain. His most popularly successful opera, *Eugen Oniegin*, was already before the world; he was even then in the throes of composing *Mazeppa*, and the last of his full-length operas, *The Queen of Spades* (produced in 1890), bears no suggestion that Tchaikovsky was prepared to revise his conception of the function of music for the stage in the light of Bayreuth. Tchaikovsky laid no claim to nationalism, but he was never so Russian as when writing for the stage (Pushkin was the prime source of all these three operas), and never so happy as when depicting in song the gentler, more refined sides of Russian life, particularly feminine refinement, as witness the scene in Lisa's room (*Queen of Spades*, Act I, sc. 2).

We have seen in Rimsky-Korsakov's description of the Balakirev circle how the conscious nationalists of Russia feared the infringement of their independence by the Wagnerian influence, and they had cause to fear. When Wagner, shortly after the Viennese episode above mentioned, visited St. Petersburg to make propaganda for his works, he was welcomed and very materially helped in making arrangements for his concerts by his one Russian adherent who had previously sought him out at Lucerne.[1] This was Alexander Serov (1820–71), composer of an opera, *Judith*, which was produced with immense success at about that time. This, it must be remembered, was a decade before the Balakirev group had begun to give tangible proof of their powers in writing for the stage on a large scale. The composers of that group were still in their artistic childhood. Serov's acceptance of the Wagnerian gospel was no apostasy from well-defined native ideals. It reflects the highest credit on his acumen as a critic, and the fact that both *Judith* and its successor, *Rogneda*, took their public by storm shows at least that he was able to make effective practical use of the ideas of stage presentation imbibed from his master. But his work also

[1] *My Life*, pp. 711, 855 et seq.

shows unmistakably what it is that the creative artist always has cause to fear from the compelling influence of a powerful personality such as Wagner's, the too easy adoption of a way of expressing himself without the personal experience behind to justify it. If Borodin and Moussorgsky had been like-minded with Serov, they would no doubt have acquired more quickly the technique which they sorely lacked, possibly in time to finish their chief works themselves instead of leaving them to be posthumously cleaned up by the devotion of Rimsky-Korsakov. But it is improbable that they would have left *Prince Igor* and *Boris Godounov* as imperishable legacies for posterity. They kept Wagner at arm's length in order that they might be themselves, and they had the more need to do so at the time when he was ranging Europe from Paris to St. Petersburg, because this was just their formative period, when they had not yet made up their minds in terms of art what 'themselves' might mean.

When we consider Latin views on Wagner we must not forget Sedan. Giuseppe Verdi (1813–1901) is now recognized as Wagner's peer in the domain of musical drama. At the time that *Tristan* and *Die Meistersinger* were setting the world ablaze he was generally regarded as a writer of a series of exceedingly popular but musically vulgar works in the conventional mould of the Italian tradition suitable for displaying the powers of a new prima donna at Mr. Mapleson's opera-house in London. As the Wagnerians of all nations increased in numbers and loquacity they showed the superiority of their taste chiefly by expressing a pitying contempt for Verdi. Abroad, Wagner in the 'sixties was becoming more and more the artistic symbol for Germanism, as was Verdi for Latinism. When in 1867 Verdi was producing his *Don Carlo* in Paris his country was carrying its arms to the assistance of Prussia against Austria. Thus politics strike across racial sympathies. Then four years passed, years which included the Franco-Prussian war, Sedan, the siege of Paris, and the ruthless triumph of Prussia, before Verdi produced another opera anywhere. This was *Aïda*, with which the opera-house at Cairo was opened on Christmas Eve, 1871. Mr. Francis Toye has summed up the effect of these circumstances on Verdi with the suggestion that at this period 'Verdi was suffering from what nowadays we should call an anti-German complex, and', he adds, 'it is not merely fanciful to link up this general state of mind with his personal attitude towards Wagner'.[1]

That is true, and it is also true that Verdi was perfectly justified in resenting the critical suggestions that *Aïda*, the opera on which he had expended his utmost efforts to produce an individual work with a style and colour all its own, was Wagnerian in tendency. But though Verdi was big enough to look Wagner boldly in the face and pass him by, as the young Russians of that time could not do, neither he nor any one else could alter the fact that Wagner had done pioneer work for the readjustment of all operatic values. *Tristan* and *Die Meistersinger* had so far changed the face of the operatic world that after them it was impossible for any composer to do what all had done hitherto from Handel to Verdi himself; that is, write music which might be transferred from one opera to another, or be fitted with a new libretto if the original one proved a failure. A great deal of the modern revival of Verdi's earlier operas has depended on such processes of reconstruction. He had accepted ready-made librettos for reasons of policy and had written music which could only be said to belong to them in the loosest sense. With *Aïda* he outgrew that casual association of words and music because Wagner had made the world outgrow it. *Aïda*, moreover, 'had the happy result of bringing together Verdi and Boito',[2] and their subsequent collaboration in *Otello*

---

[1] *G. Verdi, his Life and Works*, by Francis Toye, p. 160.
[2] *Verdi*, by Feruccio Bonavia, p. 120.

(1887) and *Falstaff* (1893) achieved the complete emancipation of Italian opera from its fetters, those alike of the tradition at which Wagner had struck, and the new ones which in the 'sixties he appeared to be forging. We will not say that Verdi, Boito, and their successors could not have reached this freedom without Wagner; all that need be pointed out is that they did not.[1]

Arrigo Boito (1842–1918) was by temperament and education the very opposite of Verdi. He was the first of the Italians to approach the problems of the lyric stage from the standpoint of literature, and in doing so his criticism necessarily proceeded on lines similar to those of Wagner. Like all who showed any reformative tendencies in the middle of the century he was labelled 'Wagnerian' by his contemporaries, but actually the musical source of his reforming zeal was not Wagner himself but Wagner's great exemplar, Beethoven. Boito's work was done as poet, critic, and thinker rather than as composer, and his influence on the art of his country would have been virtually the same had he never produced the two operas which now represent him. He was re-editing the first of them when his artistic speculations were interrupted by the war against Austria, and he volunteered among the 'Red Shirts' of Garibaldi in a campaign which, while it secured the Italian frontiers against her traditional foe, was to have as its main effect the consolidation of that Germanism in which Verdi saw the menace to the Latin tradition.

In *Mefistofele* Boito made a serious attempt to convey in his music something of the philosophy underlying the *Faust* drama

[1] No attempt is made here to re-estimate Verdi's last works in the light of later experience, although Dannreuther's summary treatment of them in vol. vi, pp. 60–6, offers temptation to do so. But the two books referred tc above by Mr. Toye and Mr. Bonavia give to the English reader all the material that he can need, apart from the scores themselves, on which to form an enlightened view of Verdi's genius, and the small space available here could add little to their information.

of Goethe. He succeeded sufficiently, at any rate in the prologue, to be ranged with the German masters, Schumann, Wagner, and Liszt, who had essayed a similar task. As originally produced at La Scala, Milan (1868), five acts followed the prologue, but Boito subsequently reduced them to four. It was a bewildering scheme of prodigious length, in which daring experiment and conventional operatic procedure jostled one another, and its immediate failure was inevitable, quite apart from the conflict of prejudice in which it was received by the audience. Boito lacked the first-rate creative musical power to enable him to weld together the divergent elements of music-drama and to surmount all difficulties as Wagner was presently to do in *Götterdämmerung*. *Mefistofele* is now treasured by Italian audiences as one of the classics of their popular repertory, much as Gounod's *Faust* is treasured by French audiences. English audiences pit one against the other, and for the most part give their suffrages in favour of the easy success of the French romantic opera. But in *Mefistofele* Boito had aimed at much more.

The rest of his musical life was concentrated on the preparation of a musical drama, *Nerone*, the text of which in five acts was published in 1901. Its production at Milan was announced for the following year but withheld, and subsequently the question of how far the music had actually proceeded was a matter of constant speculation among Boito's friends. At last, six years after his death, it was produced by Toscanini at La Scala (May 1, 1924) before an audience assembled from all parts of Europe and America to witness one of the most carefully prepared first performances of an amazingly elaborate production. Boito had abandoned the composition of the fifth act of his drama, the burning of Rome, either because after all he felt himself unequal to its completion, or because, what is more likely, he had realized that the spectacular side of the drama was in danger of obscuring deeper human issues.

'He was indeed on the horns of a dilemma. While his real desire was to depict what Wagner described as "states of the soul", his scholarship and research led him in the direction of historical drama. Consequently the realism of the theatre is too strong for him. . . . Supreme music is wanted to lift the mind above the realism of the theatre, and that suggests what has really been Boito's difficulty throughout, the one of which he was himself entirely conscious. . . .

'He could conceive his epic but could hardly embody it in words, though some of his poetry is exquisite, but the ideal music always eluded him. The instinctive composer begins always with the musical idea; Boito began with the literary one and worked through it to the music.'[1]

This last sentence points the contrast between Boito and Verdi, and suggests why their collaboration in *Otello* and *Falstaff* could achieve ideal results. Theirs was a union of brain and creative impulses, intellect and genius.

We can trace the influence of Wagner in the last decades of the century working itself out in two ways, the direct and the indirect, the technical and the intellectual. The latter played its part in breaking down the stylistic conventions of the classical types of opera which belonged to Italy and to France. The 'verismo' school of young Italy, which was heralded by the sensational success of Mascagni's *Cavalleria Rusticana* in Rome (1890), owed little directly to Wagner and can scarcely be accused of intellectual influence either from him or any one else. Mascagni, Leoncavallo, Giordano, and others were purveyors of operatic 'shockers' catering for the kind of taste which nowadays is provided for more satisfactorily by the film and the detective story. With them the Italian opera finally abandoned its classic posture and slipped down from its pedestal of high romance. From that point of view *Cavalleria*, *Pagliacci*, and other specimens of the type, represent a reaction from the ideals both of Wagner and of Verdi, yet their composers were

[1] These quotations are from an article by the author written in *The Times*, May 3, 1924, on the occasion of the first performance of *Nerone*.

indebted to Wagner for the capacity to tell their stories in music at all. He had given to the lyric stage that suppleness of musical movement which made 'tragedy', in the sense of the newspaper headline, a possible subject for opera.

In the series of operas by Giacomo Puccini (1858–1924) the traditional lyricism of Italy, the descriptive orchestral commentary of Germany, the direct theatrical expression of the 'verismo' school were blended by an unmistakably musical personality. It is interesting to recall that Boito was among those who discerned genius in Puccini's early one-act opera, *Le Villi*, and helped to secure its performance in 1884. Nine years later Puccini achieved his first decisive success with *Manon Lescaut* (Turin, February 1st, 1893). It was due to the difficulty of distilling a libretto from the novel of the Abbé Prévost (Puccini was insistent that his opera should be a fresh treatment not based on the libretto already set by Massenet) that the collaboration with Luigi Illica and Giuseppe Giacosa emerged to produce *La Bohème* (Turin, February 1st, 1896), *Tosca* (Rome, January 14th, 1900), and *Madama Butterfly* (Milan, February 17th, 1904).

The first two of these had established Puccini's reputation throughout Europe as by far the most distinguished figure of his own generation in Italian opera, when, by one of those unaccountable freaks of humour which are apt to overtake a sensation-loving public, the third was received with howls of derision on its first night. Possibly the modern dress of the European characters and the flippant conversations of the American naval officer and his consul went a step too far in departing from the romantic tradition. *Madama Butterfly*, an adaptation of a magazine story by J. L. Long, turned into a play produced in London by David Belasco, was an offence to the dignity of La Scala, and its audience showed offence by expressing an undignified derision. Nevertheless the fiasco of the first performance was speedily redeemed at Brescia in the next year, and *Madama*

Butterfly took its place with its predecessors as a representative of Puccini's art of swift characterization.

La Bohème[1] had completely outshone Leoncavallo's treatment of Murger's novel produced at Venice a year later than Puccini's work. *Tosca*, based on Sardou's play made famous by Sarah Bernhardt, had achieved a second fame by the skill with which Puccini surrounded the play with his music without destroying its vividness of action. It is evident from his correspondence[2] with his librettists that this quality was Puccini's own, that he had to insist with Illica on the elimination of long passages intended to allow space for musical expansions of the aria type which would retard the stage action. He could always make space for melodic development when he needed it. From 'che gelida manina' to the flower-strewing duet of Butterfly and her maid, Puccini showed himself at one with the tradition of his country in vocal melody. But where the action had to move through a quick interplay of conversation often trivial in itself, he liked to leave the tune to his orchestra and to work in his dialogue in the manner of the old 'recitativo secco'. Take for example the badinage between the Bohemians and the rent-collecting Benoit:

Ex. 1.

---

[1] *La Bohème* was first introduced to England by the Carl Rosa Opera Company, who gave it at Manchester in English in 1897 and at a winter season at Covent Garden in the same year. Its production in Italian in the 'Grand' Season of Covent Garden (July 1st, 1899) was primarily due to the insistence of Mme Nellie Melba, who had sung in it in New York in the previous year.

[2] See *Letters of G. Puccini* edited by Giuseppe Adami, translated into English by Ena Makin, p. 116 &c.

In this light-handed way Puccini solves the problem of conversational pace in music, and it may be noted, apropos of this
instance, that it never seems to have occurred to any one that
there was any musical impropriety in the Bohemians' offer of
Bordeaux to their landlord, though one of the shocks of *Madama
Butterfly* was Pinkerton's offer of a whisky-and-soda to the
Consul.

In more essential matters than these Puccini showed unfailing
resource in catching every suggestion of local colour without
any apparent effort. He excelled in depicting minor characters
and incidents. The toy-sellers on Montmartre, the Sacristan
surrounded by clamorous choirboys, the ceremonies of a Japanese
wedding, offered him ideal opportunities in those operas for
which he could command the services of these compliant
librettists. The association, however, was broken by the death
of Giacosa in 1906, and Puccini was never quite so happy again,
save only in *Gianni Schicchi*, his one purely comic opera, the
third of the 'Trittico' with which Giuseppe Adami provided him
(1918).

La Fanciulla del West, written for America and produced at
the New York Metropolitan Opera House (December 10th, 1910),
begins the later phase of Puccini's career, which may reasonably
be considered as belonging to the music of the twentieth
century and therefore as lying beyond our period of discussion.
Up to that time his musical language, methods of construction,
harmonic technique and the like, had been wholly that of the
nineteenth-century tradition. Such details as the 'open fifths'
in the third act of *La Bohème* suggesting the morning chill, the
disjunct chords portraying Scarpia's perverted character in
Tosca, and the ending of the first act of *Madama Butterfly* on
a tentative chord of the sixth (like a note of interrogation) each
had their eloquence, because they were rare departures from
a normal standard of well-authenticated style. It was in *La*

Fanciulla that he began to toy with descriptive noises (he had heard Strauss's *Salomé*), and though he always refused to subordinate his sense of melody to such effects, the first scene of his last opera, *Turandot* (produced posthumously), shows that he went a considerable distance along the line of sensational dissonance. Puccini's later works will form the inevitable starting-point when the history of Italian opera in the twentieth century comes to be written.

The complicated tale of French opera in the last thirty years of the century must be briefly touched on here. All circumstances combined to retard the growth of Wagner's influence there: the Parisian episodes of his own career, political antipathies hardened by the Franco-Prussian war, and the strength of the national operatic tradition in the two clearly defined styles of the 'grand' opera and the 'opéra-comique'.[1]

Despite the interruption of the war Liszt duly fulfilled his previous promise to Saint-Saëns to get his *Samson et Dalila* performed at Weimar, but that was only accomplished at the end of 1877. The introduction did not cause this now popular opera to leap into fame. There were one or two German performances, but it was not till a dozen years later that it was brought back to France, and then only to Rouen.[2] Meantime Saint-Saëns had returned to something nearer to the grand opera tradition with *Étienne Marcel* (1879) and *Henry VIII* (1883). The last-named, an unhistorical treatment of the love-story of Henry VIII and Anne Boleyn and the divorce of Catherine of Aragon, was the work with which Saint-Saëns at last gained admission to

---

[1] The distinctions are well drawn by Dannreuther, *Oxf. Hist. Mus.*, vol. vi, in his chapter on 'Romantic Opera in Paris' and 'the further development of Romantic Opera'. In the latter the story is traced up to Bizet's *Carmen* (1875).

[2] It was kept off the English stage until 1909, since in the opinion of the Censor the presentation in a theatre of Biblical incidents and characters was improper.

the Académie de Musique (l'Opéra), and it achieved success. Of it Mr. Arthur Hervey says:[1]

'The great scene in which the schism from the Roman Church is pronounced furnishes a situation not unlike that at the end of the first act of *l'Africaine*, so effectively treated by Meyerbeer, and Saint-Saëns has successfully contrived to avoid undue comparison with this.'

The clever composer had also successfully contrived to bring both these operas sufficiently within the Meyerbeer tradition to make them palatable to the taste of that day. In *Samson*, conceived originally as an oratorio with powerfully written choruses, he had seized on a situation which appealed to him, and developed it regardless of fashion. Although Saint-Saëns continued to produce operas in Paris, and later at Monte Carlo, only *Samson* attained a firm place in the international repertory. The French might ignore it and the Germans declare it to be without significance of any kind, yet it was ultimately found that beneath its superficial effectiveness there was at least the significance of sincerity.

The more serious minds in France after the Franco-Prussian war were concerned to outgrow the taste for the spectacular opera of Meyerbeer, and in this process the long series of works by Jules Massenet (1842–1912) certainly played some part. For whatever may be said, and a great deal has been said, of the weakness of sentiment and the thinness of style in Massenet's music, at any rate the general tendency of his work was to dwell on the characteristics and emotions of his personages, and not to rely primarily on sumptuousness of stage effect. Massenet had produced several operas when his 'sacred drama' *Marie Magdeleine*, given as an oratorio by Colonne (1873) with Pauline Viardot-Garcia in the name part, brought him fame. *Herodiade*

[1] See *Saint-Saëns* by Arthur Hervey, p. 60. The operas are all concisely described in this biography.

was produced at Brussels in 1881, *Manon* at the Opéra Comique in Paris in 1884, and *Le Cid* at the Opéra in the following year. Throughout the 'nineties a new opera by Massenet was almost an annual event. When *Thaïs* was produced at the Opéra in 1894, M. Adolphe Jullien wrote:

'Cette fois, la série est-elle complète ? En avons-nous fini avec ces vierges folles de leur corps, ces courtisanes rachetées par l'amour, ces saintes de boudoir, ces héroïnes d'un mysticisme lascif, que M. Massenet a fait chanter tour à tour, en leur mettant simplement dans la bouche les mélodies les plus sensuelles qu'il pût trouver, sans faire entre elles aucune différence ? Thaïs va-t-elle être enfin le dernier produit de cette fausse religiosité musicale qui nous a déjà valu Salomé, Marie-Magdeleine, Ève, la Vierge, Manon même, Esclarmonde enfin ; car toutes les femmes de M. Massenet se ressemblent, et bien malin serait celui qui distinguerait ses héroïnes sacrées de ses héroïnes profanes, ses vierges de ses courtisanes, Marie-Magdeleine de Manon !'

The series was indeed very far from being completed and was continued up to *Cleopâtre*, produced posthumously at Monte Carlo. Considering Massenet's preoccupation with erotic femininity, *Le Jongleur de Nôtre Dame* (1902), which contains no female voice at all,[1] only a vision, but which handles the theme of religious devotion with a refreshing naïveté, deserves to be singled out for mention. Among his later operas, *Don Quichotte* is a sympathetic study in the romantic idealism of Cervantes's hero, and though the impatience of M. Jullien's remarks has been shared by many to whom Massenet's lack of robustness is repellent, it must be realized that idealism combined with human interest, qualities none too plentiful in Parisian opera, pervade the best of his work.

Massenet's technical style undoubtedly owed something to Wagner, but the sameness of his melodies prevented him from

[1] In America the part of the Juggler, Jean, was, however, played by Mme Mary Garden, whose reputation was based largely on her presentation of Massenet's more sensational roles.

using leading themes in the positive manner to express distinctions of character which is Wagner's use of such themes. His pupil Alfred Bruneau (1857–1934) was much more decisively influenced both by Wagner's theories and by his experience of Wagner's handling of the orchestra. As a young man Bruneau played in Pasdeloup's orchestra and gained acquaintance with selections from Wagner from the player's point of view. He won the Prix de Rome in 1881. He occupied himself with criticism, and, like Ernest Reyer before him, may be said to have approached the opera more from the intellectual standpoint of the critic than from the instinctive one of the composer. His career as a composer virtually began in 1891 with the production at the Opéra Comique of *Le Rêve*, founded, as were most of his subsequent operas, on a story by Zola. Within the next decade he composed *L'Attaque du Moulin* (Opéra Comique, 1893), *Messidor* (Opéra, 1897), and *L'Ouragan* (Opéra Comique, 1901), which are the works on which his reputation rests.

L'Attaque du Moulin has been the most widely performed outside France. Its theme, actually an episode in the Franco-Prussian war, is an example of the tendency, not in itself Wagnerian, to base opera on contemporary life. It also shows the energy of Bruneau's mind and his love of themes, which present a conflict of physical and spiritual forces and are the very opposite of Massenet's contemplations of static types. It is curious that the composer of French opera held to have most warmly embraced the Wagnerian method at the end of the century should have chosen for his most successful work a story of the French resistance to German aggression. How far Bruneau's method could actually reflect Wagner's may be illustrated by a short extract of the instrumental music at what is really the denouement of the drama, the point at which the young Frenchman, Dominique, escaping from captivity, kills the German sentry posted outside the mill.

Ex. 2.   8ves..   BRUNEAU.

The *long cri* in the otherwise silent bar represents the death
of the sentry; in the orchestral diminuendo following it, recollections of Wagner's Norns and fate themes are inescapable.

Ernest Reyer (1823–1909), older than Bruneau by a generation, is another whose intellectual convictions served to give
a Wagnerian turn to French opera in the last quarter of the
century. His *Sigurd*, a version of the Nibelungen legend, was
planned many years before Wagner's tetralogy saw the light,
but was not produced until 1883. His reputation as a stage
composer was made in Paris with works which arrived early
enough to arouse the interest both of Halévy and Berlioz. As
critic to the *Journal des Débats* he had visited Cairo for the first
performance of Verdi's *Aïda* in 1871, and though by no means
wholly appreciative of Verdi's genius, his judgement here as
elsewhere was ranged on the side of enterprise and freedom of
dramatic expression. That he was not afraid to produce his
Sigurd, first in Brussels then in Paris, at a time when *Der Ring
des Nibelungen* was the last word in modern music-drama, is

evidence of his confidence in his own independence of thought. He knew himself to be no plagiarist. He had viewed the legend with his own eyes and translated it into his own musical terms. He submitted the results to the judgement of an audience, and the contemporary judgement both of *Sigurd* and of *Salammbo*, which followed in 1890, was favourable, even though neither work may be of the highest interest to a later generation. An extract from the passage in which Brunehild laments the death of Sigurd and accepts reunion with him in death may here be quoted as an example both of the affinity with Wagner and of the immeasurable gulf which separates it from the finale of *Götterdämmerung*:

meurs ! . . . Les dieux . . . . me font mou-

- rir, moi, la fem - me qu'il ai - me Mourir du

coup qui l'a frap-pé ! Le

glaive . . de Gun-ther   de mon sang est trem-pé

In the work of these composers we see the gradual absorption
of the major lessons of Wagner's art while on the whole they
successfully maintained the French tradition of vocal clarity
and directness of expression. César Franck himself made two
mature essays in opera, *Hulda* (1882–5), based on a Scandinavian
legend drawn from Björnson, and *Ghisèle* (1888–90), left unfinished; but they were stillborn. His disciple, d'Indy, in
Fervaal, showed himself to be almost as completely oblivious of
the traditions of the French stage as his master. Bruneau,
despite his own sympathy with Wagnerian principles, wrote
of it, 'Tout est franchement, nettement—petitement—Wag-
nérien en *Fervaal*; les personnages, les symboles, les thèmes et
l'orchestre'.[1]

One other important figure deserves consideration here.
Gustave Charpentier (born 1860) produced his highly successful
Louise at the Opéra Comique (1900) just before Debussy led
the reaction with *Pélleas*. He, like Bruneau, had passed through
Massenet's class at the Conservatoire and was also a winner of
the Prix de Rome. *Louise* is Wagnerian in the sense that it is the
fulfilment in music of a dramatic idea of its composer's own
creation. Moreover, the music in the use of leading themes owes
something to Wagner's technique. It is anti-Wagnerian, in a

[1] See *Musiques d'hier et de demain*, by Alfred Bruneau. Essay on *Fervaal*,
p. 156.

way that *Pélleas* is not, in its subject-matter. The poet-musician puts legend and fable aside and draws his characters straight from the life about him, even more decisively than Bruneau had done. The supper-table of a bourgeois family in Paris, the chatter of work-girls in a millinery establishment, are handled with extraordinary ease in Charpentier's music, yet behind these scenes of commonplace life there is a bigger theme, the struggle between youth and age, between romance and reality, between 'self-expression' and responsibility. Louise is romantic in her love for Jullien and her desire for the freedom of the life of Montmartre. Her father is equally romantic in his idealization of the domestic hearth with a newspaper and a cup of coffee. Their contrary romances clash. Realities are pictured on the one hand by the scene in which the night-wanderer moves amongst the vagrants of the streets, on the other by the uncompromising devotion to prosaic duties of Louise's mother. The realities also clash. Behind it all is the alluring, yet relentless, life of a great city. *Louise* is at once the most realistic and imaginative drama of the post-Wagnerian era, and it formed a remarkably original close to the century's development in French opera. Charpentier made the mistake of trying to follow it up with a sequel, *Jullien* (1913), but the vision had faded and *Louise* remains his one masterpiece.

We need not dwell at great length on the events of German opera after Wagner's death. There were the host of admirers who attempted to follow in his footsteps, and it seemed that in Germany at any rate Tchaikovsky's suggestion that composers must either be Wagnerian or refrain from writing operas was to be fulfilled. Two whose work stood out from the rest as showing ability to adapt the Wagnerian type of structure to individual expression were the Austrian, Wilhelm Kienzl (born 1857), and the North German, Engelbert Humperdinck (1854–1921). The former's *Der Evangelimann* (1894) and the latter's *Hänsel und*

Gretel (1893) achieved simultaneous popularity, but Humperdinck's has been the more permanent. He was fortunate; he knew a side of life which was entirely unknown to Wagner, the life of childhood. *Hänsel und Gretel*, the play written by the composer's sister, Adelheid Wette, is a child's fairy-tale; its musical matter is of a piece with the nursery rhymes of German children such as 'Du liebe Augustin', on which the curtain rises, and the composer's genius is shown in his power of drawing to scale. Here and there a Wagnerian mannerism may intrude (see for example the passage which accompanies the parents' laughter in Act I), but in general the simple diatonic tunes get the harmony which obviously belongs to them, the polychromatic orchestra rarely labours the development of them or hints at any deeper emotion than the love of games and of sweet things to eat, the fear of the dark, awe of fairies and witchcraft, and the trust in angelic protection. All is done without any hint of 'talking small' or of the patronage of the grown-up towards the child. Humperdinck's children are real in their loves and fears and fancies, and his music throughout *Hänsel und Gretel* is entirely spontaneous. A second venture in the same genre was *Königskinder* (text by Ernst Rosmer), which was first composed as continuous music to a spoken play and later made into an opera. It embodies many of the same delightful traits, but bears some traces of its changed form. *Hänsel und Gretel* was a success hardly to be repeated.

Humperdinck had taken part in the preparation for *Parsifal* at Bayreuth (1882) and to him at a later date was entrusted the musical education of Siegfried Wagner (1869–1930), whose first opera, *Der Bärenhäuter*, was given at Munich in 1899. The event naturally attracted considerable attention but the work made no permanent mark. It was not as a composer of operas but as guardian of the Bayreuth theatre that Siegfried Wagner was to continue his father's work.

A bolder claimant to the Wagnerian crown quickly presented himself. Richard Strauss (born 1864) had had a first opera, *Guntram*, produced at Weimar in 1894. He had then devoted himself to developing further his enormous orchestral sense in the series of symphonic poems which culminated in *Ein Helden-leben*.[1] He was now the complete hero according to his own conception of heroism, and ready to compose to a libretto which in its setting of the St. John's Eve festival in a medieval town would court comparison with *Die Meistersinger*. Ernst von Wolzogen supplied him in *Feuersnot* (produced Dresden, 1901) with a book designed to prove his right of succession. The high-falutin text is a reproduction of Wagner's most didactic manner. The central figure is Kunrad, a magician, who by his magic plunges the whole town in darkness until the maiden of his choice shall yield herself to his love. Using her balcony as his pulpit he harangues the benighted townsfolk, upbraiding them for having spurned his master, 'Richard the First', and having failed to appreciate the resplendent worth of himself, clearly identified by verbal pieces in the text and thematic allusions in the music with 'Richard the Second'.

The music of *Feuersnot* is much less extravagant than the composer's claims. It shows his complete competence in handling the Wagnerian technique, and its finale is conspicuous for its beauty and orchestral richness. No doubt, however, Strauss realized that the mere continuance of the Wagnerian manner would not place him where he intended to be, and his next opera, a setting of Wilde's *Salomé*, showed a complete change of standpoint. It proved to be the first and most violent shock of the new century. Into that, and all that followed from Strauss's fortunate collaboration with the poet Hugo von Hofmannsthal in *Elektra* and subsequent works, we shall not enter here. Strauss definitely closed his post-Wagnerian

[1] See Chapter V, p. 134 and p. 162.

period with *Feuersnot*, and the rest of his acts are matter for another chronicle.

It was while Strauss and von Hofmannsthal were engaged in electrifying the operatic world that the visit of a Russian company to Paris (1908) made Western Europe suddenly aware of another factor in the situation by the production of Moussorgsky's *Boris Godounov*, a work of a generation earlier. The comparative independence of western influence in which the Russian opera had been matured has already been described, and Moussorgsky's method of translating the Russian language into musical declamation will be touched on later.[1] One further element which entered deeply into the Russian sense of style in the presentation of opera in general must be taken into account.

The influence of the Russian Ballet on Western Europe, more particularly in the hands of Serge Diaghilev, is wholly a matter of the twentieth century, but its influence on native composers and on the plan of their works belongs to the nineteenth. It was at the very beginning of the nineteenth century, in the reign of Catherine II, that the famous French ballet-master, Didelot, laid the foundations of the Imperial School of Ballet in St. Petersburg. Curiously enough, it was not till very near its end (1890) that Tchaikovsky's *The Sleeping Beauty* set the fashion in the composition of independent ballets with music of a quasi-symphonic, quasi-operatic type. For that purpose the composer was supplied with a detailed scenario, describing the several scenes, the nature of the dances in which they were to be presented, even the number of bars required for each dance. The scenario of the ballet was exactly what the libretto is to the opera composer, save that the ballet-master, backed by the authority of the Imperial School, could afford to be very much more dictatorial in his attitude towards the composer than the

[1] See Chapter XI, p. 405 et seq.

author of an opera book can generally be. The Imperial School
through a century of development had established a tradition
with principles of technique and a rigorous discipline to which
all its members from the moment of their entry were committed.[1]
The School supplied all the ballets required in the operas both
of St. Petersburg and Moscow as well as weekly performances
entirely devoted to ballet. The music for these last up to the
time of Tchaikovsky's innovation was of a pasticcio kind.[2]
Tchaikovsky followed *The Sleeping Beauty* with *Casse Noisette*,
and other composers followed him in elaborating the ballet's
repertory before the time when Diaghilev launched it on its
cosmopolitan career and established the Russo-Parisian type
of which Stravinsky became the chief musician.

The ballet as a type of expression had entered very little into
Moussorgsky's schemes. It is essentially an artistic convention,
and he was obsessed with the desire to strip his art of conventions
in order to probe to realities. His 'uglinesses' were the result
of his desire for directness and his inability to confine his

[1] For an admirable account of the rigorous training which young dancers,
male or female, had to undergo, see *Theatre Street* by Mme Karsavina.

[2] The repertory of 'The Imperial Russian Ballet's' first season at Covent
Garden (1911) consisted of the following:

Cleopatra—music by Arensky, Taneiev, Rimsky-Korsakov, Glinka,
Glazounov, Moussorgsky.
Scheherazade—music by Rimsky-Korsakov.
Les Sylphides—music by Chopin.
Le Carneval—music by Schumann.
Le Pavillon d'Armide—music by Tcherepnin.
Prince Igor (Polovtsi Dances)—music by Borodin.
Le Spectre de la rose—music by Weber.
Sadko—music by Rimsky-Korsakov.
Narcisse—music by Tcherepnin.
Le Dieu bleu—music by Reynaldo Hahn.

Of these only the Tcherepnin works were originally written as independent
ballets for the Imperial troupe. Rimsky-Korsakov's were adaptations from
his symphonic suites; Borodin's dances belong to the opera; Hahn's work
was written for Paris, and the remainder are adaptations chiefly from piano
music.

imagination within any conventional framework. In *Boris* the
weak Polish scene, an afterthought, is the only one which
attempts to handle the convention of the ballet. But in later
composers the ballet helped both to develop the sense of musical
form and to intensify the sense of the stage picture. That
appears most strongly in the long series of Rimsky-Korsakov's
operas beginning with *Ivan the Terrible* and ending with *The
Golden Cockerel*. The first, like Moussorgsky's *Boris* and Borodin's
Prince Igor, is an epic of Russian history; the last, when it was
first given in England, was described as a 'ballet-opera'. This
was not Rimsky-Korsakov's intention or designation, but the
whole subject-matter and style lent itself readily to the adaptation. Between the two, a long series (there are fifteen operas in
all) shows the composer turning away from the naturalism of
the historic drama to the symbolism of the pictorial stage, of
which ballet is the ideal presentation. Vocal melody was not
Rimsky-Korsakov's strong point as it was Tchaikovsky's.
Rather the keen-edged instrumental phrase in appropriate
colouring of violin, trumpet, or oboe, the counterpart of gesture,
the incisive rhythm, and the languorous arabesque were the
groundwork of his musical inspiration. In *A Night in May*
which followed *Ivan* in 1879 the music of the lovers is less to the
point than the dance music of the Gopak and the night scene
in which the Burgomaster is befooled. In *The Snow Maiden,
The Christmas Eve Revels*, *Sadko*, *Tsar Saltan*, and *Kastchei*, folk-
lore and legend pictured in action are the bases of his drama.
Mlada (1889) was his individual treatment of a ballet-opera
which originally was to have been composed by Borodin,
Moussorgsky, César Cui, and himself. Mrs. Newmarch writes
of it:

'In the ballet the shade of Mlada was represented by the famous
"ballerina" Petipa, and the shade of Cleopatra by Skorsiouka. The
subject is taken from the history of the Balkan Slavs in the ninth

century; but although in this work he returns to an historical episode, the composer does not go back to the declamatory style of the *Maid of Pskov* [*Ivan the Terrible*]. . . .

'The scenes representing the ancient pagan customs of the Slavs are highly picturesque, and, except on the grounds of its expensive setting, it is difficult to understand why this work should have passed out of the repertory of the Russian opera.'[1]

Rimsky-Korsakov's musical versatility led him to make occasional experiments in other styles; *Mozart and Salieri* (1897) has become the most famous of them through Chaliapin's dramatic characterization of the part of Salieri. It is a perfect short specimen of the declamatory duologue owing nothing to the pictorialism of the ballet, a study in human character and the clash of impulses expressed through voice and orchestra. In the main, however, if we say that it was Rimsky-Korsakov who gave form and consistency to the Russian opera, we must also say that it was the Russian preoccupation with the ballet which imbued Rimsky-Korsakov with a distinctive sense of those qualities.

The lack of them in the Czech opera has kept it at home while the Russian has gone abroad. No country has based its national musical education so directly on the repertory of the National Opera House as have the Czechs.[2] The foundations laid by Smetana were carried on by Dvořák, Joseph Bohuslav Foerster, and Karel Kovařovic. The last-named was musical director of the National Opera House for the last twenty years of his life (1900–20).

Dvořák's operas, excluding the early *Alfred*, which was with-

[1] See *The Russian Opera*, by Rosa Newmarch, p. 304.

[2] One has only to attend a Saturday matinée of one of the larger operas of Smetana, *Dalibor* or *Libuša*, to realize the strength of their hold on all classes of the people. Women wearing shawls over their heads bring small children in from the country, clubs of young men and women, artisans and shop assistants, take up the cheap subscription. They listen to these long and, to the outsider, tedious works with the closest attention and with every evidence of keen appreciation.

drawn, number nine.[1] His best work is that which follows the
model of peasant opera set by Smetana in *The Bartered Bride*.[2]
In *The Peasant a Rogue* a brilliant overture leads to a bright
comedy of intrigue in which, after the manner of *Figaro*, a Duke
makes love to a lady's-maid and a plot to fool him involves a
series of disguises. But it is in the peasant scenes, the revels
round the Maypole, that Dvořák is most in his element. *The
Jacobin*, a romantic tale of an heir disinherited for political
views (which however are made of little interest to the audience),
contains the most delightful studies in village life. The old
schoolmaster and organist with his youths and maidens (who
are given to love-making during singing lessons) are drawn true
to life in Dvořák's naïve melody. It is here that those reminiscences of his own youth at Nelahozeves alluded to in connexion
with the 'New World' Symphony make their appearance. But it
is only in individual scenes such as this which touch him nearly
that Dvořák displays anything like an operatic style of his own.
The larger his canvas the more uncertain is his touch.

Dimitrij, an opera in four acts on the grand scale, has for its
subject the phase of Russian history immediately following the
death of Boris Godounov, that is the conflict between the
usurper and Boris's children. It opens with a sombre orchestral
Largo which has something Beethoven-like in the way it arouses
a sense of imminent tragedy by insistence on plain bold themes
(Ex. 4).

The opening double chorus of peasants before the Kremlin,
with its conflicting rhythms, carries further the dramatic

[1] The complete series, *Král a uhlir* (King and Collier) (1874), *Tvrde
palice* (The Pigheaded Peasants) (1874), *Vanda* (1876), *Selma Šedlak* (The
Peasant a Rogue), *Dimitrij* (1883), *Jakobin* (1888), *Čert a Kača* (The Devil and
Kate) (1899), *Rusalka* (1900), and *Armida* (1903), was given in the Národní
Divadlo (National Opera House) in Prague in the summer of 1929 in
commemoration of the composer twenty-five years after his death.

[2] See *Oxf. Hist. Mus.*, vol. vi, p. 77.

Dvořák. *Dimitrij.*

impressiveness of the prelude. The Patriarch of the Church and
Shiusky as representative of the Boyars declare for the children
of Boris, while the army has gone over to the support of the
pretender from Poland. The people shout for both sides (Ex. 5).

These things show Dvořák attacking his subject in something
of the spirit of Moussorgsky but with a higher technical equipment in the disposal of voices and orchestra. But the scale was
too large. In spite of much fine music and some strongly dramatic
moments interest wavers for lack of definite proportions in the
plot, and definite constructive principle in the music.

Ex. 5.

Dvořák. *Dimitrij.*

1st Chorus.

f Slá - va Fe - do - ro - vi ca - ru,

2nd Chorus.

f Nač nám Go-du-nův? nač nám ty-ra-nův?

ve - li - ké - mu go - su - da - ru,

Di - mi - trij pra - vý syn je I - va - nův,

When it first appeared *Dimitrij* was complained of as being
'more Meyerbeer', and its plan, so far as it has one, is certainly
nearer to the old-fashioned grand opera than to the modern
musical drama. Its elaborate ensembles, involving much verbal
repetition, are, for an opera composed in the year of Wagner's
death, curiously oblivious of the lessons of Wagner's life.

AFTER WAGNER 353

The rough comedy of *The Devil and Kate*[1] and the picturesque romance of *Rusalka*, both of them a return to Czech folk-lore in differing moods, secured a local popularity, but Dvořák's last opera, *Armida*, was a failure. He was by far the strongest genius of the Czech school, perhaps the only one after Smetana whose right to the name of genius is indisputable, but he failed to establish a type. By the end of the century only the Latin culture of Europe had been strong enough to digest the Wagnerian feast.

[1] This work was given in England in the autumn of 1932 by the Oxford University Opera Club.

CHAPTER X

SONG. I. BRAHMS

BRAHMS's published works contain two hundred original songs for single voice with piano accompaniment, exclusive of the *Deutsche Volkslieder* (seven books of seven songs each), and the set of fourteen *Volkskinderlieder* written for the Schumann children. There are also two dozen or so of duets with piano accompaniment (Opp. 20, 28, 61, 66, 75, 84), and with them may be named certain works for larger combinations of voices with accompaniment, the songs for women's choir with two horns and harp (Op. 17), the vocal quartets with piano accompaniment (Opp. 31, 64, 92, 112), the two sets of *Liebeslieder Walzer* (Opp. 52, 65) for vocal quartet and piano duet, the *Zigeuner Lieder* (Op. 103) for vocal quartet and piano. The numerous unaccompanied part-songs may be considered, for the purpose of the moment, to belong to a different category even though they have much of the same lyrical quality as the accompanied songs. One must draw the line somewhere. If we draw it between songs with instrumental accompaniment and without we still have the embarrassment of Op. 44, 'Twelve Songs and Romances composed for women's choir *a cappella*, or with optional piano accompaniment.' This, like the better-known set of four songs with horns and harp, is one of the instances in which Brahms applied his lyrical gift to the needs of the Ladies' Choir which he conducted at Hamburg in 1859. They are, moreover, conspicuous among the few instances in the whole of Brahms's large output of works written for the immediate purpose of performance.

In the songs proper, which range from the six of Opus 3 (with *Liebestreu* at its head, in which Schumann first discovered the deep song-melody of Brahms's genius) to the *Vier ernste*

Gesänge (Op. 121) which are his epilogue, there is little to indicate that any special singer or even a special type of voice was thought of in the act of composition. Opp. 3 and 6 were published as 'for a tenor or soprano voice', and the *Vier ernste Gesänge* are for a bass voice. But the customary subheading is merely 'for a single voice with piano accompaniment' and Brahms's correspondence with publishers shows that he was not usually particular as to the actual pitch, and was quite willing that his songs should be transposed into any convenient key.

About 1880 he seems to have developed a predilection for a low voice and several of the sets are described as 'für eine tiefere Stimme'. It is noteworthy that each of them contains one or more of his most widely acknowledged masterpieces, *Feldeinsamkeit* (Op. 86, No. 2), perfect presentation of summer serenity, *Sapphische Ode* (Op. 94, No. 4), a melody as inseparable from contralto tone as that of the slow movement of the Violin Concerto is from the oboe, *Immer leiser wird mein Schlummer* and *Auf dem Kirchhofe* (Op. 105, Nos. 2 and 4), both of which probe to the inner recesses of the human heart. If the singers who delight in *Sapphische Ode* would look a little deeper into the *Fünf Lieder* of Op. 94, recital programmes would be richer. Op. 94 begins with *Mit vierzig Jahren*, originally written in the bass clef and intended for Stockhausen, who sang it with Brahms and broke down under the stress of emotion. Third in the set is *Mein Herz ist schwer*, one of the amplest in harmonic colour of all Brahms's songs. The whole set, appearing as it did just about the time of the Third Symphony, marks that turning-point noticed in connexion with the symphonies from what was there called the heroic period to the 'autumnal mood'. With that turning-point the use of the low voice is associated, and besides those instances already mentioned we have the two exquisite songs for alto voice, viola, and piano, *Gestillte Sehnsucht* and *Geistliches Wiegenlied* (Op. 91), which form as delicate a combination of dark tones, vocal and instrumental, as the women's choral songs with horns and harp are of light, ethereal tones.

We might take these two (Opp. 17 and 91) as dividing lines between the three seasons, spring, summer, and autumn, of Brahms's song-writing career. Happily he never had to suffer the chills of winter as did both Schumann and Hugo Wolf, the leading representatives of German song in the generations before and after him. His power remained undiminished right up to the date, 'Wien, Mai. 96', which stands at the end of the manuscript of the *Ernste Gesänge*.[1]

The early songs by no means all live up to the promise of *Liebestreu*, *Weit über das Feld* (Op. 3, No. 4), and *Nachtigallen schwingen* (Op. 6, No. 6). As Mr. Fuller-Maitland has pointed out, the influence of such traditional German distinctions as between the *Volkslied* and *volksthümliches Lied*, the *strophisches* and the *durchcomponiertes*, have to be taken into account.[2] To those not bred in the tradition, some of the strophic settings of Opp. 6, 7, and 14 may seem inadequate, and the square tunes and rhythms characteristic of German popular song are apt to be prosaic. What has been said of the influence of such songs as a disintegrating, because unassimilable, factor in Brahms's early piano sonatas, must be borne in mind here.[3]

Brahms and his contemporaries did not regard the folksong, as we are apt to do, as an interesting survival among the unlettered classes of society, but as a type of simple song which might as well be written by one of themselves as by an unknown and forgotten singer by the wayside. When therefore he labelled

[1] See facsimile of the manuscript reproduced by Drei Masken Verlag. The original is the property of the Gesellschaft der Musikfreunde, Vienna, to which Society Brahms bequeathed his manuscripts.

[2] See Fuller-Maitland's *Brahms*, p. 157 et seq. In that work the whole series of Brahms's songs is passed in review, briefly noting details of all the more important songs. Max Friedlaender's *Brahms's Lieder* (Eng. trans. by Leonard Leese), Oxford University Press, covers the same ground in greater detail.   [3] See Chapter II, p. 26.

Vor dem Fenster or *Vom verwundeten Knaben* (Op. 14, 1 and 2) with the description *Volkslied* he did not mean that he had heard the tune sung at the plough's tail, or that he had dug it out of some collection such as that of his favourite Zuccagmaglio. He means it to be a song for the people to sing, one written in a style which will be familiar to them and which they can both sing and play on the piano fairly easily. This sort of song was the ground plan as it were from which his more expansive and individual style of expression sprang. From that point of view the humbler examples of his art of the spring-time period have an inherent interest and value for the historian if not for the recital-giving vocalist.

It is to the long summer-time of the twenty years which began with the publications of 1862 that we must turn to get a comprehensive view of Brahms's personal attitude towards the song form. From the *Fünf Gedichte* of Op. 19 onwards, the songs are poured out in an almost continuous stream. Neither opus numbers nor dates of publication represent accurately the order of composition, but from here up to Op. 85 (i.e. stopping short of the first of the low-voiced groups) we have a hundred and ten songs published in groups of any number from four to nine. These groups were made up on no principle save that of effective contrast, and were sent off to press whenever he had finished one and desired to get it off his hands.

Brahms's choice of poets baffles classification; his literary taste was far from impeccable. He never set great poetry because it was great poetry, and he could be attracted by very poor poetry if it would make a song. He even seemed to fight shy of the great poets. He set only seven of Goethe's songs,[1] minor lyrics all of them, and none of them amongst his most famous songs. No doubt he realized here how Schubert had been before him.

[1] In addition to the seven there is the *Heidenröslein* of the *Volkskinder-lieder*.

His chief indebtedness to Goethe appears not in solo song but in the *Harzreise Rhapsodie* for alto voice, male chorus, and orchestra (Op. 53), which shows, more particularly in the declamation of the opening pages, to what heights Brahms could rise in conjunction with a great poetic theme. From Heine he picked out scarce a handful of lyrics, five in all, and they all belong to the later period. *Es liebt sich so lieblich im Lenze* (Op. 71, No. 1) does not inspire him to the height of Hölty's *Die Mainacht.* The most deeply felt of the Heine songs is *Der Tod, das ist die kühle Nacht* (Op. 96, No. 1), which has curious though remote affinity with Wagner's *O sink' hernieder* (*Tristan*); Uhland, Rückert, Eichendorff, Mörike, and others of the acknowledged German lyricists are drawn on impartially but only occasionally, and among the many poets of small account in themselves Brahms declared a special affection for Ludwig Hölty, who, if he had no other claim to fame, had that of making Brahms produce exquisite melody.

Ludwig Tieck and Georg Friedrich Daumer take specially prominent places among Brahms's poets, as the only two to whom he devoted a complete opus. The series of fifteen songs from Tieck's romance of *Die schöne Magelone* are an exceptional essay in the cyclic treatment of song. G. F. Daumer was Brahms's own discovery in the sense that his fame as a poet was spread by Brahms's settings of his works, both original and translations from oriental sources. Op. 32 is in the nature of a song cycle; it consists of poems by August von Platen and Daumer grouped together, with Daumer's *Wie bist du meine Königin* as finale to a tale of love longings, doubts, fears, and resistances. Op. 57 is entirely given to Daumer's poems, and to him also Brahms owed the texts for both sets of the *Liebeslieder Walzer*. Among the poets who were Brahms's personal friends Klaus Groth, Professor of German language and literature at Kiel University, is of more than ordinary importance to us, because to him we owe the *Regenlied* and *Nachklang* (Op. 59, nos. 3 and 4), and consequently the finale of the Violin Sonata in G, if not indeed the idea of the whole Sonata.

But there is no need to catalogue all. The important point to note here is that Brahms generally accepted a poem not for any merit in itself but because he felt a song to be lurking behind its rhythm, its fantasy, or its imagery. It is clear too that the influence of the poem varied in kind and in degree. He, like every other great song-writer, required it to provide him with the first impulse to compose, but that impulse might come from the whole poem, its thought, its mood, its quality of human emotion, its rhythm, and the verbal images used as means of expression, all together, or out of any one of these things singly. While it is possible, speaking theoretically, to postulate that the perfect song will be that which illumines every aspect of the poem with musical beauty, yet, practically speaking, inspiration of that order, alike in the poet and the musician, is exceedingly rare, and the great musicians have not allowed themselves to be dependent on their poets to anything like that extent. They have realized that while the poem is their starting-point, the music is the singer's and the hearer's starting-point, that it is with the singer that the life of a song begins, and that its life is primarily a musical one. The composer's main task then is to discover a musical form which will embody what he has got from the poem. It may be less or more than a literary judgement would discover in the poem, because what he has got is a musical conception, and according to the quality of his musical conception aided by his subsequent craftsmanship his song will stand or fall, be judged great or little, weighty or trivial. If the composer is a man of fine literary taste he will naturally find what he wants only in poems of fine literary quality, but most of the great song composers have not been men of fine literary taste. Some of them have even been

notably deficient in it, but their deficiency has not prevented
them producing great songs, even from words which a fine taste
regards as deplorable. It is no very high commendation of a
song-writer to declare that his taste in poetry is good, though we
may regard it as an added merit; nor is it certainly a final
condemnation to discover that his taste in poetry is bad. It is
his taste in music which matters.

Brahms's taste in poetry was that of the average German of
the mid-nineteenth century whose reading was more or less
bounded by his own language and whose literary education had
been slight in youth but improved by converse with men and
women, friends like the von Herzogenbergs, of wider culture
than his own. He reacted readily to the accepted types of
German romantic poetry, saw nothing banal or absurd in the
conventional imagery of may-flowers, breezes and swallows,
summer moonlight and nightingales. These were the proper
surroundings of lovers in ecstasy or despair, hope or doubt, and
love, as the emotion most common to mankind, was the theme
most congenial to the singer and to the maker of songs. It is the
constant theme of the folksinger and Brahms was of the folk.
He never married, and so far as we know, was never deeply,
passionately in love with any woman, but he poured out love
songs, because the inexhaustible theme with its myriad facets
stirred the impulse to make melody, and, as it were, set his
musical nature in vibration. He was the aeolian harp swept by
the breeze.

For other phases of human emotion, those of religion
for example, he had other musical resources. It was only
in the last phase (*Auf dem Kirchhofe* and more definitely the
Ernste Gesänge) that religious aspiration began to show itself
in his songs. He wrote no liturgical church music because
he was not of any church, and complete sympathy with the
implication of any words, great or little, which he chose was of

the essence of the contract. He could no more have published a Mass than he could write an opera. The motets and the Biblical work which he called *Ein deutsches Requiem* are the fullest expression of the religious side of his nature. The song, a small form, was in his view best suited to the simpler emotions in which intellectual questioning finds no place. Brahms refused to risk overstraining the song form. There is in the whole of his output of song no poem of the scale of Goethe's *Prometheus* on which both Schubert and Hugo Wolf alike expended their full powers.

The five songs of Op. 19, the beginning of what has been called Brahms's summer period of song, may be taken as an index of certain broad characteristics. It at once affords an example of the musical variety which he brought to the love-song. *Der Kuss* (Op. 19, No. 1) is the first of his settings of Hölty's little lyrics.

> Unter Blüthen des Mais spielt' ich mit ihrer Hand;
> koste liebelnd mit ihr, schaute mein schwebendes
> Bild im Auge des Mädchens;
> raubt' ihr bebend den ersten Kuss.

Here is the usual may-blossom imagery but Brahms is not more conscious of it than the lovers themselves looking into one another's eyes and tasting the wonder of the first kiss. There is no luxuriating in either the scene or the sentiment. The melody is mostly on conjunct degrees of the scale; the harmony is diatonic and there is no pianistic figuration. The whole charm and freshness of the song are derived from its rhythm, a subtle combination of phrases in 5, 4, and 3 bar lengths; it is not implicit in the poetic metre but is Brahms's way of conveying the sense of an unforgettable moment. This is the very opposite of his method in *Die Mainacht* (Op. 43, No. 2), in which the lonely lover is deeply affected by the shimmer of moonlight and the nightingale's note. In that case the whole movement is under the sway of the arpeggio, and the sensuous modulation of key contributes to the mood of luxuriating in melancholy.

Following *Der Kuss* in Op. 19 come the pair *Scheiden und Meiden* and *In der Ferne* (Uhland), two quite different developments of a single musical theme, which, it may be noticed, starts on the voice without any preamble on the piano. *Der Schmied*, also by Uhland, is a peculiarly refreshing version of the love theme and also of Brahms's dealings with arpeggio shapes. The student who goes carefully through Brahms's songs (not the listener to a well-chosen group in a recital programme) must feel that he falls back too readily on the easily effective arpeggio figures of accompaniment, the type found in the Uhland pair just named. It is his way of using the piano part as a neutral-tinted background serving to throw the voice into high relief. Though always done with artistry it is possible to feel that the piano is too often put into this position of neutrality, and that some of the lesser songs might have been turned into great ones by a more enterprising handling of the accompaniment. *Der Schmied* is arpeggio-wise both in tune and accompaniment, but the piano arpeggios are the hammer-strokes of the forge, and the vocal ones (note Brahms's favourite form of two notes out of the three contained in the chord) are the girl's exultation in her lover's strength. Every note speaks to the point.

A 'forte' is marked at the beginning of each verse of *Der Schmied* and that is the only mark of expression (loud or soft) written in the voice part of this opus. That is an indication of a deep underlying principle of Brahms's mature song writing. In the earlier songs p's and f's and the hairpin marks $\diamondsuit$ are scattered almost as freely through the voice parts (particularly in Opp. 6 and 14) as they are in all his instrumental works. From Op. 19 onward they virtually disappear. Song after song has merely an indication of tempo or of mood at the beginning and every nuance of tone is left to the singer. When marks of the kind are given they are used to avoid possible misunderstanding, for example, at the words 'Rund um ihn Freuden' in the first part of the *Magelone Lieder*, where the voice must enter 'poco forte' at the moment when the piano part sinks through a diminuendo to a pianissimo. Or again in *Von ewiger Liebe*, where the lover 'redet so viel und so mancherlei', and Brahms wants the tone kept up so that it may lead to the lover's outpouring of words in the forthcoming verse, he puts in a long crescendo mark, the only one in a song which must obviously end in a tremendous tonal climax left otherwise without any marking as far as the voice is concerned.

This is not only a refusal to indicate the obvious; Brahms's practice in such things means that he held that the singer's expression should be spontaneous, the outcome generally of his own feeling for the song as a whole, words and music, not of the composer's. Moreover, he knew that expression in song is a matter not so much of degrees of tone as of qualities of tone, which are infinitely variable within the same degree by the human voice, and for such variations of quality musical notation cannot devise any code of symbols. It is easily possible to tell the singer to make crescendo to f, ff, and fff through the last verse of *Von ewiger Liebe* (every singing teacher can pencil it in, and does, for the benefit of his mechanically trained pupils), but that in itself gets no nearer to the expression of a love stronger than steel. Brahms knew that in this matter the composer is at the mercy of the singer's temperament or lack of it. Consequently he preferred to leave the singer unhampered to do his best, or his worst.[1]

Op. 19 is concluded with *An eine Aeolsharfe*, the only one of Brahms's songs which begins with a passage marked '*Recit*'. The fact in itself is no more than a reminder of how completely

[1] The same reticence in regard to vocal marks of expression is to be noticed in Wagner's operatic scores.

lyrical as opposed to dramatic was Brahms's treatment of song forms. Here the opening words of the poem set the scene, as it were, before the music of the wind-swept harp begins to be heard and consequently vocal speech, merely supported by held chords, is the natural treatment. Hugo Wolf does the same thing. The whole song shows Brahms dominated by the delicate colouring of the poem. He responds to its influence instinctively alike in this unusual opening, in the pulsing chords in slow triplets which accompany the latter part of the recitative, and in the rhythmic and harmonic texture of the long-drawn aria. The rhythm is disturbed by an incursion of the recitative where the wind stirring more strongly brings from the harp 'ein holder Schrei'. Brahms has been given a bad mark[1] for not suggesting the 'holder Schrei' itself by some new musical feature, as Wolf does by a change of tonality; but the fact is that the one does with a change of rhythm what the other does with a change of harmony, and this sort of textual comparison of the two masters is apt to be misleading. The contrast in their general approach to the song form will be discussed later.

From these prolegomena it will be gathered that Brahms's songs are primarily melodies in the mouth of the singer, that the piano part, however significant it may be, is ancillary to the vocal, and that, while in Brahms's view the poem is the parent of the song, he considered that there must be limits to the binding force of the fifth commandment if the child is to enjoy a full and unfettered life. This view is opposed alike to those of his elder contemporary Robert Franz[2] and of his younger contemporary Hugo Wolf. It remains to examine some of the more important results of it.

Op. 32, the nine songs already mentioned as a series (if not exactly a cycle) of the poems of von Platen and Daumer, opens

[1] Ernest Newman's *Hugo Wolf*, p. 188.
[2] See *Oxford History of Music*, vol. vi, p. 275.

with *Wie rafft' ich mich auf in der Nacht*, one of those peculiarly searching, dark-toned melodies which could have been written by nobody but Brahms. Exactly how the words are fitted to it, their repetitions in the first verse, is a matter of no great consequence; the essential point of the poem is the restless wandering of the wakeful and troubled spirit and that is fully brought out in the music. The participation of the piano in the development, its transference of the melody from the bass to the treble in the two verses about the mill-stream below and the stars above, gives the song an unusually symphonic character. If, as seems to be the case, Brahms expected these songs to be sung in sequence, it is natural that the first of them should have a 'first movement' character, that is to say should strongly pose the problem which is to be resolved in the finale. That is what *Wie rafft' ich mich* does consummately. None of the numbers between it and *Wie bist du meine Königin* is on as large a scale. It is impossible here to discuss them individually, but one quotation shall be made of the second for the instruction of those who, knowing little of Brahms's methods in general, lay particular emphasis on the fact that the melody of *Wie bist du meine Königin* has the effect of turning a comma into a full stop at the end of the first line. *Nicht mehr zu dir zu gehen* is a song in which the melody grows unerringly out of the implications and accents of the poem. It can be cited as that rare thing, the perfect song from the constructional point of view. The broken melody not only serves to accentuate the words, 'Beschloss ich und beschwor ich', but gives the sense of the impotence of the resisting lover's resolution. Moreover, it is a case in which the accustomed ternary form, accustomed indeed but never used thoughtlessly by Brahms, has a special appropriateness. No matter how he protests, the lover is brought back to his allegiance. The first stanza only can be given here, but the student who will study the whole will be repaid by the discovery that the idea is carried out even to the last bars of the piano's peroration.

Ex. 1.

The fifteen *Romanzen aus Magelone* (Op. 33) take a peculiar place in Brahms's output of song. Tieck's story was one of the books of his childhood and the associations of his childhood were never really outgrown. But the music is very much the music of manhood. The extravagant adventures of the young knight, the highly coloured orientalism, the Arabian Nights atmosphere which would have made such an appeal to the typical romantics of Brahms's epoch, Rimsky-Korsakov for example, find practically no reflection at all in this music. The story is the thread on which the poems are strung and remained a sort of connecting link in Brahms's mind[1] which he took no pains to make evident to the hearer, so completely without 'stage sense' was he. Save for the cantering rhythm to which the knight rides forth on his quest in the first number, there is scarcely a touch of local colour anywhere. And the poems being originally insets in the romance do not tell their own story, as, for example, the songs of *Die schöne Müllerin* do. There is not even any outward indication as to who is the singer of each number, and four characters, the Minstrel (No. 1), Magelone (No. 11), Sulima (No. 13), and the knight, Pierre, himself (the remainder) are in fact represented. Consequently the songs, presenting no composite picture to the listener, do not make a satisfactory cycle, while at the same time their musical contrasts are so well considered that they lose a good deal when they are sung as detached numbers. They have a context, but the listener is never told what the context is. Some of the numbers, too (No. 3, *Sind es Schmerzen*, No. 6, *Wie soll ich die Freude*, No. 10, *Verzweiflung*, No. 14, *Wie froh und frisch*), are unusually expansive. In numbers 3 and 6 more particularly Brahms adopts a free rhapsodic manner very different from the compact

[1] Brahms told Friedlaender many years later (1886) that 'he would like to introduce in a new edition a few words on the poems in order to convey to the singer and the player something of the mood in which he himself had composed the songs' (Friedlaender's *Brahms's Lieder*, Eng. ed., p. 40).

lyrical shapes in which he generally worked, and they require
the contact of the smaller songs to set them off. *Traun, Bogen
und Pfeil*, and *Sind es Schmerzen* belong to one another. They
are the counterpart to Wagner's young Siegfried and the Siegfried
who has known fear at the sight of Brünnhilde (no musical
parallel is intended here); again the gentle *Liebe kam* and the
exuberant *So willst du des Armen* are two contrasted aspects
of the knight's successful love. The exquisite *Ruhe, Süssliebchen*
stands alone as the most subtle, as it is also the most extended,
of Brahms's lullaby songs, but *Verzweiflung* certainly gains in
effect if we turn straight on from Book III to Book IV. Magelone's only song, *Wie schnell verschwindet*, is in charming contrast
with its surroundings. It adds one to the gallery of feminine
portrait-studies (*Der Schmied, Von ewiger Liebe, Des Liebsten
Schwur*) which can be collected out of Brahms's songs, but the
other feminine song, *Sulima*, must be written down a failure.
Perhaps it is a part of Brahms's childish association with the
story that he is unable to bestow any real sympathy on the
Sultan's daughter whose glamour imperilled the course of true
love. He seems to be labouring to give it a distinctive character
which he cannot realize. He recovers his mastery, however, in
the two concluding songs, and the serenity of *Treue Liebe*, with a
theme anticipating the Third Symphony, ends the series ideally.

The *Romanzen aus Magelone* were in fact written in two series
published separately (the first six in 1864 and the remainder in
1868), and all were dedicated to Julius Stockhausen, who was
to Brahms's songs very much what Joseph Joachim was to
his chamber music. The later of these two years was one of the
richest in song publication. In addition we have the four songs
of Opus 43, including *Von ewiger Liebe* and *Die Mainacht*, the
four of Opus 46 in which the gipsy rhythm of *Magyarisch* makes
a welcome incursion amongst the more sentimental poems of
Daumer and Hölty, the five of Opus 47 in which are *Botschaft*,

O liebliche Wangen, the seven of Opus 48, mostly written in the strophic form and beginning with the favourite *Es glänzt der Mond*, and the five of Opus 49 wherein is the popular *Wiegenlied*. Passing over the more famous examples we must here only touch on two, *Herbstgefühl* (Op. 48, No. 7) and *Abenddämmerung* (Op. 49, No. 5), both poems by Friedrich von Schack. They are examples of that pensive autumn mood which, as has been suggested, became a more personal matter with Brahms at a later stage of his career. In the former, it should be noticed how delicately the harmonies colour the image of the burnished autumn leaf clinging to the tree; in the latter, the shimmering accompaniment in thirds and sixths creates the twilight picture. Brahms's scenic sense, which responded so little to the orientalism of the Magelone romances, was readily aroused to sensitiveness by such familiar suggestions as these.

Among the innumerable songs of Brahms's middle life which, like the above, are conspicuous for some subtle trait of feeling or expression, the eight of Op. 57, all of them settings of poems by G. F. Daumer, stand apart. Like Op. 32, they may be considered as a series knit together by a sequence of ideas in the poems, but they do not arrive in the end at anything like the calm security of *Wie bist du meine Königin*. They may be regarded as Brahms's rebellion against himself, at any rate against that part of himself which was ready to resort to the comfort of beautiful melody. He seems to have chosen these poems for their direct expression of a personal passion, and indeed of a physical passion which some of his admirers were inclined to think passed the limits of good taste, and he clearly aimed here at an intensity of emotional expression beyond that of the conventional love lyric. He did not, however, abandon his melodic method for a declamatory one. He does not concentrate feeling into those stabs of poignant harmony which belong to Wagner's *Tristan*. Indeed it is noticeable that where the dramatic composer would instinctively shorten his phrases Brahms tends to lengthen his, as in the following, which is the vocal climax of the first, a woman's song:

Ex. 2.   Op. 57, No. 1.

To quote the melody alone is to give the essence of the song. That is not always so. The fourth of the set, in which the man struggles to free himself from the toils of his love, is more dependent on texture. Here is its opening motive:

Ex. 3.   BRAHMS.   Op. 57, No. 4.

The central passage, in which he summons all his energies to resist the fevered impulse of the senses, is a piece of extraordinary musical concentration. It deserves comparison with the passage quoted from Op. 32 (Ex. 1), but instead of suggesting a wavering indecision it is filled with a tense determination to resist. Here are none of the easy outlines of arpeggio movement, but a gripping melody moving forward step by step.

Ex. 4.   Op. 57, No. 4.

Wenn ein - mal   die ge - quäl - te

See - le ruht,   und mit so

fie - be - ri - scher Wil - de nicht in mei - nen

A - dern, in mei - nen A - - dern

rollt   das heisse   Blut.   Ein

Strahl, ein flüch-ti-ger, von dei - nem Licht,

An unsatisfied longing is the theme of all this series, and it
reaches its most graphic expression in the last song of all in

which the quiet of the garden at night, the 'tiefe Ruhe der Natur' is contrasted with

> Aber im Gemüthe schwillt
> heissere Begierde mir.

Brahms has, however, given a turn to the ending which is not explicit in the words. Did he after all seek to spiritualize the feeling of the poet whose physical ardour had at first attracted him? He gives the song a soft coda in which the bass (E, F natural, the original key is E major) reasserts that peace of nature and stills the cry,

> Komm, O komm, damit wir uns
> himmlische genügen.

But this softened reflection comes only after the fervent appeal has been fully realized in the development of the song.

That the same poet should supply the composer with material both for these songs and for the *Liebeslieder Walzer* at about the same period is not a little astonishing. In Opus 57 Brahms strained every nerve to reach the essence of the matter, in the waltzes (Opp. 52 and 65, both from Daumer's *Polydora*) the formal grace of the waltz rhythm holds passion at arm's length and tosses the love theme lightly to and fro. There is a difference between the two sets. The first, 'Im Ländler-Tempo', are piano duets with voices *ad libitum* (which does not mean that the pianists are free to hammer away to their hearts' content, leaving the voices to pursue them breathless and discomforted), while the second is for vocal quartet with piano duet accompaniment. The first set is the more gracious because more under the spell of the dance with that lilt which Brahms could free entirely from its tendency to vulgarity by his subtle cross-rhythms. Each works out its delicate pattern on instrumental lines similar to those of the piano waltzes of Op. 39, and the voices add colour, the very opposite of what we have seen to be

Brahms's normal relation of voice and instrument in the song. The following is typical:

Ex. 5.   Liebeslieder Waltzes.

lie - - - - blich   schau - et,

It is because of the peculiar relationship of voice and instrument that the *Regenlied* and *Nachklang* (Op. 59, Nos. 3 and 4)
may be singled out from among the many beautiful specimens of
Brahms's art which fill that Opus and its companion Opus 58.
They are unique as the one instance in which Brahms deliberately
quoted himself and turned the matter of a song into one of his
major instrumental works, the Violin Sonata in G (Op. 78). It
should be noticed that the essential musical substance of these
songs is twofold, like the chamber works for piano and strings,[1]
and it is its twofold nature which made it amenable to the
larger treatment of the sonata independent of words. The
first half-phrase (four bars) of the tune with its pattering
raindrop accompaniment is the principal theme of the Finale
of the Sonata completed quite differently in the second half-
phrase, which in the Sonata leads to a free development nowhere

[1] See Chapter III, p. 49.

hinted at in the song. The hesitant rhythm (♩ 𝄽 ♪ | ♩) which pervades both voice part and accompaniment in the song is present in the Sonata from the first notes of the first movement, and more than that, the very curve of the violin's initial theme in the Sonata, which seems as spontaneous a thought as any theme in the whole range of chamber music whether by Brahms or by any one else, is actually implicit in the introduction to the *Regenlied*. Note the brackets (*a*) in the following example:

Ex. 6.   Violin Sonata.   Op. 78.

Regenlied.

(Voice.)

The point is of importance only as showing how the song theme of piano as well as voice was lurking in Brahms's mind from the first in the composition of the Sonata. He did not fall back on a favourite song to finish off a sonata begun independently of it. Mr. Fuller-Maitland has pointed to the closeness of the development from the seminal idea of both songs, *Regenlied* and *Nachklang*.

If the later songs of this period in Brahms's career are here passed over with but slight reference it is not because they are any less interesting in themselves than those which have been already discussed, but because those of Opp. 63, 69, 70, 71, and 72 are for the most part further essays in types which the earlier series have made familiar. With Opus 63 Brahms discovered fresh poetic material in the *Gedichte* of Max von Schenkendorf, and among the settings to broadly defined melodies with rich arpeggiando accompaniments *Erinnerung* stands out as a master-piece. It would have been a joy to Robert Schumann to know that his son Felix had impelled Brahms to the young exuberance of *Meine Liebe ist grün*, which, with a companion song of less distinction, is included in the second part of this opus. The *Lieder und Gesänge* of Opus 69 take several texts from the Bohemian and other Slavonic ballads and revert to the strophic treatment. The nationality of the poem does not specially colour the music, but the ballad style with its half articulate human feeling always stirred Brahms to peculiar sympathy. *Mädchenfluch*, the last of the set, is one of the most finely wrought of his ballads. Opp. 70, 71, and 72 for the most part lie more in the region of the songs of Op. 63, and, though almost each one discloses some sensitiveness to a poetic suggestion, *Lerchengesang* (Op. 70, No. 2), *Minnelied* (Op. 71, No. 5), *Alte Liebe* (Op. 72, No. 1), and *Sommerfäden* (Op. 72, No. 2) are outstanding, their subtleties are all within that method of eloquent vocal melody backed by hints of pianistic expression which is Brahms's own. In *Verzagen* (Op. 72, No. 4) the piano part is more than a hint; it comes near to direct representation of the perpetual breaking of waves on a desolate shore.

It has been necessary to pass without special remark the earlier duets which, charming as many of them are, do not greatly differ in style from the slighter songs. The dialogue duets of Op. 75, beginning with the Scottish ballad *Edward*, in which the voices for the most part do not join in harmony, and the five songs for 'one or two voices' of Op. 84, where they never so join, are different in style from the duets proper. Among the latter is the very popular *Vergebliches Ständchen*. In all of them Brahms's idea is to use the voices semi-dramatically, carrying out the conversational structure of the ballads and making use of varied tone colour, alto and tenor in *Edward* and alto and soprano in the several dialogues between mother and daughter. In *Vergebliches Ständchen* there is not, as in the others of its series, any difference of tessitura for the two voices. That fact, together with the suggestion of naughtiness in the ballad, accounts for its superior attraction as a single-voiced song in recital programmes.

Four years separate these two sets of dialogue songs (1878–82) and within them there are no song publications, but amongst the larger works of that time, the Violin Concerto, the Violin Sonata in G, and the two orchestral overtures, are the piano pieces of Op. 76 which contain much of the lyrical impulse characteristic of the songs. With Op. 86 began, as has been said, the songs 'for a deeper voice'. In contrast with this mood we have in the following years the *Zigeuner Lieder* for vocal quartet and piano (Op. 103), and four more of the same type among the six quartets of Op. 112, all to poems translated from the Hungarian by Hugo Conrat. Eight of the first series were also arranged for a single voice and piano by the composer. Brahms's fondness for the incisive energy of the gipsy idiom, first stimulated by the arrangement (or composition) of the early Hungarian dances for piano duet, has been already discussed in connexion with the chamber music. The only wonder is that it found so small a place in his songs until the late period. Friedlaender has examined the influence of the original folk melodies on Brahms and finds it to be mostly of the indirect kind, that is, it is more an affinity of rhythm than a quotation of melody. The songs are original compositions, and extraordinarily delightful ones.

The *Vier ernste Gesänge* (Op. 121) hold a place apart from all other songs of Brahms, but by no means apart from all his previous compositions. They are a personal document. His mind towards religion and more particularly that part of it which is concerned with the immortality of man was of that kind prevalent among the intellectuals of the last century, more particularly in protestant countries. He was no materialist but he could subscribe to no religious system. The crude presentation of religious dogma stood between him and an assured faith. Christian aspiration still swayed him, and his philosophy of life was rooted in the thought and language of the Bible. Moreover, though a physically healthy man, he was much preoccupied, rather as Samuel Johnson was, by the idea (perhaps by a repressed fear) of death. It first shows itself in his compositions in the sombre *Begräbnissgesang* (Op. 13), for six-part choir with wind instruments (1859), the opening theme of which has a marked affinity with that of the first of the *Vier ernste Gesänge*. It may well be that that dark brooding character in Brahms's work, the Ballade for piano, *Edward* (Op. 10, No. 1), the first movement of the Piano Concerto in D minor, and much else even in the 'Young Eagle' period of his youth, was the result of this preoccupation. Joachim declared that *Ein deutsches Requiem* was a memorial to Brahms's mother, and Kalbeck would attribute its inception to Schumann's death ten years earlier. Both are right, and both wrong. No doubt both these events helped to concentrate Brahms's mind on the problem of human sorrow and the hope of immortality. Without them the *Requiem* might not have been the deeply moving experience which it is, but some work of the kind was bound

to come from an artist whose mind was set from the first in its
direction.

In the last year of his life, when illness was already threatening
the body, it was inevitable that such thoughts should recur with
redoubled force. The songs were written in the month that his
friend Clara Schumann died. That event is said to have 'inspired'
them, but again they are not accounted for by it.

For the last phase of his thought Brahms would not burden
himself with the paraphernalia of choir and orchestra. He took
the simplest means at disposal; the voice of his friend, Stockhausen, and his life-long companion the piano. He chose as
texts,

Ecclesiastes iii. 19–22,
Ecclesiastes iv. 1–3,
Ecclesiasticus xli. 1–2,
1 Corinthians xiii. 1–3, 12, 13;

a sequence which passes from a gnawing agnosticism, dwelling
on death as the fate common to man and beast, through the
scepticism which regards death as a welcome oblivion, or as a
release from the troubles of the world, to the Pauline conception
of the remedy in 'faith, hope, and charity'. By the description of
the cycle as a personal document is meant chiefly that it is not
a moral tract. Brahms does not, like second-rate oratorio composers, set up false gods for the pleasure of knocking them down.
Nothing could be more completely and sincerely felt than the
pessimistic mood of the first three songs. The first, with its
heavy reiterated figures and plodding pedal notes, is the music
of a soul in bondage. It has that stark character which Brahms
seemed to associate instinctively with the key of D minor
(compare the third movement of the *Requiem*). The repeated
bass notes persist throughout that passage (akin to the *Schicksalslied*) where a flying arpeggio suggests the ephemeral nature
of all life. The second song gleans no real comfort from its

cynicism, even though the music turns to a major key with the thought that it is better to be dead and not see the evil that is done under the sun. The apostrophe to death in the third begins on a note of passionate bitterness. Here, however, the change from minor to major does bring a measure of relief, but it is the relief of tears, not of consolation.

It is with an effort that Brahms braces himself to rise to the level of the Pauline gospel. It is for him no glib and easy doctrine but one which calls for all his energy of mind and heart to realize. It is not until he breaks away from the key of E flat into the broad B major melody of 'Wir sehen jetzt durch einen Spiegel' that he seems to have brought himself into entire consonance of spirit with his text. It is typical of him that at this point there is no following of the text word by word. Not the darkened glass but the confident upward gaze is the inspiration of this melody, which is also that of the climax, 'Aber die Liebe ist die grösste unter ihnen'. That is Brahms's last love-song.

CHAPTER XI

SONG. II. WOLF AND OTHERS

THE one figure to stand beside Brahms here, that is the one composer who developed the German song in directions which were not those of Brahms, is Hugo Wolf (1860–1903). Historically it may be claimed that his songs are of greater importance than Brahms's in the sense that the first essays in a new style of art are more important than late masterpieces in a classic manner. However this may be, it is important here to emphasize the fact that there is between them so essential a difference of view-point in their approach to what on the face of it seems to be the same task, the writing of songs for voice and piano, that comparison of their results is liable to be singularly mis-leading. Indeed, most of the bad criticism of both has been due to the error prevalent to-day of treating Brahms as though he ought to have been Wolf, and that of yesterday which viewed Wolf as though he were trying to be Brahms.

But before illustrating this difference it is necessary to recall a few facts about the new-comer. Wolf was a boy of fifteen, a student at the Conservatorium of Vienna, with a passion for music and a great hope that somehow or other he might some day add to its content, when in 1875, the year before the first Bayreuth Festival, Wagner came to Vienna to supervise pro-ductions of his earlier works. The boy forced himself into the great man's presence and begged him to glance at some of his compositions. Wagner was kind and non-committal, but his kindness was sufficient to turn admiration for the master into hero-worship of the man. This was the time of Wagner's triumph over his detractors; it was also the time when the Viennese Wagnerians were beginning to discover in Anton Bruckner a symphonist more to their liking than Brahms, who had not yet produced his first symphony. The young Wolf embraced the Wagnerian faith. After leaving the Conservatorium he clung to the skirts of Viennese musical life, encountering the poverty and hardship which a young man determined on an artistic career without having discovered the right line for himself to follow was bound to suffer. At last (1884), to give him a means of livelihood, a place was found for him as music critic to a paper, the *Salonblatt*. The name does not suggest devotion to the higher types of critical journalism, but Wolf took his duties seriously. His articles were read, more especially when they began to include a clear exposition of his thoroughly Wagnerian view of Brahms's music. Wagner himself was dead, but Wagner Societies lived, and Wagnerians in Vienna, who had not forgotten Hanslick's critical maltreatment of Wagner, became increasingly interested in Wolf. Nor did the Brahms party forget what Wolf had said of their master when at last Wolf's own compositions began to come up for judgement.

Distasteful as the record of this local partisanship necessarily is, it cannot be completely ignored, because it was the first stage in that misapplied comparison from which even the best of the criticism of Wolf's art still suffers. It has put off anything like a balanced estimate of his work. As his songs had only just begun to be known when the tragic insanity set in which put a stop to composition and shrouded the last six years of his short life, his reputation before the world had to be established by a process of posthumous propaganda, and that process necessarily entails a good deal of over-statement. Those who have not studied the matter try to improve on the high estimates formed by those who have, with lamentably distorted results.[1]

---

[1] This kind of thing: 'It is only within recent years that the recognition of his genius has become at all general. Now, however, there are many who declare that he is greater than Schubert and consequently the greatest of all song-writers.' *Radio Times*, July 29, 1932.

Wolf enjoyed only ten years of full creative vigour. They began with the publication in 1887 of two sets of six songs each, by various poets including samples from two, Goethe and Mörike, on whom he was presently to fasten a more concentrated attention. These songs are gleanings from the comparatively thin harvests of the previous ten years. Early in 1888, having given up his journalistic work in Vienna, he settled for the time being in the house of a friend at Perchtoldsdorf, a village on the road between Vienna and Mödling, and there his genius for song declared itself in his absorption in the poems of Mörike. The whole of the fifty-three *Mörike Lieder* were completed in the spring and autumn of that year, with a break in the summer, when he revisited the Bayreuth Festival. In September he stayed with another friend at Unterach in the Salzkammergut, and it was there that the *Mörike Lieder* were completed and many of the poems of Eichendorff were set. Then he plunged into Goethe, and on his lyrics together with the poems from the *Spanisches Liederbuch* of Heyse and Geibel, and the *Italienisches Liederbuch* of Heyse, Wolf's creative energy poured itself out, chiefly in the winter months up to the end of 1891. By this date the Mörike, Eichendorff, and Goethe volumes had all been published, but only through the smaller houses and by means of personal subscriptions. Wolf, if he made some enemies, certainly found good friends, but this method of publication never brings a composer's work before a wide public as quickly as the commercial method does. Composers often like to think that they do not care about the wide public; whether they care or not, the fact remains that it is only after their work has been submitted to the rough sifting process of presentation to all and sundry that a permanent assessment of it can begin to be made.

After 1891 Wolf went more slowly. The sets of songs named above are the bulk of his work in that kind. His enthusiasm for Wagner had fired him with the ambition to write opera. He encountered difficulty in finding a libretto, a difficulty common to all composers who begin by wanting to write an opera and then cast about for an opera to write. Eventually he accepted one based on the German translation of a short story by the Spanish novelist Pedro Antonio de Alarcón (1833–91).[1] He was attracted by the German version at the time when he was composing the *Spanisches Liederbuch* and tried to fashion it into a libretto for himself. A conspiracy among his friends to help him was first scornfully rejected and only accepted some years later. The result was *Der Corregidor*, which eventually saw the light at Mannheim in June 1896. A second Spanish opera, also based on Alarcón, *Manuel Venegas*, was in process of composition when all prospect of future work was cut short by illness. However, after the composition of *Der Corregidor* and before its performance, Wolf was able to indulge in a further bout of song-writing, and, back at Perchtoldsdorf in the spring of 1896, he added a second volume of twenty-four songs from the *Italienisches Liederbuch* to that of twenty-two composed more than four years before. Wolf's opera was well received and then dropped out of the repertory. The student who would discover its quality must do so through a vocal score. It is the songs and the songs alone that assure his place in musical history.

These facts point the contrast of Wolf's case with that of Brahms in a number of ways. Most important of them is his attitude towards his poets. From the first Perchtoldsdorf sojourn onward, he is seen steeping himself in one poet at a time in order to identify himself as closely as possible with that poet's mind and matter and manner. This is a very different thing from merely accepting from the poem the impulse to

---

[1] Alarcón's story is known to musicians to-day through Falla's ballet, *The Three-Cornered Hat*. Wolf's opera was given for the first time in London by students of the R.A.M. in 1934.

compose. It is a conscious intellectual concentration on the poetry in order that the resultant song, whatever else it may or may not be, shall be a musical embodiment of the poem.

To clinch the difference as one of principle, not one of degree, we may place Brahms's and Wolf's settings of Goethe's *Phänomen* beside one another. This is not done to show that one is better than the other. Both are songs of only minor interest, and on neither can any part of the composer's reputation be supposed to depend. The little poem from the *Westöstlicher Divan* is a simple parable.

> Wenn zu der Regenwand
> Phöbus sich gattet,
> gleich steht ein Bogenrand
> farbig beschattet.
>
> Im Nebel gleichen Kreis
> seh' ich gezogen;
> zwar ist der Bogen weiss,
> doch Himmelsbogen.
>
> So sollst du, muntrer Greis,
> dich nicht betrüben:
> sind gleich die Haare weiss,
> doch wirst du lieben.

Brahms's Op. 61, No. 3, is a duet for soprano and alto voices. The three stanzas give him a song in ternary form, the third exactly repeating the first; in the middle one the voices move in canon, beginning from a phrase which is a strict inversion of that which begins stanzas 1 and 3. Stated like this the scheme seems severely academic, but Brahms had a way of using such traditional devices as though for his private entertainment. No one else need notice them; the music flows over them unchecked and the lyrical beauty of the result is undeniable. The structure is only described here to show that the contrasting section grows out of the initial musical idea, in fact that the whole form is a musical and not a poetic one. To the same purpose is the fact that no one of the three sections fits the stanza. The first, for example, sets a four-line stanza to a five-phrase tune, thus—

Ex. 1.

and what occurs with 'farbig, farbig beschattet' is made a
little worse from the poet's point of view by 'doch wirst, doch
wirst, du lieben' at the end.

Wolf sets the singer to recite the poem 'very slowly' with
due care for 'just note and accent'. Generally one line of the
poem occupies one bar of music, but if we count the vocal bars
we find that they amount to twelve and a half in all because the
last word, 'lieben', being the point of the whole poem, is lengthened
to secure its pre-eminence. This is in itself an extension of the
only licence in the matter of setting the words which Wolf has
conceded to his musical sense, a dotted-note figure of two notes
used on the penultimate syllables of the lines. Even this, it may
be argued, has a poetic justification in helping to suggest the
rhyme of 'gezogen' and 'Himmelsbogen' and the imperfect rhyme
of 'betrüben' and 'du lieben'. The anticipation of the word
'farbig', giving a touch of 'colour' and incidentally avoiding the
possibility of a comma where no comma should be, the descending chromatics on 'muntrer Greis', and the ascending accent on
'nicht', are further indication of how one may go over Wolf's
vocal declamation with a microscope and find him living up to
his principles. The piano part, too, though apparently its chief
function is to support the declamation with suitable harmony,

yields results from the same process. The song begins in A major
and ends in E; between these points Wolf has handled tonality so
freely that key definition is impossible, but at the end of each
stanza he gives one bar of piano music to clarify the position.
Moreover, it is through the harmonic scheme that the imagery of
the poem is reflected in the music. As the harmonic scheme is so
closely knit that quotation must destroy the sense, and as the
song is so short, it will be best to give it in its entirety (Ex. 2).

To arraign either composer before a jury packed with the
partisans of the other side would be to secure a verdict of
guilty. The Brahms jury would find that Wolf's song has no
tune and no rhythm of the musical kind worth mentioning,
that it is nothing but an aimless harmony exercise in chromatic

Ex. 2.

So sollst du, muntrer Greis, dich nicht be - trü - ben:

sind gleich die Ha - are weiss, doch wirst du lie -

- - ben.

modulation, such as every student writes and every master marks with a blue pencil. That was, in fact, very much the verdict of no less a person than Max Kalbeck when some of Wolf's songs first came before him, and it is one not to be lightly dismissed. From the standpoint of classical song, a standpoint summed up in the one word 'melody', Wolf's *Phänomen* is undeniably deficient. The wrongness of the verdict is not in the finding, but in what the jury has failed to find.

On the other hand, Brahms before the Wolf jury, a situation of which we see much more at the present day, fares equally ill, and this is a grosser miscarriage of justice than the other. The prisoner is entitled to plead not merely that he did not know the law but that the law was not in force at the time the offence against it was committed. The 'Poetic Supremacy Act, 1887' had not reached its first reading by a long way when Brahms wrote his duet. How little its provisions were accepted then is shown by what so devout a Wagnerian as Hermann Levi, the conductor, wrote to Brahms about this very song. 'If only I could tell you how the song has impressed and moved me,' he wrote, and beyond a doubt it was the melody itself, its own beauty of contour over and above its expressive treatment of the poem, which had power to move the musician as it still has power to move the singer and his audience.

Composers had in fact always acted on the assumption that the presentation of the poetic form in a song was a matter of quite secondary importance in comparison with the necessity for creating a musical one. Even Herman Goetz, a composer whose works at one time were frequently cited as displaying more modern tendencies than Brahms's, in setting Mörike's *Das verlassene Mägdlein,* had no compunction at all in repeating the last lines as a means of picturing the girl's weary longing. It was only after Wolf's setting that it occurred to any one to question the propriety of Goetz's.

It may well be questioned how far Wolf's success in his own special method should have been allowed to set up a 'Poetic Supremacy Act' for subsequent composers. Is it to supersede the immemorial prerogative of melody in song? In any case it is merely ridiculous to attempt to apply it as a law acting retrospectively. To do so is to condemn practically all the great song-writers of the world.

The unconditional surrender of the musical form to the poem will clearly be a very welcome doctrine to composers of small originality, which is one reason why it has been embraced with such ardour by the earnest but uninspired composers of our own day. Thousands of 'art songs' have been produced on the principle of getting the declamation right and surrounding it with a more or less involved texture of piano music of which the composer may say 'that is how I feel it'.[1] It is as easy to write bad songs on that principle as on any other rule of thumb that a Beckmesser may lay down as unchanging law. It may also have its dangers for even a gifted composer like Hugo Wolf. The *Mörike Lieder* are full of exquisite things, but the fifty-three numbers can be pronounced to be fifty-three masterpieces of song only by people who are obsessed by the poetic supremacy idea. Wolf responds very readily to that vein of a slightly morbid religious sentiment which runs through a good many of Mörike's poems; it calls out a sympathy from him

---

[1] At the beginning of the war, in August 1914, the writer found himself marooned in a Swiss château, with an excellent German musician as a fellow-castaway. The time was passed in making music. When he had listened to a number of modern English songs of that date played from memory on the piano, with croakings and hummings to indicate the voice part, the German remarked, 'I see that you in England still think of the song as melody. We do not; we think of it as a piece of music surrounding the poem declaimed by the voice.' He proceeded to illustrate his principle by examples of his own compositions. He was not an innovator and his compositions have attained no subsequent eminence. The point of quoting him here is to show that a decade or so after Hugo Wolf's death Wolf's method had become axiomatic with the rank and file of German musicians.

which may find expression in very questionable musical terms. It accounts for his tendency to drop into that kind of chromatic harmony, passing-notes, and accented appoggiaturas which he, in common with Bruckner and others of the post-Wagnerians, had inherited from their master. What had been an occasional weakness becomes a *cliché* with his followers when they have nothing particular to say. Wolf uses it both well and ill; well in *Im Frühling*, which contains such lines as

> Ich denke dies und denke das,
> ich sehne mich, und weiss nicht recht,
> nach was,

and where the chromatic wavering is worked into a consistently developed figure with a character of its own; but very ill surely in the opening to *Gebet*, which is like the village organist improvising an 'in voluntary'. (Cf. Ex. 9 below.)

Ex. 3.

The word 'getragen' brands him with his sin. But whether used well or ill, Wolf certainly uses the device too much. It trails through the more sentimental of the *Mörike Lieder*. It smirches the purity of the Christmas rose and invests the opening of *Karwoche* with an atmosphere painfully akin to that of Gounod's 'There is a green hill far away'. Even the favourite melody of *Verborgenheit* derives some of its pathos from the chromatic use of the fourth note of the scale (the same which belongs to Wolfram's evening star), and the salient progression of *An eine Aeolsharfe* is one of easy sensuousness which, it may be noted,

Wagner seems to have associated dramatically with the characters of light-minded women.[1]

This defect in Wolf is part-product of his time, the post-Wagnerian era; it is accentuated and encouraged by the comparatively loose hold he keeps on the continuous line of vocal melody. When a tune has to move at all costs a composer either forgoes harmonic luxuries or finds that they are kept in their place by the discipline of rhythmic movement. It is, indeed, only a musical discipline, not the discipline of literary taste, of following the words, or of entering into the poet's psychology, which can save him. Happily, in the more vigorous songs Wolf is saved by this rhythmic discipline, though often it is imparted more through the piano than through the voice. Clearly it is the piano which sets the pace in the swaggering lilt of the drummer's song *Wenn meine Mutter hexen könnt'*, and its jubilant onrush in *Er ist's* cannot be checked by the length of the poem. The instrument must sing its spring song when the voice has finished.

It is only occasionally that Wolf essays anything of the *volksthümliches Lied* type, and then he is not conspicuously successful. *Jägerlied* (5–4 time) is too tightly tied to its bar rhythm rather in the manner of Schumann, and the tune of *Fussreise* a little overdoes the conscious plodding simplicity. In *Auf einer Wanderung*, on the other hand, where again the piano leads the way, the pilgrim treads on air, and the whole piece is a thing of exquisite fantasy. It is unnecessary to dwell on the filigree texture of the *Elfenlied* and *Nixe Binsefuss*, on the prancing paces of the Princess's steed in *Der Gärtner* and the shivering motions of *Citronenfalter im April*. The wealth of Wolf's imagination is shown in the contrast of these delicate things with scene painting of such compelling energy as *Lied vom Winde*, *Der Feuerreiter*, and *Die Geister am Mummelsee*.

But these last are more in the nature of tone poems for the piano with vocal commentaries than songs in the hitherto accepted sense of the word. In them we may even see the poetic supremacy law brought to defeat by its own action. The music must have its outlet somewhere. If the singer may not elaborate the melody, using verbal repetition for the purpose, he must give way to his colleague the instrumentalist. The practical effect of the words in *Der Feuerreiter* is of a series of agitated exclamations, more or less detached from one another, interjected through the continuous music of the piano. They might as well be in prose as in verse as far as the listener is concerned.

Wolf's songs of the Goethe series naturally take a wider range and employ more forcible terms of expression than do those of the *Mörike Lieder*. They include many of Goethe's most famous lyrics which have been set by all and sundry from Beethoven and Schubert onward, and so tempt to those comparisons which it has already been suggested are best avoided.

In the Goethe songs we see Wolf's grip of his own point of view becoming firmer. It may be that he has still not quite outgrown his Wagnerian discipleship. He seems himself to have recognized that one of the largest of them, *Prometheus*, is a setting which could only have been made in the post-Wagnerian era.[1] But if certain of the figures and turns of expression recall Wagner there is an intense individuality of thought underlying Wolf's use of them. Most striking is the suggestion of impotence behind the wrathful defiance expressed through the reiterated chord of the opening of *Prometheus* (Ex. 5).

The quotation gives a concrete example of that instinctive realization of the psychology of a situation which is Wolf's special contribution to the song form. Incidentally it will be

---

[1] The extraordinary thing about Schubert's setting of *Prometheus* is the extent to which it anticipates Wagnerian methods. It is worth while to compare Schubert's song with the Wanderer's scene in the first act of *Siegfried*, as something clearly independent while tending in the same direction. To compare Wolf with *The Ring* is to raise some doubts about his originality. Schubert at many points suggests doubts about the originality of the Wagnerian method.

Ex. 5.

Be - de - cke dei - nen Him - mel, Zeus,

mit Wol - ken - dunst,

noticed that here is a case where he seems to be thinking in terms of the orchestra rather than of the piano. Such cases are more numerous among the Goethe songs than elsewhere, and

Prometheus (with some half-dozen others, including the three Harper's and two Mignon songs) was in fact scored for orchestra by the composer later. But if Wolf is consciously post-Wagnerian in his approach to the greatest of the German poets, his contact with greatness seems to have enabled him to outgrow the unconscious Wagnerisms which mar some of the most delicate of the *Mörike Lieder*. Along with his power of entering into the poet's deeper thought comes that of finding a perfect shape for a hint expressed in the tiniest of lyrics. The ability to put a thought in a nutshell is certainly not a Wagnerian attribute. It is not indeed commonly possessed by the German mind or the greatest of the German composers, but it is something which Wolf learnt to share with Goethe. To show it at its finest point of concentration we must quote one more whole song, *Gleich und Gleich* (Ex. 6).

There is no need to underline with appreciative comments the merits of such a miniature. Wolf had shown himself on the way to the miniature style early in the *Mörike Lieder* with such things as *Ein Stündlein wohl vor Tag* and *Das verlassene Mägdlein*, but there it is done romantically for the expression of girlish sighs and tears. Here it is the perfect shapeliness which is the song's complete justification. It prepares us for the notable

Ex. 6.

Blu - men - glöck-chen vom Bo - den her - vor   war

früh   ge - spros - sen in   lieb - lich-em Flor;

da kam ein Bien - chen und nasch - te fein:

8va...

Die müssen wohl bei-de für ein-

- an - der sein. . .

change which takes place in Wolf between the German songs proper and those of the Spanish and Italian Song-books.

The moment we turn to the latter we feel ourselves in a

VII   D d

different atmosphere, and that is not the difference of local colour, southern sunniness, though some signs of such colour will naturally appear, but a difference in Wolf's ideal of song. It is much more lyrical even though the lyricism is still not generally that of an independent vocal melody, but of a sustained line of musical thought in which both the participants have a share. The voice part frequently moves by small steps, and monotone takes a larger place not only in the religious songs of the Spanish book but in those of human passion. With few exceptions the songs of both books are short, the Italian especially so, and frequently a single figure or instrumental device is taken as a sort of text from which the whole song is developed. This last is not always done with equal success. It depends on the nature of the chosen figure and the pliability of its handling. A stiffly harmonic one like that of *Nun bin ich dein* is apt to get too much into the foreground, as is also that of *Die du Gott gebarst*, through over-insistence again on the accented appoggiatura. On the other hand the four-note figure of *Selig ihr Blinden* (Italian Book, No. 5), used both diatonically and chromatically, bends supply to its expressive purpose while maintaining continuity through the short length of the whole song, and there are many other examples of this order. Another device which binds together several of the Christmas songs in the Spanish book beginning with St. Joseph's song, *Nun wandre, Maria*, is a movement of the piano part in thirds not confined to the repetition of one figure either rhythmic or harmonic. It wreathes a delicate decoration round the group of the Holy Family and endows the songs with something of that serenity which belongs to the classical treatment of the subject in painting. Needless to say the guitar, the mandoline, the pandora, and the rhythms which their several techniques induce, find their places in the lighter numbers of the Spanish songs. *Klinge, klinge mein Pandero* obviously calls for such 'colour', and the more sensuous use of it in *Auf dem grünen Balkon* accounts for the superior popularity of that song over its companions. But more remarkable than the use of such things is the extent to which Wolf is able to make his points without them in a series of thirty-five ostensibly Spanish songs.

Again, in the Italian book the one characteristic of Italy one would expect to find, the unrestrained outpouring of vocal melody, is the one thing which Wolf will not allow. His principles of song forbid it him. Little poems will only make little songs, and to these little Italian rhymes, some of them witty with a touch of cynicism, the Italianate melody, if used at all, must be laid on only with a fine brush. In the 1896 set, beginning with *Ich esse nun mein Brot*, Wolf's brush-work has become unerring. The difference in maturity between these songs and the *Mörike Lieder* is so marked that one is tempted to speak of the early and the late Wolf, forgetting what a very small period of time passed between them. He no longer pleads fidelity to his poet as an excuse for musical vagueness. He has found his own means of reconciling the claims of music and of poetry, and in doing so has acquired style, which is a different thing from a style.

In setting Spanish or Italian songs Wolf is not concerned to adopt a Spanish or an Italian idiom in the way that Brahms, for example, uses the gipsy idiom in the *Zigeunerlieder* and Dvořák a Slavonic one in the *Moravian Duets*. Indeed the mention of these is a reminder of how remote Wolf was from any folk tradition, either of his own or any other country. It is largely because Wolf's idea of the song does not begin with the folk melody in any shape or form that comparisons with Schubert or with Brahms are futile. Because of that too the majority of his songs remain a rather hardly acquired taste. Popular judgement of them is apt to be summed up in the phrase, 'there seems nothing to take hold of'. His recondite art carried German song, which up to his time had been more directly based on folksong than that of any other nation or language in Europe, into a new and sophisticated phase, just at the time when the national ideal was asserting itself most strongly elsewhere. Grieg in Norway, Dvořák in Bohemia, each developing an intensely personal style rooted in his country's melodic inheritance, in local customs, associations, and even scenery, are really closer to the classical tradition of which Brahms was the last German representative than was Wolf himself or any of his followers. Moreover, practically all German song since has followed Wolf, though often at a considerable distance. Max Reger, for example, who is generally spoken of, and indeed apparently regarded himself, as a disciple of Brahms, is very much nearer to Wolf in his conception of the song form. A study of the simplest of his songs, the *Schlichte Weisen*, shows how far Reger's mind had travelled away from the *Volkslied*.

It is obviously impossible to trace here the evolution of the innumerable song types all over Europe which sprang from the renewed interest of cultivated musicians in the folksongs of their own and other countries. The interest was pursued in the latter part of the nineteenth century through the length and breadth of Europe with varying degrees of consciousness and conscientiousness. While Grieg was garnering into his own music the characteristics of Norwegian folk melody, Felipe Pedrell[1] was making for the instruction of his pupils his *Cancionero* of traditional songs from all parts of Spain. While Borodin was bringing the method of the scientist to bear on the study of his native Russian folksong for the purposes of his own composition, J. B. Weckerlin's bibliographical mind was devoting itself to the collection and arrangement of French 'chansons' and 'ballades'. Even Dvořák, a Czech peasant whose own unpremeditated style was that of the songs his mother-country taught him, cast

---

[1] See *Manuel de Falla and Spanish Music*, by J. B. Trend.

an eye of interest on those of Serbia in his youth and of the negro Americans in his age.

Political ambitions, social and ethnographical considerations, all combined to further that fervour of musical nationalism which was alluded to at the beginning of this volume as one of the causes contributing ultimately to the disintegration of the accepted tonal system. On leaving the discussion of Hugo Wolf we may notice parenthetically that his own harmonic style did not proceed one inch in the direction towards dis-integration. On the contrary, his later style, retreating from the chromaticism of his post-Wagnerian starting-point, seems to find increasing scope within the limits of a simple tonal and rhythmic system. It was left to his successors in German song to seek expression of the poem by means of a new musical language.

There is one figure in the Russian nationalistic movement whose songs must be considered with some closeness here, and who is designedly placed after Wolf although he died when Wolf was only beginning to feel his way as a composer. Vienna and Western Europe generally knew nothing of him until many years later. This was Modeste Moussorgsky (1835–81), who in his songs apart from opera was a pioneer in the exploration of those delicate problems of vocal declamation which were even then occupying Wagner in the German language and later would be Wolf's *point d'appui*. Moussorgsky's songs are not many. Some of them, such as the four *Songs and dances of Death* (words by Count A. Golenistchev-Koutouzov), are in the nature of narrative ballads. The folk-song influence is obvious here particularly in *Trepak*, where Moussorgsky seems beset by that morbid desire to make the flesh creep which is symptomatic of the immature romanticist. His sardonic humour in the setting of the Mephistophelian *Song of the Flea* and in the trivial jest which gained currency in England under the name of *The Musicians'*

Peepshow[1] do not represent the deeper side of his character. That is found in the six songs for baritone or mezzo-soprano called *Sans Soleil* (words by Golenistchev-Koutouzov), the seven *Nursery Songs* for which Moussorgsky wrote his own poems, and a few others. Here his desire for the closest declamation of the words was pushed to the point of making the voice part reproduce not only speech rhythms but even the intonations of the speaking voice in its rise and fall.[2] This side of Moussorgsky's nationalism is independent of folksong influence. As the Russian talks so he should sing, is the argument. It is an evocation of music from speech, not of cultivated music from uncultivated song.

The tender little pictures of nursery life are not those of a happy childhood. The Russian child's voice is generally plaintive and often whining. True to life, perhaps, at any rate a complete contrast with the English conception of child-life, expressed in such lines as,

> And when you look back it's all a puff,
> Happy and over and short enough.

Moussorgsky is not looking back, but living the child's life. He is not writing for children or for grown-up people about children; his little series of miniatures is a faithful portraiture of the particular kind of child-life he saw and knew, set down without

---

[1] *The Musicians' Peepshow*, a skit on the professed critics and other musical panjandrums of St. Petersburg in Moussorgsky's day, was translated into English by Mrs. Rosa Newmarch, who had been a pupil of Stassov to whom the work is dedicated. Scored for orchestra by Sir Henry Wood, and supplied with explanatory notes by Mrs. Newmarch, it became a popular number at the Promenade concerts at Queen's Hall, when it was first sung by Mr. Thorpe Bates in the summer of 1909.

[2] This was proved to me by the following experiment. Not knowing Russian, I asked a Russian lady who did not know Moussorgsky's songs to read aloud to me his poems of childhood, so that I might get the rhythm of the language. I followed the voice part with my eye while she read. To my surprise I found that unconsciously her voice took not only the rhythm but frequently the rise and fall of Moussorgsky's musical phrases.

any gloss. The child pesters its nurse for a story, is put in the
corner, is frightened by a cockchafer, plays with dolls and
rocking-horses, patters a prayer for all its tedious, elderly
relatives. Through it all the one thing Moussorgsky cares about
is truthfulness to the child's voice. All musical sense of rhythm,
of melody, harmony, and figuration in the piano part, must
contribute to this or be left out altogether. A few bars, the end
of the first one, with the French text of M. Delines, will serve
to show both the style and the lack of it. It should be compared with the scene of the children with the nurse in *Boris
Godounov* (Ex. 7).

This is the method in its nakedness; elsewhere it is often
given more musical clothing so that it appears to conform to

Ex. 7.

Mais dis - moi ce conte, ha! si

a - mu-sant!

more normal standards of tonality and rhythm. The *Cockchafer*, for example, is all in common time, and presumably it is the shape of the creature, its wings and legs and buzziness, which leads Moussorgsky to find a more consistent shape for his music in the manner of the following opening:

Ex. 8.   Moussorgsky. *Nursery Songs.*

Nia - nia, nia - niouch-ka!

Viens, é - cou - te,   chè-re nia - niouch-ka

Con 8ve ....

In such instances Moussorgsky's instinct for musical illustration, of the kind which we know in the piano pieces called *Pictures from an Exhibition*, comes to reinforce the principle of speech in song. But it never modifies that principle. Alike in the nursery songs and in the gloomy broodings of the sunless singer Moussorgsky is as chary as Wolf is of repeating words or of allowing more than the one required note to the syllable, and he never reached the certainty which Wolf reached of satisfying musical requirements in the act of pursuing his principle. Everything which Moussorgsky wrote, from the tiny children's songs to the music-drama of *Boris*, was left in the condition of a sketch for something greater.

Whither the *Sans Soleil* [1] songs led will be suggested at once by a quotation from one of them (Ex. 9).

The figure brings instantly to mind the first of Debussy's orchestral Nocturnes (*Nuages*). The latter may even be a case of unconscious reminiscence, but if it is, that is of no particular

Ex. 9.   MOUSSORGSKY. *Sans Soleil.*

et j'y res - pire   un lent   poi - son . . .   Prin -
Con 8ve

---

[1] The French text quoted is that of Mr. M. D. Calvocoressi.

- temps pas - sés,   ar - deurs,   ex - ta - ses re -

- vi - vent dans   mon   cœur trou - blé.   L'es -

- poir,   les rê - ves,   les chi - mè - res.

consequence. What is of consequence is the fact that this treatment of language in song was passed from Russia to France by the influence on Debussy of Moussorgsky's pioneer work. With the appreciation of Debussy's subtle personal style of artistic treatment it lost the crudeness of manner which is characteristic of Moussorgsky, but with Debussy's handling of the song form we are not here concerned.

It remains merely to note that before Debussy's influence asserted itself in Paris that renaissance of French music after the Franco-Prussian war which has been more particularly described in connexion with Chamber Music (Chapter IV) had its effect on song. Where formerly the opera song had held undisputed sway, what may be called the chamber music song, the concise setting of a lyric for voice and piano, began to take a place of increasing importance. The facile and eclectic talent of Saint-Saëns contributed comparatively little to it, though he began setting Victor Hugo in the 'fifties and published songs at intervals throughout his long career. His *La Fiancée du Timbalier* (Victor Hugo) is an extraordinarily effective ballad for mezzo-soprano voice with orchestra. César Franck wrote only a few stray songs, taking up a poem here and there which happened to appeal to him in some personal way. Happily among them was Brizeux's *La Procession*, a picture of the village priest carrying the Host through the cornfields, which Franck could colour in music with that reverent restraint which came naturally to him. It is his one little masterpiece in song. Others such as *Le Mariage des Roses* and *Lied* are trifles, and his church solos such as *Panis Angelicus* belong to the weaker side of his church music. The opening of this last is worth comparing with what has been described as the manner of the village organist in Wolf's *Gebet* (Ex. 3).

Ex. 10.   FRANCK.   *Panis Angelicus.*

Franck's pupils, however, took the song more seriously. The short-lived amongst them, Alexis de Castillon (1838–73), whose *Six Poésies* were held to have pointed the way to his friend Henri Duparc, and Ernest Chausson (1855–99), who left a score or so of songs of rich and varied interest, amongst them four *Chansons de Shakespeare* (translated by Bouchor), deserve mention. The longest lived, Henri Duparc (born 1848), had the

most distinctive genius in this direction, although his published
songs are fewer than Chausson's. Illness caused his retirement
in 1885. The dozen songs produced show an ampler style, an
altogether higher and more serious handling of the song form
than is found amongst any of his countrymen of that date.
Duparc's chief poets were Théophile Gautier, Charles Baudelaire,
and others of the romanticists, and with each poem he threw
himself into the spirit, though not necessarily the form, of his
words in a way which reveals the instinctive song-writer. From
the delicately 'atmospheric' style of *L'invitation au voyage* and
Chanson triste, he ranges to the rich harmonic expression of
Lamento, the more positive descriptive character of *La vague et
la cloche*, and the powerful expressive climax of *La vie antérieure*,
probably his greatest song. Duparc gave promise unfulfilled.
Gabriel Fauré (1845–1924) more than fulfilled the promise of
his early work. The *Vingt Mélodies*, contemporary with Duparc's
songs, seem much more limited. He chose more or less from
among the same poets, though the twenty contain five by Victor
Hugo. He set them to well-defined melodies, graceful, neat, and
tending to triteness, with generally only a serviceable backing
of clear harmony and facile arpeggio figures of piano accompaniment, typical *salon* songs of the more refined type. Later, in
contact with poets of his own day, notably Verlaine, he acquired
more suppleness of melody and a finer feeling for texture. Such
songs as *D'une prison*, *Après un rêve*, and *Les Roses d'Ispahan*
could hardly have been expected to come from the composer of
the *Vingt Mélodies*. His last songs, such as *Le Jardin clos*, eight
poems by van de Lerbughe, and the four *Mirages* (de Brimont)
seem separated from the early ones by a whole generation of
musical development. Fauré entirely escaped that tendency
to thicken and overload detail from which so many of the
German song-writers after Wolf have suffered. Although his
youth had been influenced by Schumann he retained his French

precision, indeed he intensified it, as his style developed. His song accompaniments remained slight in texture as compared with Duparc's, and they remained accompaniments. He never allowed the piano to usurp the prerogative of the voice. One small example from *Mirage* may serve to illustrate this precision from the last phase of Fauré's song writing. It is the beginning of *Danseuse*. The pianistic figure is carried with delicate enrichments through the whole development of the song.

Ex. 11.   FAURÉ. *Danseuse.*

Having touched on the leaders in the revival of French song, one which may be considered as the emancipation of song from the tradition of the opera, it would be natural to cross the Channel and consider their contemporaries in a country in which there was no operatic tradition from which to seek emancipation. English song, however, whether for one voice or for many, is the prime factor in that renaissance which was led by Parry and Stanford, and therefore special consideration of it is best deferred to the end of this volume, where an attempt is made to view the whole situation of the revival in English music. The songs of Duparc and Fauré are a by-product of a new era, while those of English composers are its very foundation.

CHAPTER XII

CHORAL MUSIC

IF we touch on choral music here only as a brief addendum to the above discussion of song, it is because the most distinctive work of the kind during our period may be regarded as an emanation from song, the application of its principles to a larger canvas, using a larger brush and a fuller palette.

Choral music has the longest tradition of all developed forms of the art. To sort and classify the innumerable works for combined voices with or without instruments composed within any fifty years between 1500 and 1900 would be a task to fill a volume larger than this one. The last half of the nineteenth century was certainly by no means the least prolific. A great deal of its product in church music, oratorio, and the like continued habits of thought ingrained by the traditions of earlier centuries, and is in consequence of comparatively slight historic significance.

The church, the chamber, and the theatre had provided successive nurseries for choral art. The nineteenth century added the public concert-hall and with it the choral society of mixed voices as a permanent institution for the pursuit of such music.[1] Almost all the composers of central Europe we have named, and a vast army who need not be named, have made

---

[1] This is broadly true of the Continent, although such institutions as the Concerts Spirituels in Paris and the Gewandhaus Concerts of Leipzig were founded in the eighteenth century. England, having less interest in the musical theatre, began its concert life at an earlier date. Choirs of mixed voices began to make tentative appearances in England in the latter half of the eighteenth century. The choruses of Handel's oratorios were first sung by choirs of men and boys drawn from the Cathedrals, the Chapels Royal, &c. In the large choir formed for the Handel Commemoration in Westminster Abbey, 1784, there were, according to Burney's list, six women sopranos, the remainder being boys, and no women contraltos, only male altos.

some contribution to its repertory. Outstanding works are Brahms's *Ein deutsches Requiem*; Dvořák's *Requiem, Stabat Mater*, the oratorio *St. Ludmila*, and secular cantatas such as *The Spectre's Bride*; Verdi's *Requiem, Stabat Mater*, and shorter pieces; César Franck's *Ruth* (an early work) and, in the period of his fuller activity, *Rédemption* and *Les Béatitudes*; all of them bearing the stamp of their composer's personal outlook towards their several subjects.

In a lower rank are the composers of what may be called repertory music for choral societies, some of it much admired in its day, but having little permanence. This sort of music was poured out in Germany. Ferdinand Hiller (1811–85), friend of Mendelssohn and conductor successively of the Gewandhaus concerts and the Lower Rhine Festivals, could even feel a little offended with Brahms for producing a setting of Goethe's *Gesang der Parzen* which superseded his own. Max Bruch (1838–1920) believed himself to be doing more than supplying a popular demand when he wrote his cantatas on such themes as *Odysseus, Arminius, Achilleus*, and a number of other heroic characters. He even expressed a belief that in the dramatic cantata lay the hope for the future of the art. Bernhard Scholz (1836–1916), conductor of the Gesang-Verein at Mainz, went to Schiller for the texts of his two most successful works, *Das Lied von der Glocke*[1] and *Das Siegesfest*, as did both Brahms and Goetz in their settings of *Nänie*.

In these specimens, great and small, and still more directly in Hugo Wolf's fugitive choral pieces, *Christnacht, Der Feuerreiter*, and *Elfenlied*, we can discern the tendency of the time to handle the chorus with orchestra on the principles of the song with piano. A poem, more or less complete, is taken as the text and

---

[1] When Scholz looked to Brahms for commendation of his *Lied von der Glocke* the latter merely made some remark on the quality of Schiller's poem.

the composer applies himself to the expression of its character in his music. A line can be drawn between works of this kind and the oratorios and cantatas, religious or secular, written to librettos fashioned for the concert-room as an opera libretto is fashioned for the stage. Until the later part of the nineteenth century little had been done with modern poetry, surprisingly little considering the age-long popularity of liturgical texts such as *Stabat Mater* and *Te Deum*. The German composers with their devotion to Goethe and Schiller led the way to new types of choral music, the ode and the choral ballad. Dvořák similarly drew on his Czech poets, Halék and Erben, for the texts of his *Hymnus*[1] (*The Heirs of the White Mountains*) and *The Spectre's Bride*. These examples had an important effect on that English renaissance which we are to discuss in a final chapter.

Choral music of this kind poses the problem of the relation between words and music in a peculiarly subtle way. A rigid application of what has been called the poetic supremacy law to the case of many voices singing in counterpoint would be paralysing to composition. Only a part-song written in block harmony of the baldest description can possibly obey such a law, and criticism of the result primarily from the point of view of the composer's faithfulness to the poetic form is soon reduced to absurdity. Judged by such a standard Barnby's *Sweet and Low* would be a perfect specimen and Elgar's *Go, Song of mine* a deplorable travesty.

In taking a poem for choral setting, whether with instrumental accompaniment or not, the composer claims the right to ignore its structure of metre and rhyme in the interests of his own art. He is concerned only with the content of the poem. He replaces poetic form with musical form. Any less freedom would deprive

[1] This, Dvořák's first public success, it is worth noting, was produced at the first public concert of the mixed choir, 'Hlahol', which Karel Bendl founded in Prague (1873).

him of the greatest resource of choral music, contrapuntal
design. A composer with a tender literary conscience will never
get very far with choral music. He must be inspired by words
but not held captive by them. His business is to fulfil his own
inspiration in his music, not to prate about the poet's inspiration.[1]
This, it has been already suggested, holds good of all song, but,
as Hugo Wolf proved, it is just possible in certain instances
of solo song for the composer to fulfil his inspiration while
leaving the poem intact. The nature of the technique forbids
that forbearance to the choral composer.

Brahms understood the nature of the case more fully than
any other composer of his day. His circumstances and upbringing had kept him away from the older traditions of choral
music derived either from the church or the theatre. To the
one belonged the Mass, the Requiem, and the other texts of
the Latin liturgy; the narrative oratorio owed its existence to
the other. With neither of these types was Brahms concerned at
any time, save for purposes of study.[2] Mr. Fuller-Maitland has
commented on the tentative nature[3] of what remains of Brahms's
early choral music as compared with the direct expression of
himself in piano music and solo song. With the choir, as with the
orchestra, he was deliberate in acquiring technique. Many of
his early short pieces were written for the Ladies' Choir which he
conducted at Hamburg. Some, the *Ave Maria*, Op. 12 (Detmold,
1858), and the *Psalm xiii*, Op. 27, for instance, might have

---

[1] While the proofs of this volume were passing through the press the late
Robert Bridges's Preface to his *Ode for the Bicentenary Commemoration of
Henry Purcell* was brought to my attention. Originally published by Elkin
Mathews (1896), it is now to be reprinted with other essays by its author
having a bearing on music. The Preface is in fact a cogent statement of the
relations between the poet and the musician in song, stating the case for the
musician's independence with all the weight of a great poet's authority.

[2] Among Brahms's many vocal studies of his earlier years was a five-part
Mass, in canon throughout. See Kalbeck, i. 227.

[3] See *Brahms*, by Fuller-Maitland, p. 196.

gone the way of his other preliminary essays had they not been
perpetuated by this choir's performances.

The *Begräbnissgesang* for choir and wind instruments is the first
choral work in which we can be certain of the authentic tones of
Brahms's voice. Its place in his psychology has already been
suggested. The two motets of Op. 29, *Es ist das Heil* (Choral) and
Schaffe in mir, Gott, ein rein Herz (from Psalm li), are primarily
essays in the choral technique of J. S. Bach, and, as such, declare
the ground on which Brahms took his stand for his larger choral
works. The first begins with the Choral harmonized in the manner
of Bach, and both contain strict fugues. Both are fine specimens
of their types. He carried further his control of the canonic treatment of voices for musical expression in the *Geistliches Lied* (Paul
Flemming) for four-part mixed choir and organ, which is his Op. 30.

Very different in manner are the *Drei Gesänge* for six-voiced
choir unaccompanied, which are Brahms's Op. 42 (1868). These,
Abendständchen (Clemens Brentano), *Vineta* (W. Müller), and
Darthulas Grabesgesang (after Ossian von Herder), are part-songs
pure and simple, the application to combined voices of the
lyrical style which Brahms had developed so richly in his solo
song-writing. Only in the last does he make much use of the
independent movement of the voices in imitative counterpoint.
In the best-known and most beautiful of them, *Vineta*, the
writing is all of the smooth spontaneous type which is shown by
the final cadence here quoted:

Ex. 1.

BRAHMS. *Vineta.*

Und   mir   ist,   als   ob   mich   En - gel

Incidentally the quotation shows how little Brahms was prepared to sacrifice the flow of his melody to such a verbal consideration as getting the principal word in a sentence to coincide with the climax of the musical phrase. That is an altogether secondary matter compared with the need of the part-song to fulfil its own musical form. It is that form, and no mere question of verbal accentuation, which makes it an intimate expression of the content of the poem.

All these diverse studies may be regarded as preparatory to that series of works for solo voices, choir, and orchestra, which is headed by *Ein deutsches Requiem*, Op. 45. Since so many English people still have little knowledge of what a Requiem, properly so called, means, it is necessary to insist that this work has nothing to do with the numerous Latin Requiems which composers have produced often with little or no regard to liturgical use in the rite of the Mass for the Dead. Brahms's title may not be a very fortunate one. It tends to link his work with a tradition in which it has no real part. The several movements composed at different times[1] represent a prolonged contemplation of the enigma of death and mankind's hope of consolation through the idea of immortality. In choosing his words from different parts of the Bible[2] Brahms had no idea of compiling an oratorio book. Save for the musical link existing between the first and last movements, the several movements are related to one another only by this all-pervading contemplation of the one idea from different angles, as it were. It does not make an entirely satisfactory cantata scheme. It has often been remarked, and with justice, that movements II, III, and VI together traverse too often the same emotional ground from gloom and fear to confidence and joy. Nevertheless, these three movements are strongly contrasted one with another.

No. II, beginning with the orchestral march rhythm (in triple time), pictures the inexorable fate of all things living, with, however, in its Trio, the hope of salvation. Suddenly, Isaiah's prophecy, 'The redeemed of the Lord shall return and come to Zion', flashes out, but the exuberant fugal chorus fades into a soft ending. No. III, begun with the baritone solo, is more personal. The aspiring mood, which emerges from the demand, 'Lord, let me know mine end', is reached only through prolonged struggle. The curious conception of the pedal fugue may be intended to

---

[1] The first three movements were first heard at a concert of the 'Gesellschaft der Musikfreunde' in Vienna on Dec. 1st, 1867. It was given complete, save for No. V, in Bremen Cathedral on Apr. 10th, 1868 (Good Friday). The completed and published work was given at a Gewandhaus concert in Leipzig on Feb. 18th, 1869.

[2] The scheme is as follows:
  I. *Chorus* Matt. v. 4; Ps. cxxvi. 5, 6; Matt. v. 4.
  II. *Chorus* 1 Peter i. 24; James v. 7; 1 Peter i. 24, 25; Isaiah xxxv. 10.
  III. *Baritone solo and chorus* Ps. xxxix. 4–7; Wisdom iii. 1.
  IV. *Chorus* Ps. lxxxiv. 1, 2, 4.
  V. *Soprano solo* John xvi. 22, Eccles. ii. 27, with *chorus* Isaiah lxvi. 13.
  VI. *Chorus* Heb. xiii. 14.
      Baritone solo and chorus 1 Cor. xv. 51, 55.
      Chorus Rev. iv. 11.
  VII. *Chorus* Rev. xiv. 13.

represent the immutable security of the righteous souls in the hand of God; certainly the tonic pedal sustained throughout excludes anything like the exuberance of the preceding number. The aspirant remains standing on earth looking upward into clouds, which, however, do not part to reveal the heavenly vision. It is the baritone solo of No. VI which pierces the clouds with the Pauline vision of resurrection, completed in words from the Apocalypse. This the fugal chorus carries to a point of ecstasy nowhere previously attained.

Together the first and last choruses form prologue and epilogue, and in the midst of them No. IV, 'How lovely is Thy dwelling place', and No. V, the exquisite soprano solo and chorus, 'Ye now are sorrowful', stand like Allegretto and slow movement respectively.

Indeed *Ein deutsches Requiem* is a choral symphony of gigantic proportions. The more it is regarded symphonically and the less it is thought of as a cantata the more its splendour appears. It is to be remembered that it was composed several years before the First Symphony. Brahms's only previous orchestral work on a large scale had been the Piano Concerto in D minor, in which his orchestration was manifestly immature. His command of the large orchestra in the *Requiem* (using trombones and tuba, three drums and harp) is surprising, and shows him to be anything but oblivious of the value of 'colour' in its effect on design. For example, note the opening of the march movement No. II, with the violins, 'con sordino', in the top octave, the violas in three parts ('senza sordino') an octave lower, and the horns, trumpets, and harp softly emphasizing the second beat in each bar; compare this with the enriched scoring of the same phrase where the full chorus enters, the trombones bodying out the vocal unison in their harmony and the string and harp parts more widely spaced. Throughout, the score is full of felicitous touches in the instrumentation. Despite the great breadth of the choral writing, *Ein deutsches Requiem* is by no means exclusively a choral work. The last movement is the most richly imaginative of all in this respect. Here Brahms approaches the spirit of the Italian fresco painters. 'I heard a voice from Heaven saying unto me, Write'; in a spacious opening melody, moving down from a long, poised, high note wreathed round with the paired quavers on the strings, he draws his great winged figure sweeping earthwards through a troubled sky. Its image pervades the whole movement.

To establish the points both of the essentially symphonic structure and the subtle blending of voices and instruments, a passage from the coda of this finale is here quoted in score. It should be noticed how the modulations to remote flat keys (E flat, A flat, D flat) are unified by the main key (F major), making an extension of the principal modulation in the first movement. Every bar illustrates the delicate blending of tones, but special attention may be drawn to the two violas and the violoncellos of the last bar of the quotation taking their chord from the pianissimo trombones (Ex. 2).[1]

It is natural to consider the *Triumphlied* (Op. 55, 1872) beside the *Requiem* because it too takes its subject from the Apocalyptic vision.[2] But it is distressing to do so, because the later work disappoints the hopes of the earlier one. To it Brahms brought the full panoply of his contrapuntal skill in choral writing. Orchestra and choirs hurl themselves on the theme of triumph in massed formation. There is not only a lack of musical contrast, that perhaps is inevitable in a work designed

---

[1] Brahms's use of the trombones throughout *Ein deutsches Requiem* especially in pianissimo is noteworthy. He had used trombones only in one previous score, the *Begräbnissgesang*.

[2] Rev. xix:
    I. *Double Chorus*, parts of verses 1 and 2.
    II. Ditto, parts of verses 5 and 6.
    III. *Baritone solo and chorus*, verses 11, 15, 16.

Ex. 2.

BRAHMS. *Requiem.*

Ex. 2 *cont.*

Ex. 2 cont.

Ex. 2 *cont.*

Ex. 2 *cont.*

Ex. 2 *cont.*

in a mood of untempered exultation, but one misses any suggestion that the composer has really seen behind the external
implication of the subject. It brings from him no single melody
which can be placed beside that of the 'Voice from Heaven'
in the *Requiem*. For once Brahms seems to have fallen into the
sin of spilling notes on music-paper, and, since the *Triumphlied*
was written to celebrate the victory of Germany in the Franco-
Prussian war (it was dedicated to the Emperor, William I),
the fall is easily accounted for. Brahms was less moved
by the Apocalyptic vision than by the spirit of the racial
war-god.[1]

Between the *Requiem* and the *Triumphlied* come in order of
publication the cantata, *Rinaldo*, for tenor solo, male-voiced
choir, and orchestra (1869), the *Harzreise Rhapsodie* for alto
voice, male-voiced choir, and orchestra (1870), and the *Schicksalslied* for mixed choir and orchestra (1870). A second group of
choral works is formed, between the appearance of the first and
second pairs of symphonies, by the two Motets Op. 74, for mixed
choir 'a cappella' (1879), *Nänie* for choir and orchestra (1881),
and the *Gesang der Parzen* for six-voiced choir and orchestra
(1883). The *Fünf Gesänge* for mixed choir (Op. 104) (containing
the two beautiful *Nachtwache* songs), 1889, the *Fest- und Gedenksprüche* (Op. 109) written for Hamburg (1890), and the three
Motets for four- and eight-voiced choir, Op. 110 (1890), make a
third group produced after Brahms's list of orchestral works had
been completed with the Double Concerto.

Rinaldo is Brahms's only cantata. Its text was originally

---

[1] It is only right to record here that there is an opposed point of view
which many admirers of Brahms strongly maintain. Mr. Fuller-Maitland,
writing in 1911, deplored the neglect of the *Triumphlied* in England and
declared that 'it sorely needs frequent revival, for it is a noble song of
victory, and among other things it reveals a spirit of grave exultation and
thankfulness to God, which is a salutary corrective to certain forms of
popular elation which have occasionally been seen in England'.

written by Goethe for musical treatment in that style,[1] and it seems to have captivated Brahms's imagination very much as Tieck's *Magelone Lieder* had done. His music indeed has something of the same romantic quality, and his general outlook is bounded by the same limitations. It is known that after its composition he was occupied for a time with the idea of operatic composition, but the cantata shows how far removed from the quick action of the stage was Brahms's leisurely development of lyrical song.

The *Rhapsodie* from Goethe's *Harzreise im Winter*, the *Schicksalslied*, poem by Friedrich Hölderlin (1770–1843), *Nänie*, a sonnet in hexameters by Schiller, and the *Gesang der Parzen* from Act IV of Goethe's *Iphigenie auf Tauris*, may be regarded as conspicuous examples of that extension of the song style to choral music which has been spoken of as a characteristic of the century. The *Rhapsodie* indeed is a contralto scena with no more than a background of choral voices added to its final movement. The vocal writing of the others is purely choral, but still primarily lyrical. In none of these works does Brahms make any display of technical elaboration. In each it is easy to discern that his attractions to the several poems lay in the fate motive which actuates them all.

None of the words, save those of the *Rhapsodie*, give any hint of that consolation through faith which is so richly given in the *Requiem*, and Brahms does not go beyond his texts in his music. The suggestion that the return to the opening symphony of the *Schicksalslied* is meant to suggest the final beatification of storm-tossed humanity has nothing to support it. Indeed, the re-creation of the picture of serenity may equally well have been undertaken in order to heighten the contrast between the condition of gods and men. Brahms's devotion to musical

[1] Brahms substitutes the male choir for Goethe's two knights who come to the rescue of Rinaldo.

recapitulations at all times is sufficient to explain it. The *Schicksalslied*, because of the beauty of its musical themes, the directness of its emotional contrasts, and the conciseness with which they are presented, is Brahms's masterpiece in this genre.

The Motets Opp. 74, 109, 110 carry further that type, partially dependent on the example of Bach, which began with the two of Op. 29; the *Fest- und Gedenksprüche*, written for a civic occasion, bear less of the stamp of Brahms's own personality than the others, but are the most famous. Because of their occasion they have some of that assertiveness which destroys the more sensitive qualities of music, and which is heard at its worst in the *Triumphlied*, but behind this there is a real nobility of design and great power in contrapuntal execution of the design. Both the sets of motets of Opp. 74 and 110 cut deeper, and if their prevailing moods are sombre, they reflect those of Brahms's own life, the alternations of doubt and hope, conflict and tenderness, which are at the root of his finest work, from the First Piano Concerto to the *Vier ernste Gesänge*.

To turn from Brahms to any other choral composer among his contemporaries is to realize the chasm which divides him from them in the matter of vocal texture. In his capacity to create varied depth in the texture Brahms is undeniably the greatest master since Bach, whose technique he assimilated. The Viennese masters, who owed their style to Italy, relied less on the subtler devices of counterpoint. Mozart himself rarely lavished that contrapuntal skill on his chorus which flows so readily in the Finale of the 'Jupiter' Symphony and the vocal ensembles of his operatic finales. Brahms's northern descent is proclaimed in his choral writing more than in any other phase of his composition.

At first sight one might expect to find in César Franck's

Les Béatitudes a work more or less comparable to *Ein deutsches Requiem*. It is contemplative, the outcome of deep and serious conviction, and its general plan, a prologue followed by a series of eight choral tableaux, each one depicting the troubles of a distracted world lulled to rest by the pronouncements of the Saviour's voice, bears a certain analogy to that of Brahms's work. But unfortunately it shows the composer to be so completely devoid of any sense of choral texture that, despite many beauties of detail, *Les Béatitudes* becomes intolerably monotonous.

It may be suggested that the sense of texture developed by the contemplative attitude towards music is the compensation for lack of the sense of drama exhibited in swift action and compelling phrase. Brahms may have been deficient in the sense of drama, though not devoid of it, as certain passages, particularly the baritone solos of the *Requiem*, attest. But the *Béatitudes*, with its eight scenes all leading to one solution, is defective in both directions. There is no drama, and without the variety of texture to support the progress of the scenes their movement lags heavily.

César Franck's experience of choral music was that of a Parisian church choir, and the music, a Mass and many motets, which he wrote for it is negligible for any purpose outside its immediate one of parochial worship. The French had little choral tradition, and their productions add little or nothing to the history of our period. One of the best ecclesiastical works for choir and orchestra was the *Requiem* by Alfred Bruneau which was given its first performance in London at a concert of the Bach choir in 1896. Fauré had produced a *Requiem* at the Madeleine at an earlier date, and a choral cantata by him, *La Naissance de Vénus*, reached England at the Leeds Festival of 1898. Gabriel Pierné, Franck's successor at St. Clothilde, achieved some success both at home and abroad with his picturesque children's pieces (French counter-part to the operas of Humperdinck) *La Croisade des enfants*, a musical legend, and *Les Enfants de Bethléem*, a Christmas mystery.

The vogue of Dvořák in England rather over-emphasized his importance as a choral composer in the 'eighties, and his oratorio *St. Ludmila*, an exceedingly elaborate work on which he had expended his utmost efforts, fell flat after its production at Leeds (1886), and its repetition in London. His no less portentous *Requiem*, produced at Birmingham (1891), has shared a similar fate, immediate success and subsequent oblivion; the earlier *Stabat Mater* has been saved by the beauty and spontaneity of its melody and that evidence of an untutored devotion which also informs his *Biblical Songs*. The *Te Deum* in G (Op. 103), which he took with him to America, is sufficiently described by the fact that its text is supplemented by an 'Alleluya' chorus in order that the work might end in the mood of unreflecting jubilation appropriate to a festival in honour of Christopher Columbus. In fact the discoverer of America was to Dvořák very much what Wilhelm I was to Brahms, but with more excuse.

The liturgical text of the Requiem Mass has held a peculiar attraction for composers ever since Berlioz, because of the opportunity for vivid scene-painting provided by the Sequence, *Dies irae*. All through the nineteenth century it, even more than the Ordinary of the Mass, was becoming increasingly dissociated from its proper function, and most of these musical settings of it were written for the concert-room, and with little or no idea of presentation as part of an ecclesiastical ritual. What most distinguishes Verdi's *Manzoni Requiem* from such works is that while force of circumstance has made it a concert piece, and its whole style and proportions are completely at variance with modern ecclesiastical requirements as laid down

in the Motu Proprio of Pius X,[1] it is animated from first to last
by the spirit of Catholic devotion, as Italians conceive it, and
the spirituality of the music can be only fully realized when it
is performed liturgically. It is that which makes it by far the
most outstanding church work of its age.[2]

Viewed in this light, the admiration which the Austrians extend
to the church music of Anton Bruckner is explicable. He left
three Masses, No. 1 in D minor, with orchestra (1864), No. 2 in
E minor for eight-voiced choir with wind or organ accompaniment (1866), No. 3 in F minor, *Grosse Messe* for soli, choir, and
orchestra (1867–8), and the *Te Deum* in C for soli, choir, and
orchestra (1881–4), with sundry other settings of ecclesiastical
texts. These are emphatically not concert pieces but designed for that type of church service which belongs to the
Viennese tradition, to which Haydn, Mozart, and Schubert each
made their distinctive contributions. None of Bruckner's Masses
have that inflated character which his symphonies, under the
influence of the Wagnerian orchestra, exhibit. Even the *Grosse
Messe* employs an orchestra of only normal dimensions, and
the general method of its use is that of weaving decorations
round a simple outline of vocal music declaiming the text. The
expression of the text is the primary purpose of these works,
and generally Bruckner achieves his purpose quite definitely
and sometimes with distinction. In Bruckner's Masses there
is none of the rudderless wandering which is the defect of
his symphonies. One might almost say that he thought of the
symphony as a Mass with the voices left out, not realizing
the stronger principle of internal structure which must direct
the course of purely instrumental music, but which may be a

[1] For text of the Motu Proprio see *Catholic Church Music* by Sir Richard
Terry.
[2] Verdi's *Requiem* is appreciatively, if somewhat dispassionately, discussed
by Dannreuther, *Oxf. Hist. Mus.* vi, pp. 221–2.

positive interference in music which is ancillary to some ulterior purpose.

The best church music, like the best stage music, loses much of its point when it is divorced from its original surroundings, and while we may say that the best music is that which is self-sufficient, in fact the symphony, music which insists on its self-sufficiency when it is intended to serve the purposes either of religious devotion or of dramatic representation, is, if not bad, at any rate misplaced. Bruckner's church music is well-placed. It may not be of the highest type, but there can be no doubt of its seriousness, of its insight into the particular situation it was designed to fill, and of its many singular beauties from a purely musical point of view.

That he was well able when he desired to do so to create an impression solely from the contact of voices moving in a contrapuntal design may be shown by a quotation from the 'Christe Eleison' of the Mass in E minor (No. 2). Actually the passage is accompanied on the organ but the accompaniment adds nothing to the texture (Ex. 5, below).

It displays the characteristic Bruckner *crescendo* so prevalent in the symphonies, but the device is relevant here, and it has not the mechanical effect of merely adding more instruments, in the manner of organ stops, which it has throughout the instrumental music.

In the *Grosse Messe* in F minor, a work of larger scope and freer expression than the earlier Masses, Bruckner is seen at his best. Its greatest contrapuntal efforts are the two fugues at the end of 'Gloria' and 'Credo'. The one has a bold subject,

Ex. 3.   BRUCKNER. *Mass in F minor.*

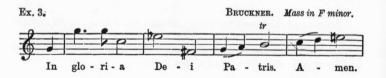

In   glo - ri - a   De - i   Pa - tris.   A -   men.

the other a less distinctive one, which, however, has been the principal theme for the *Credo* throughout.

Ex. 4.   BRUCKNER. *Mass in F minor.*

In   vi - tam ven - tu - ri   sae - cu - li. A - men.

From both Bruckner succeeds in generating a considerable amount of heat as the result of contrapuntal friction, and his fugal movements show him to be by no means entirely dependent on those resources of chromatic harmony on which he too readily falls back in his more sentimental moments.

Bruckner's church music as a whole, considered as the outcome of his national tradition, appears to give him a higher place as a composer than that to which his symphonies entitle him. It is true that it will not readily bear transplantation either into the concert-room or into the ritual of any other form of Christian worship than that which inspired it. We in England, who have a tradition of church music of our own equally incapable of transplantation, should appreciate the value of local art forms within the borders of the Christian Church.

Ex. 5.   BRUCKNER. *Mass in E minor.*

Ex. 5 *cont.*

Ex. 5 *cont.*

Ex. 5 *cont.*

Ex. 5 *cont.*

Ex. 5 *cont.*

Ex. 5 *cont.*

Ex. 5 *cont.*

Sempre ff

CHAPTER XIII

ENGLAND

1850–1900

U<small>P</small> to this point the discussion of composers and their works in these pages has avoided strict classification according to nationality. The avoidance has been with intention. The aim has been to show men of genius working along parallel lines, influenced no doubt by race and environment, but primarily bringing their personal temperaments and abilities to bear on art-forms which were more or less a common interest to the artistic society of Europe. Wagner, Verdi, and Moussorgsky wrestling with the problems of the musical drama, Brahms, Tchaikovsky, and César Franck reshaping symphonic music, are not merely to be regarded as the products of their several national 'schools', though each was that to some degree. They were master-minds contributing, however unconsciously, to the completion of an epoch closed with the end of the century.

If we consider England here apart from the Continent, it is not done in order to make pretensions, which would be manifestly false, to any position of peculiar importance for English music of the period. Quite the reverse. It is because while the Continent was reaping its rich harvest of music, and incidentally exporting it across the channel, English music was represented only by some rather thin sowings in a soil, rich enough indeed, but very poorly tilled. A future chronicler will probably be able to discuss the English product of the twentieth century on parallel lines with that of other countries. To attempt to do so in regard to that of the last half of the nineteenth century would be merely to confirm the prevalent view that England was a country unaccountably barren of music of her own but the wealthiest purchaser of continental music.

About 1850 the operatic stars were illuminating London with uncommon brilliance. Benjamin Lumley had been successful in securing the brightest of them for Her Majesty's Theatre, and the extravagant enthusiasm which Jenny Lind aroused had enabled him to face the powerful opposition of the new con- stellation at Covent Garden. Then Jenny Lind had forsworn opera (as Alberich forswore love), and the American showman, P. T. Barnum, had carried her off to America in that very year. Barnum's venture was the exceptional enterprise of a very exceptional man, but it began the process of extending the orbit of the international stars to the other side of the Atlantic. As the century progressed, London, and especially Covent Garden Theatre, became increasingly recognized as the first objective of singers and other executants who aimed at world power. To have made a success at Covent Garden was a passport to New York.[1]

This was the time when Grisi and Mario were making the reputation of the Royal Italian Opera started at Covent Garden by Charles Lewis Gruneisen and conducted by Costa. During its first seasons Edward Delafield, its financier, lost something like £60,000 over the 'Costamongers', as Lumley nicknamed them, but the more astute management of Gye, begun in 1851, turned the huge deficit into a small profit. The novelties were Italian versions of Meyerbeer and Gounod, Spohr's *Faust*, conducted by the composer, and Verdi's *Rigoletto* (1853).

All this shows London still playing the old game which had brought Handel to bankruptcy a hundred years earlier. It was to be played out in alternating periods of excitement and depression right up to the time of the war (1914). Even after this London failed to realize how completely the game had been played out, and lost. After the management of the Gyes, father

[1] Now the position is reversed.

and son, came Augustus Harris, followed by the Royal Opera Syndicate. After Grisi came Patti, Albani, Melba, the last two, despite their Italianate names, both of British origin. The Royal Italian Opera became the Royal Opera under Harris, not because it was becoming more indigenous, but because it had to accommodate the German and French languages. Enough money was poured out on these transient entertainments to have founded several times over the permanent society for the development of native opera which has been the unattainable dream of English musicians.

More than that, native opera proved that in those more prosperous times it could be a profitable undertaking. Louisa Pyne and William Harrison began giving seasons of 'English Opera' at Covent Garden, which had been burnt down and rebuilt by Gye, in 1858. Balfe's *Satanella or the Power of Love* ran to something like fifty performances. A year or so later Wallace's *Lurline* brought these managers a fortune of £50,000. They recovered from a native opera very nearly what Delafield had dropped over the 'Costamongers'. That versatile and cosmopolitan person, Julius Benedict, enriched their repertory in 1862 with *The Lily of Killarney*, which still clings to life in the occasional performances of travelling companies. But though these composers were men of talent and with considerable stage experience they all allowed English opera to remain weighed down by a ridiculous convention of false romanticism. Of the English opera of that time Mr. Cecil Forsyth says:

'It is an opera of no-where and no-time: of men and women who never have existed and never can exist: an opera of sham sentiment and sham motive, of artificiality and bunkum. Its dwelling-place is a fantastic Nightmareland, peopled, not by human beings, but by dismal theatrical ghosts and corpses, each one of whom seems to have borrowed a moral rig-out second hand from Pecksniff.[1]

[1] See *Music and Nationalism, a study of English Opera*, by Cecil Forsyth, 1911. In this work a thorough study of English opera books is made, and

New hopes for English opera were opened up in the 'eighties by D'Oyly Carte and Carl Rosa. The former had discovered genius for a new genre in comic opera when *Trial by Jury*, 'a dramatic cantata', words by W. S. Gilbert and music by Arthur Sullivan, was produced at the Royalty Theatre on March 25, 1875. The latter had realized that a new group of composers had arisen who were not content with the old 'artificiality and bunkum', who were determined to handle dramatic subjects seriously in their music, and were equipped with the knowledge of the newer technical methods of combining voices and orchestra for dramatic expression. Amongst them genius might be found. Carte formed a syndicate for the production of operas by Gilbert and Sullivan, and Rosa founded the opera company which bore his name, both in the year of *Trial by Jury*. Carl Rosa included the production of Frederic Cowen's first opera, *Pauline*, in his season at the Lyceum of the following year. At the theatre called the 'Opera Comique' *The Sorcerer* began the famous collaboration of D'Oyly Carte, Gilbert, and Sullivan in 1877; *H.M.S. Pinafore*, *The Pirates of Penzance*, and *Patience* followed in the same theatre, until in the course of its long run the last-named was transferred to Carte's newly built theatre called 'The Savoy' in 1881.

Gilbert, even more than Sullivan, took London, and presently the whole country, by storm, because for the first time English opera was talking sense. That the sense was disguised as hilarious nonsense made the attraction all the more piquant. No more the warriors with impossibly small armies marching to and fro, the stealthy bandits doing nothing in particular, the death-dealing heroes and the distressed damsels of the Pyne and

---

the fashion of writing operatic English as though it were a bad translation of a foreign libretto is exposed.

The judgement quoted above suggests an interesting parallel with certain aspects of the present-day film industry.

Harrison repertory; instead, Gilbert regaled his public with a chorus of British jurymen, a squad of the Metropolitan police, the crew of a battleship, ordinary figures of everyday life, no less real because every line of them was subtly caricatured. Good music, partly no doubt because of the strength of the oratorio tradition, had hitherto seemed to the ordinary Englishman to demand a mood of preternatural solemnity. It was even questioned whether Sullivan's music, which joined in the laughter and partly caused it, could be really good. Serious musicians were a little concerned lest their art should be degraded by popular favour. Sullivan himself was apt to be restive at the decree of fate which devoted him to the comic muse. Fate, however, was irresistible, and the long series of Savoy operas[1] was started from which English audiences were to learn that music is for laughter as much as for tears, that fantasy is futile unless it springs out of reality, that the English language can be sung, that the English song is among the most beautiful in the world when 'music and sweet poetry agree', and a host of other lessons, in learning which they were not to be conscious that they were being taught anything.

Meantime, Carl Rosa was doing his utmost to place the larger types of English opera on an assured footing. In the course of his several seasons at Drury Lane he produced Mackenzie's *Colomba* and Goring Thomas's *Esmeralda* (both in 1883), Stanford's *The Canterbury Pilgrims* (1884), Goring Thomas's

---

[1] Sullivan's Savoy operas, all with Gilbert save where another name is given, were:
Iolanthe (1882), *Princess Ida* (1884), *The Mikado* (1885), *Ruddigore* (1887), *The Yeoman of the Guard* (1888), *The Gondoliers* (1889), *Haddon Hall* (Sydney Grundy) (1892), *Utopia Limited* (1893), *The Chieftain* (F. C. Burnand, originally *Contrabandista* in 1867) (1894), *The Grand Duke* (1896), *The Beauty Stone* (Comyns Carr and A. W. Pinero) (1896), *The Rose of Persia* (Basil Hood) (1899).

The Emerald Isle (Basil Hood) was begun by Sullivan before his death (Nov. 22, 1900); it was finished by Edward German and produced at the Savoy in 1901.

Nadeshda (1885), Frederick Corder's *Nordisa* (1887). Cowen's *Thorgrim* (1890) was produced by the company after Carl Rosa's death.

Of these, Stanford's work alone, taking one great theme from English literature, and another, the melody 'Sumer is icumen in', from English music, made a definite move in the direction of a national type. He had had two operas, *The Veiled Prophet* and *Savonarola*, previously produced at Hamburg, a fact which gave him a certain prestige with English audiences. Probably Stanford's intellectual refinement a little overshot the mark in *The Canterbury Pilgrims*, as elsewhere. He designed to catch the medieval atmosphere of the subject by writing modal music which may well have been rather too recondite for the opera-goers of the 'eighties. Nevertheless if Rosa, instead of giving it four performances and then dropping it out of the repertory, had insisted on certain recensions in the plot and form of the work, and then given it a renewed hearing, it is more than probable that it would have made a permanent mark. Many a continental reputation has been made from stuff of a much poorer quality than that of *The Canterbury Pilgrims*.

Ill fortune, however, continued to dog English opera. Carl Rosa had attempted to give everybody a chance and had given nobody a sufficient chance when he died. D'Oyly Carte had observed from Rosa's experience that there might be possibilities for opera on a larger plan than that of the Savoy. Having succeeded where Rosa had failed, in finding a composer who could immediately captivate a large public, and obsessed with the idea engendered by the Savoy of an opera which could be run for hundreds of nights without cessation, he proceeded to build his Royal English Opera House in Cambridge Circus and to open it on January 1, 1891, with Sullivan's *Ivanhoe*. It was the death-blow to the hopes raised a decade earlier.

Ivanhoe, lavishly mounted and fitted with a double cast, ran for 160 performances, an unprecedented achievement for an opera in the grand manner. It was received on all hands with enthusiasm and drew crowded houses from the first. Carte seems to have supposed that opera scores would fall like manna from heaven on a house which could secure so remarkable an initial success. They did not fall, but the English Opera House did, for after an effort to carry on with Messager's *La Basoche*, it was sold to become the Palace Theatre of Varieties, and Carte and Sullivan returned to the Savoy. English opera has been in the wilderness ever since.

This fluctuation of affairs is bound up with the fact, so surprising to foreigners, that England has never made any public provision for the practice of the art of music, either in the theatre or in the concert-room. In a few cases a more or less grudging support for a local orchestra at seaside resorts and inland spas has been wrested from town councils, but there is not to this day a city in the British Isles which owns a Municipal Theatre for the performance of spoken drama and of opera such as is to be found in every German town with pretensions to civilization. There is not, and has never been, an Opera House maintained by the State in the capital, and the term 'Royal Opera' has never meant anything more than the hope of such favours from royalty as the occasional occupation of a royal box, not always as much as that. Everything in opera that has been done has been due to the enterprise of private entrepreneurs, who have risked their own fortunes and those of any one else whom they could persuade to join them in the venture, and the same has been the case, though generally with a smaller outlay of capital, in the concert-room. It does not follow from this that England is an inherently unmusical country, any more than it can be said to be devoid of medical science because its hospitals are supported by voluntary contribution. But it does argue a curious mentality with regard to music. The English people have never made up their minds that music is more to them than a pleasant recreation for leisure hours; they are in fact incorrigible amateurs.

To find English music at its best, therefore, we have to turn to those forms of music which are most amenable to cultivation by amateurs, the many varieties of choral song. That in the middle of the century English music was in a bad way is shown less by the fact that opera in London and the professional concert-room were given over to the exploitation of continental art than by the paucity of institutions for the cultivation of native choral music and the obliviousness of its past glories. Madrigal singing was almost dead. The Madrigal Society (founded 1741) kept alive the social character of madrigal singing in its meetings at which a few gentlemen supped and sang. The Bristol Madrigal Society (founded 1837) was beginning a revival in the provinces which, however, tended to copy the concert-room by adopting the habit of singing madrigals in chorus under the beat of a conductor. Robert Lucas Pearsall (1795–1856) had added something to the store of such music by his madrigal compositions, of which 'Great God of Love' is the most famous. This was, however, the post-Mendelssohn era in which the goal of ambition for most composers was to produce a second *Elijah*. The Sacred Harmonic Society (founded 1832) was devoting itself to the performance of oratorios, old and new. When Spohr arrived to conduct his *Faust* at Covent Garden, he was seized on to listen to his own *Calvary* (*Des Heilands letzen Stunden*), performed by this Society under Costa at Exeter Hall, and was constrained to remark that the effect 'in many points, especially that of the powerfully imposing choruses, was more immense than the composer himself had ever conceived'.[1] Thus the Society

[1] *The Sacred Harmonic Society, a thirty-five years retrospect, from its commencement in 1832, to the five hundredth concert, in Exeter Hall, 13th December, 1867.* Printed for private circulation.

furthered that ideal which had begun with the Handel Commemoration of 1784 in Westminster Abbey and was to be
upheld in the subsequent Handel Festivals of the Crystal Palace,
the ideal of the Snark who

> Summed up so well that it came to far more
> Than the witnesses ever had said.

A successor to *Elijah* seemed to have been found when Costa
produced his oratorio, *Eli*, at the Birmingham Festival in 1856,
and the Sacred Harmonic Society annexed it and reproduced it
in repeated triumphs at Exeter Hall. True to its name, the
oratorio, however, ultimately proved to be but half *Elijah*, the
worse half.

Michael Costa (1808–84), of Spanish birth and Neapolitan
education, was, as we have seen, at this time king of the opera
at Covent Garden; he was also supreme in the concert-rooms of
London through his conductorship of the Philharmonic and the
Sacred Harmonic Societies, and a great power at the provincial
festivals of which Birmingham was the most important. He
was an autocrat who had banished Sterndale Bennett from the
Philharmonic, because Bennett had dared to express views of
his own about the tempi of his own overture. He conducted
with the iron hand in the white kid glove, 'and the children of
Israel sighed by reason of the bondage'.

William Sterndale Bennett (1816–75) was the most brilliant
of the early pupils of the Royal Academy of Music (founded
1822), disciple of Mendelssohn and friend of Schumann, whose
early success in playing his own concerto at Leipzig had given
him something of an international reputation not possessed by
any other Englishman of his generation.[1] Costa's insolence
proved to be a public service. Without it Bennett might have
gone on playing concertos to Philharmonic audiences. Instead,

[1] See Dannreuther's estimate of Bennett as composer. *Oxf. Hist. Mus.*
vol. vi, pp. 310–12.

his mind turned to the idea of making his countrymen sing Bach. When one day he walked home from the Royal Academy, talking with his friend Charles Steggall of his project, he had little thought of what a weapon he was forging for the breaking of the bondage. A few days later, in October 1849, half a dozen friends met at Bennett's house and founded 'The Bach Society', not with a view to any immediate performance, but for the study of J. S. Bach. Other musicians were quickly co-opted, among them W. H. Holmes, John Goss, Henry Smart, C. E. Horsley, John Hullah. Older worthies, Sir George Smart and Cipriani Potter, were induced to give the young society their distinguished countenance, and when the august *Mr. Punch* honoured it with some bad puns about '*Bach*-ing up its friends' in a '*Bach* attic', it was clear that the Bach Society had taken its place as an English institution. The Society was just in time to celebrate the centenary of Bach's death with a private concert which included chorals and motets, and to negotiate on that occasion with Messrs. Ewer for the publication of six motets. The great movement was started. It was to be furthered, as all the best of amateur music in England since has been furthered, by the untiring efforts of a woman who made the cause her life-work. In this case it was Miss Helen Johnston, one of Bennett's pupils, who later became responsible for the first English version of the text of the *St. Matthew Passion*.

The production of the *Passion* by Bennett at St. Martin's Hall on March 22, 1858, was the crowning achievement of his personal work in that direction. In collaboration with Otto Goldschmidt, husband of Jenny Lind, he prepared *The Chorale Book for England*,[1] but it was left to his collaborator to found the Bach Choir and achieve the first performance in this country of the

---

[1] *Lyra Germanica* (2 vols., 1855 and 1858) contained translations by Catherine Winkworth of German hymns. *The Chorale Book for England* (1859) was announced as the musical edition of *Lyra Germanica*.

B minor Mass in 1876, the year after Bennett's death. S. S. Wesley introduced the *St. Matthew Passion* at the Three Choirs Festival at Gloucester in 1871, and a little later John Stainer made its annual performance in Holy Week a feature of the drastic reform of cathedral music which he carried out at St. Paul's Cathedral. Bennett had indeed lit such a candle as should never be put out.

But the importance of the Bach movement to English music was not merely the introduction once again of the best of continental art to this country. Rather it was that Bach roused the English amateurs from their lethargy, and set them new tasks of varying magnitude. Bach's music called for the highest efforts of all classes, from the Leeds Festival Choirs glorying in the eight-part polyphony of *Sing ye to the Lord*, to a village choir compassing with difficulty a four-part choral. It broke down the obsession with oratorio and opened the minds of English choralists to a myriad of musical forms great and small, and of English audiences to a new delight in texture, a delight which they had lost in forgetting their own classics of Byrd and Weelkes and Purcell.

In tracing this revival we cannot afford to ignore the humblest evidences of a new life. John Hullah's singing-classes began at Exeter Hall in 1847, and the concerts resulting from them at St. Martin's Hall (built for him by his friends); John Curwen's propaganda of the system of Tonic Sol-fa notation and his foundation of a College for teaching the system (1863); these and similar efforts opened up choral singing as a recreation to large numbers of people who hitherto had had no possibility of partaking in any kind of musical activity. It was the Tonic Sol-fa notation which made possible the choral singing of Yorkshire mill-hands and Welsh miners. With this easily acquired system of reading vocal music all and sundry could join in the artistic rendering of choral music on a large scale.

Without it the Leeds Festival Choir could scarcely have been formed on the scale which it assumed in 1874, and it was at about the same time that Henry Coward, an elementary school-master, founded a Tonic Sol-fa association in Sheffield from which in process of time he would build up a choral union to rival that of Leeds.

Nor can the hymns of the people be passed over in a country in which the Church was the only established institution charged officially with the duty of making music. The publication in 1861 of the first edition of *Hymns Ancient and Modern* is a more important landmark in English musical history than the formation of many a famous concert-giving institution. That volume contained:

'Latin hymns, and in a few cases their old melodies also, from the *Hymnal Noted* . . . the traditional English hymns from Watts onward with some of the old Psalm tunes and church tunes recovered by Havergal and others; the German translations of Miss Winkworth and the German tunes from the *Chorale Book* and elsewhere, with others newly adapted:—all these found a place with the new school of English writers inaugurated by Keble, and, with seven of the new tunes of Dykes, to represent the latest musical development.'[1]

It is the fashion of to-day to speak slightingly of the Victorian hymn-tune and particularly to base the poor opinion of its quality on the tunes of the Rev. J. B. Dykes. He is spoken of as if he had debased a noble tradition of English hymnody by supplying melody of weak quality made attractive by over-sweet harmony. Dykes was an amateur musician who wrote too much and too readily, and his defects became more apparent when a greatly enlarged edition of *Hymns Ancient and Modern* was called for in 1875. But the injustice of the estimate is at once apparent when it is recalled that his modest contribution of seven tunes to the book of 273 hymns published in 1861 included

[1] Introduction by the Rev. W. H. Frere to the *Historical Edition of Hymns Ancient and Modern*, published 1909.

six which have become inseparable from such favourite hymns as 'O come and mourn', 'Our blest Redeemer', 'Holy, Holy, Holy', 'Nearer, my God, to Thee', 'Jesu, lover of my Soul', and 'Eternal Father, strong to save'.[1] The book began a new era of English hymnody, one which, in both words and music, was to reflect the weakness as well as the strength of the English conception of the Christian faith; but good or bad, strong or weak, it was to play its part in re-creating the sense of national possession in the heritage of song, and in this, Dykes, along with more cultivated musicians such as Ouseley, Stainer, and Barnby, played a considerable and worthy part.

The greatest defect in the amateur's equipment is invariably his inability to sift good from bad, and to form for himself a critical estimate of quality. It is this that professional institutions for music-making help to remedy. Without them the amateur is peculiarly liable to accept everything which comes his way, to remain inchoate and undeveloped in his tastes. That was the misfortune of the popular revival in England. Without settled institutions for opera and concert-giving the amateurs greeted with extravagant enthusiasm the meteoric appearances of international stars; professional musicians, having to earn their livings precariously, played down to the supposed low level of taste of the half-educated amateurs. Commercialists exploited professionals and amateurs alike. There followed all the artistic degradation of the 'royalty' ballad, the cheap church music, and the paltry cantatas turned out for the use of the newly founded choral societies.

It is from this confused background that the work of Parry and Stanford stands forward in the 'eighties. Together they made a firm stand for the best and only the best. They were impatient of the second-rate but not too impatient for the needs

---

[1] In fact only one, a tune written to the *Dies Irae*, now invariably sung to its traditional plainsong, cannot be said to have become a classic.

of their time. They saw their contemporaries vacillating between art and artifice: Sullivan with his lyrical genius confusing the public mind, and perhaps even his own, with such drivel as *The Lost Chord* and *The Chorister*; Cowen debasing the currency with *The Children's Home* and *The Better Land*; Stainer setting a dignified standard for the cathedral, and writing *The Crucifixion* for parish churches. Their motto from the first, therefore, was 'No compromise', and to it they held through evil report and good report. Their service to their generation and to those which have followed them was inestimable quite apart from the abiding value of the best of their own compositions. With them in their general attitude must be mentioned Alexander Mackenzie, whose influence as composer and teacher, especially from the time that he became Principal of the Royal Academy of Music (1888), was exerted in a similar direction. Mackenzie, however, did not participate in the most distinctive service which Parry and Stanford together did for English vocal music, that is its liberation from the trammels of the hack librettist and its reunion with the highest expressions of the language in literature and poetry.[1]

One other factor which dates from the beginning of our period must here be taken into account. After the Great Exhibition of 1851 its principal building, the Crystal Palace, was re-erected at Sydenham, by a company formed for the purpose, as a place of popular instruction and entertainment. It was entirely due to George Grove (1820–1900), who was appointed Secretary to the Crystal Palace, that from the first its entertainment and instruction took an enlightened line in regard to music. August Manns, an efficient German bandmaster, was appointed to conduct a wind band in the centre transept of the Palace. He might have remained there doing nothing else for

[1] For a discussion of this aspect of the case see the author's *Voice and Verse*, particularly Chapter IX, 'The British Renaissance'.

the term of his natural existence had it not been for Grove. Once more it was the amateur who shaped the future of English music. Manns was presently put in command of a full orchestra and a portion of the building was fitted up as a concert-room. The weekly Saturday orchestral concerts began on Dec. 1, 1855, and were continued through the winter months of each year till the end of the century,[1] and the first care was to form a repertory round the classics of the symphony, beginning with Beethoven. The credit for the high standard of performance attained belongs to Manns; the means of attaining it were given him by Grove, and it was Grove who set the course of the repertory and secured its enrichment from contemporary works, especially those of the young English school. Manns might have been merely another Costa had it not been for the ameliorating influence of Grove.

Thus, week by week for over forty years, the opportunity for becoming familiar with a wide repertory of the great works of orchestral music of every kind was afforded to Londoners, even though they had to endure the tedium and discomfort of a railway journey to a southern suburb to enjoy the privilege. The Crystal Palace did more to supply the place of a permanent orchestra to London than the more exclusive societies, which from 1858 onward had their home at St. James's Hall, Piccadilly, could do. It was at about the same period, and as a result of the Manchester Exhibition of 1857, that the Hallé Society was formed in Manchester, and Charles Hallé (1819–95) began a parallel work for orchestral music in the North of England. But Hallé had not a George Grove at his elbow, and the Hallé orchestra, though it extended its performances to other towns, hardly achieved the wide influence of the Crystal Palace. Both under Hallé and subsequently under Richter, the Manchester orchestra addressed itself to a distinctively musical clientele and

---

[1] A catalogue of the principal works performed from Oct. 1855 to May 1895 was issued, with a preface by Manns, in 1900.

was supported primarily by the wealthier classes, largely of foreign extraction, engaged in trade in Manchester and elsewhere.

The work of the Crystal Palace concerts was transferred to London itself when, after the building of Queen's Hall (1893), Robert Newman conceived the idea of a summer series of 'Promenade Concerts' there. Such concerts, given in various theatres, had long been popular; but now the repertory was based on the standard upheld at the Crystal Palace. With a young Englishman as conductor, Henry J. Wood (born 1870), the now famous Promenades began a new era in the musical life of London in the summer of 1895, one which was to bring innumerable new experiences from abroad, particularly of Russian music, but also immeasurably to widen the appreciation of native works.

Almost simultaneously with the formation of the Newman-Wood partnership another young English conductor began a similar work in the Winter Gardens at Bournemouth. Dan Godfrey (born 1868) came of a family of British military bandmasters. His father and his grandfather had been bandmasters in the Brigade of Guards, the former attaining that position as early as 1825. When it is remembered with what complacence the British army placed its music in the hands of foreigners throughout the last century, it will be realized that the Godfrey family were pioneers in a patriotic reform of considerable importance to British music.[1] When Dan Godfrey accepted the commission of the Bournemouth Corporation to convert their more or less derelict Winter Gardens into a 'Temple of Music'

---

[1] Regimental bands were commonly maintained at the expense of the regimental officers, who, being themselves drawn from the British aristocracy, regarded music as something which only foreigners could understand. They were anxious to buy the best for the honour of their regiments and therefore naturally imported foreign bandmasters.

The general change of attitude began with the official recognition of Army bands and the establishment of the Royal Military School of Music at Kneller Hall (1857), due to the efforts of the Duke of Cambridge; this was another seed for the revival of native music sown in the 'fifties.

his employers little thought what music would be worshipped in that 'Temple'. They had had Signor Something-or-other conducting an Italian band there before. Young Godfrey might be better or not as good; at any rate they would let him try to brighten up the place a bit. In the summer of 1895 he was allowed an orchestra of thirty-three performers (an unprecedented size for Bournemouth). In the following year he was appointed General Manager of the Winter Gardens, so that all its varied entertainments were under his control, and during his long office in that capacity, till 1923, he was able, by unremitting effort, to see to it that the interests of orchestral music were not swamped by the theatrical and variety shows which were a necessary part of the undertaking.

'In January, 1897, by rare good fortune, Mr. August Manns paid a visit to the town and very kindly consented to conduct performances of two symphonies, which were great favourites of his—Schubert's C major and Schumann's D minor.'[1]

Thus the torch was passed from the Crystal Palace to the Winter Gardens, and Grove's 'great favourites', both of them first introduced at the Crystal Palace in 1856, reached Bournemouth forty years later.

But Godfrey was not content with the classics. He concentrated particular attention on the effort to create a wide repertory of British music. To works which were heard once in London and laid aside he insisted on giving repeated hearings. Everything which had any individual quality found a place in his schemes, and when eventually he resigned the general managership though not the conductorship of the orchestra, a list of such works was compiled which included the names of no less than 163 contemporary native composers.[2] Possibly Henry

---

[1] *Memories and Music*, by Sir Dan Godfrey.

[2] Ibid. Appendix B. 'Selected list of Works by British composers performed at the Bournemouth Symphony Concerts from October 14th, 1895 to December 31st, 1923.' Compiled by Hadley Watkins.

Wood's Promenade programmes in the same period could show a similar record, but certainly no other institution in the British Isles could approach it.

By the end of the nineteenth century, then, this country had with infinite struggle attained to the possession of two regular orchestral institutions, both maintained more or less precariously, the one by private enterprise, the other by a grudging municipal support, but both commanded by British-born conductors with a high sense of responsibility towards native music. It was not a magnificent victory, but it was a position gained and held, to be consolidated in the new century. It proved at any rate that English musicians could make their own music with an orchestra, just as the English amateurs had proved that they could make their own music with their voices. Moreover, the amateurs were being taught to listen as well as to sing.

The orchestral problem was in its nature entirely different from the choral one. Beethoven's Ninth Symphony can be adequately played only by a body of highly skilled professional instrumentalists; its choral Finale can be superbly rendered by people with good voices, natural musical aptitude, and a smattering of knowledge sufficient to enable them to read a part. Manns is reported to have said that an orchestra, by which he meant a professional orchestra, will play as badly as the conductor lets it. It is the conductor's business to secure the best from his players. But the conductor is powerless to secure the best unless it is already there. It is only when every individual player has a complete technical equipment plus a long experience of ensemble playing behind him that the conductor can secure the great performance.

This was the real significance of Hans Richter's work in London and Manchester, the training of a new order of orchestral player. He came with Wagner to take part in the concerts at the Albert Hall in 1877 which were designed to contribute to the establishment of the Bayreuth theatre. He returned in subsequent years to conduct 'Orchestral Festival Concerts' which presently became the regular series known as the 'Richter Concerts'. He took over the direction of the Hallé Orchestra in Manchester in 1897.

It has already been pointed out that not the least part of Wagner's revolution was that he moulded the orchestra into a new instrument and established a new standard of orchestral playing. It was Richter who taught this to English orchestral players, doing so primarily through his interpretations of the works of Beethoven and Wagner. Other able conductors, notably George Henschel, Felix Mottl, and Felix Weingartner, made their contributions to this training, but it was Richter, himself an orchestral player with an intimate knowledge of the technique of every instrument, who founded the new race.

When Henry Wood began his work of initiating a wider public into the wonders of orchestral music he inherited Richter's players. The first Queen's Hall Orchestra, which provided both the Promenades in the summer and the Symphony Concerts in the winter, was virtually that of the Richter Concerts and the London Symphony Concerts which Henschel had directed. The distinctive character of Wood's work was twofold, the widening of the repertory and the education of new audiences. In the matter of players Wood in London had the advantage over Godfrey in Bournemouth. The latter had to begin from scratch, working with military bandsmen, some of whom were 'double-handed', that is, could play either a string or a wind instrument at need. To make such material capable not only of playing the enormous repertory demanded, but in a way which would satisfy the modern requirements of interpretation, was the almost superhuman task which Godfrey undertook. He was beginning in the 'nineties where Manns had begun in the 'fifties.

Meantime, the need for training artists and more particularly instrumental artists, had been realized, and a great educational movement to meet it had been set on foot almost at the time of Richter's first entrance into the London concert-rooms. On July 13, 1878, the Prince of Wales (afterwards King Edward VII) presided at a meeting held at Marlborough House,

'for the purpose of taking into consideration the advancement of the art of music in the United Kingdom by establishing a College of Music on a more permanent and extended basis than any existing institution.'

The Prince of Wales headed the movement; he devoted an enormous amount of personal work to its furtherance, and presently became the first President of the Royal College of Music opened at Kensington Gore in 1883. But again it must be noted that Royal patronage did not mean endowment with public funds allocated to it by the Government. Here, as elsewhere, if people wanted music they must show themselves individually ready to pay for it. The promoters had to stump the country. George Grove was once more the moving spirit. He spoke for it, wrote for it, begged for it.

'At the special request of the Prince of Wales he undertook the task of organizing the subscriptions for a period of six months. This was the outcome of a conference of Mayors and distinguished representatives of religious and educational bodies convened by the Prince of Wales and held early in 1882, and led in turn to the successful movement for the establishment of local and colonial scholarships.'[1]

Thus the appeal was made a national one. The plan was to found a large number of open and local scholarships endowed by public subscription; to comb the whole country for the most promising musical talent, holding preliminary examinations at local centres and the final ones in London; to bring the successful candidates to the College, where they would be admitted to a

[1] See *Life of Sir George Grove*, by C. L. Graves, p. 280. *The Royal College of Music—A Jubilee Record, 1883–1933*, by the author, gives a full account of the foundation.

rigorously pursued system of education covering at least three
years in their special branches of singing or instrumental playing,
in *ensemble* work of all kinds, and in matters of general musical
culture.

It was a greatly conceived scheme and it was magnificently
accomplished when the Prince of Wales formally opened the
College on May 7, 1883, with Grove as Director, a staff of pro-
fessors all carefully chosen by him, fifty scholars selected from
all parts of the kingdom and representative of all classes of
society, and forty-two paying students. It was to widen its
borders in the eleven years of Grove's directorate, so much so
that when the foundation-stone of the new and more spacious
building in Prince Consort Road was laid in 1890, the scholarships had increased to sixty and the paying students to two
hundred and eighty-five.

But the immediate success of the Royal College of Music as
a place of education is not the point which most concerns us
here. Rather it is the fact that the movement which created it
marks a stage in the realization of music as a matter of national
concern. When, after the centenary of the Royal Academy of
Music, Sir Alexander Mackenzie was entertained at dinner by the
younger institution, he jokingly remarked to his hosts that if
the Academy had done its duty the College would never have
existed. The remark perhaps bore a little hardly on the institution which had produced Sterndale Bennett, Sullivan, and the
speaker himself. But the Academy, struggling on through the
middle of the century in a make-shift building in Tenterden
Street, and supported by inadequate funds, had not been able
to impress itself and its aims on the country at large. Moreover,
despite the good work done successively by Bennett and Mac-
farren at its head, it was not till Mackenzie himself took charge
of it in 1888 that its type of education began to meet the requirements of the modern art. Mackenzie with his wide experience

of music and musicians, gained through his long sojourn abroad, his personal contact with such men as Liszt, Hans von Bülow, and Verdi, was the very man to sweep away the dust of ages and to put the place in order for training on modern lines. It is more difficult to effect a reform than to initiate something new. The Academy had been unable to reform itself when it was invited to join hands in the educational enterprise of 1880. That movement was started without its co-operation. Mackenzie's task was to bring the organization of the Academy into line, and with his Scottish persistence added to great artistic gifts he succeeded beyond all expectation. When at last in 1911 he carried the Royal Academy of Music to its new and splendid home in the Marylebone Road, he had given it a teaching staff, a curriculum, and a type of student equal to that which had been demanded for the College thirty years before.

Unfortunately the educators of the 'eighties grappled with only one side of the problem. While the College was training its first group of scholars, Carl Rosa was making his spirited experiments in English opera; the walls of the new building in Prince Consort Road were rising when D'Oyly Carte's project of the Royal English Opera House was collapsing. Probably Stanford realized more acutely than any one else how inseparably the interests of these different institutions were bound up together. At any rate he expressed it succinctly when he wrote a good many years later,

'. . . without doubt England has been putting the cart before the horse. Elsewhere the national stage is founded first, and the schools for training successions of artists for it afterwards. The date of Lulli's control of the State Opera of Paris was 1672, that of the foundation of the Conservatoire was 1795. England has begun by providing the schools to educate artists, and founds no institutions to employ them when they are educated. We are beginning to reap the inevitable harvest of this short-sighted policy.'[1]

[1] See 'The Case for National Opera' in *Studies and Memories*, by C. V. Stanford, 1908.

Quite apart from the stage, it would certainly have been well if the 'Mayors and distinguished representatives of religious and educational bodies' called together by the Prince for the founding of the College had been reminded that if they made young people take up a musical career the responsibility for finding employment for them in after-life would be theirs. It might also have been explained to the Mayors that if their municipal music was to be made in the future by highly trained artists the scale of payment for their services must be higher than that demanded by double- or single-handed military bandsmen. Similarly, the representatives of religious bodies might have been reminded that if their village schoolmasters were to be replaced by gifted organists trained under a Sir Walter Parratt their budget for church expenses would have to undergo revision. Apparently this was not done. Perhaps, had it been done, the Mayors and distinguished representatives would have declined to co-operate, and the Prince's educational movement would have gone no farther.

As it was, composers, pianists, organists, singers, and orchestral players were, and still are, turned out in large numbers to earn their living by teaching others, by playing in theatre bands, restaurants, and later in cinemas, by anything but those higher forms of art for which they have been trained, often at the public expense. The economic side of the situation need not be examined here. The consequence to artistic perspective was that by first generating power and then neglecting to use it, the English people still remained at the end of the century what they had been before the revival began, interested amateurs of music.

We turn from this catalogue of struggles, failures, and achievements on the executive side to consider a few of the positive results in musical composition which were the product of this era. The instrumental music has already been touched on, because what British composers achieved in that direction was done independently of any local conditions, in fact in defiance of the innumerable deterrents which local conditions placed in their way. The chamber works and the symphonies of the last century have not taken their places as the classics of this one, because when they were produced there were so few native artists ready to perform them that public taste could not be said to have been cultivated by means of them. A great deal of the best work of the Parry-Stanford group was laid on one side before it had been put to the test of presentation to a wide and miscellaneous public. British orchestral music lacked its own audience until Wood and Godfrey began to create one for it. Moreover, with so few orchestras to play the music, publishers were naturally chary of embarking on the expensive publication of scores and parts, and no Belaiev came forward to take British music in hand.[1]

With vocal music, however, the case was different. The renaissance in amateur choral singing begun in the 'fifties had proceeded some distance by the 'eighties, and the enterprise it had shown was rewarded in the choral works of Hubert Parry (1848-1918). The date (September 7, 1880) on which the first of them appeared has been spoken of as the birthday of modern English music.[2] The choice of subject, 'Scenes from Shelley's

---

[1] It was only in the twentieth century that patronage comparable to that which Belaiev brought to the Russian composers began to be exercised on behalf of British music. Early in the century Walter Willson Cobbett instituted the 'Cobbett Competitions' for chamber music compositions, commissioned a number of works, encouraged the younger composers to write in concise single-movement forms of the kind described as 'Phantasy', and furthered chamber music composition and performance in every way possible. Ernest Palmer founded his Patrons' Fund at the Royal College of Music to encourage the work of British composers by performance and to a limited extent by publication. Later the Carnegie Trust embarked on a comprehensive scheme for the publication of works not likely to appeal to the commercial publishers.

[2] *History of Music in England*, by Ernest Walker, 2nd edition (1924), p. 300. In a chapter on 'Later Victorian Music' the characteristics of the principal composers of the time are acutely summed up in an appreciative though discriminating commentary.

Prometheus Unbound', itself proclaims a new freedom, and the opening prelude declares the composer absorbed in the imaginative spirit of the quasi-dramatic poem, while the first monologue of the enchained and rebellious Prometheus shows a sense of forceful declamation which English music had not known since Purcell. Contrast it with the opening words of Lucifer in the prologue of Sullivan's *Golden Legend,* so much admired for its dramatic quality when it first appeared at Leeds six years later. Beside Parry's Prometheus the declamation of Sullivan's Lucifer is flaccid and nerveless.

Ex. 1.   PARRY. *Prometheus Unbound.*

one . . . . who throng these bright and roll - ing

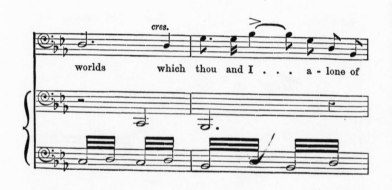

worlds which thou and I . . . a - lone of

liv-ing things be - hold with sleep-less eyes, Re -

hearts   with fear   and self-con-

-tempt   and bar-ren   hope.

SULLIVAN.   *Golden Legend.*
LUCIFER (*quasi recit.*)

Has-ten,   has-ten . .

... O ye spi - rits!

From its sta - tion drag the pon'drous

Cross of i - ron, that to mock us is up -

- lift - ed high in air !

In mobilizing the forces of choral voices for dramatic expression Parry at once shows a rich variety of resource. The choruses of furies and of spirits of the air have none of the formal patterns of the old oratorio types. Their phraseology grows straight from the poetic idea and they are borne forward on the wings of the words. It is little wonder that *Prometheus* was something of a shock to its first audience at the Gloucester Festival, who responded to the shock by putting it aside. Parry never quite recovered the rapturous fervour of the mood in which *Prometheus* is couched, and particularly its blend of his innate strenuousness with a delicate sensitiveness to the effects of colour in the combination of voices and instruments. His later choral works show increasing reliance on the voices, and in some of them he is undeniably guilty of perfunctoriness in regard to instrumentation. The circumstances in which he worked partly accounted for this; most of his works were written for increasingly well-drilled amateur choirs combined for festival purposes with practically unrehearsed professional orchestras.

Shirley's ode, *The Glories of our Blood and State*, Parry's setting of which Gloucester produced at its next festival three years later, offered no scope for the rich imaginative variety which Shelley had inspired, but the grave elegiac beauty of its main theme contrasted with the vigorous chorus, 'Some men with swords may reap the field', is perfect in its kind, and makes it a work to be compared with Brahms's *Schicksalslied*. The return to the broad opening tune of the orchestra supporting the voices in unison may be quoted as a sample of the dignified utterance which was to become typical of Parry's personal tone of voice.

A similar eloquence appears again in innumerable later works, in the 'Hail, thou Goddess' of *L'Allegro ed il Penseroso* (1890), in the 'Blow Trumpets' of *War and Peace* (1903), and in the chorus 'For everything there is a season', of the cantata *Beyond these voices* (1908), to name instances from various periods. The famous setting for double choir and orchestra of Milton's ode, *Blest Pair of Sirens* (1887), is instinct with the life of the words from first to last, and possibly this choral-singing country is right in treasuring it as Parry's supreme contribution to the national art, but its frequent performance half a century after its birth and the complete neglect into which his many other noble works have fallen is a symptom of the less admirable side of the English amateurism.

In 1888 Parry disappointed those who had regarded him as the apostle of the new freedom in English music by producing a full-length oratorio, *Judith*, at the Birmingham Festival. They had no difficulty in detecting the individuality of the composer in the broadly planned and massive choruses, in the vivid declamation of the solos, and in the lyrical delicacy of the scene of the children of Manasseh. But the whole plan of the work, using words partly written by Parry himself and partly culled from the Apocrypha, seemed a throwback to the Mendelssohn tradition against which he and others with him had hitherto waged successful war.

If *Judith* is placed beside Mackenzie's *The Rose of Sharon* (1884), it is clear that the latter is the richer in suggestions of oriental colouring appropriate to the subject. In such things as the orchestral Intermezzo, 'Spring morning on Lebanon', the solo and chorus, 'Who is this coming up from the Valley', and the sleep scene of 'The Sulamite's dream', we find Mackenzie anticipating something of that sensuous charm which belongs to 'The Dawn' in Elgar's *The Apostles* and the more piquant details of Bantock's *Omar Khayyam*. There was scarcely a touch of local colour anywhere to lighten the rather plodding progress of Parry's *Judith*. But Mackenzie had depended too exclusively on his sense of the picturesque, and after a first successful production at Norwich *The Rose of Sharon* soon dropped out of the repertory.

Parry in *Judith* depended on his purpose of illustrating the 'force of character' behind the exploit of his heroine and on 'popular movements and passions and such results of them as recur a hundred times in history'.[1] It was in fact the spiritual significance behind the narrative which impelled his return to the oratorio form, and he showed himself undismayed by censure in following up *Judith* with *Job* (1892) and *King Saul* (1894). For all of them he compiled the books himself. *Job*, the first work by a native composer to be performed in successive years at each of the Three Choir centres (Gloucester, Worcester, and Hereford), is the most concise and the most completely individual of the three. There are few finer things in English music than

[1] See preface to vocal score of *Judith*.

the baritone solo, the Lamentation of Job, and the subsequent chorus, the answer of 'the Lord out of the whirlwind'. One short quotation from the former is given here, both as a further instance of Parry's eloquence in handling words of deep human import, and because the weight of its impressiveness is shared by the orchestral instruments.

He com-eth forth . . like a

V'Cello.   cres.

flower, and is cut   down :   he fle-eth al-so as a

sha-dow,   and con - tin-ueth not.

p cres.

Parry's period of oratorio composition, which included also the spacious *De Profundis* written for Hereford in 1891, more or less closes that part of his career which belongs strictly to the nineteenth century. The production of *King Saul* at Birmingham coincided with his acceptance of the Directorship of the Royal College of Music in succession to Sir George Grove, and though the cares of that office did not check his composition to anything like the extent that similar cares at the Royal Academy checked Mackenzie, his output from that time became slighter. It is scarcely surprising, too, that his later compositions showed increasing signs of hasty workmanship and similarity of idiom. The majestic epic, *War and Peace*, another work for which Parry wrote his own words, followed the South African war. It is as far removed from the 'Mafeking' spirit which characterized the national rejoicings of that day as it is from the imperial posturings which had affected Brahms in the *Triumphlied* thirty years earlier. It was little regarded after its first performance at the Albert Hall.

Though Parry turned from time to time to instrumental work, notably the delightful Symphonic Variations (1897) and the later symphonies, as a holiday task composed music for undergraduate performances of Greek plays at Oxford and Cambridge, as well as the popular cantata, *The Pied Piper of Hamelin*, he was occupied in the main in his later years with choral composition of an increasingly introspective kind. He summed up his philosophy of life[1] in the allegory of four Biblical cantatas produced at the Three Choirs Festivals (*Voces Clamantium, The Love that Casteth out fear, The Soul's Ransom,* and *Beyond these Voices*), and, more directly if less intimately, in the setting of his own poem, *A Vision of Life* (Cardiff, 1907). In the last year or two of his life his original genius was able to shine clear in a series of six motets for unaccompanied voices called *Songs of Farewell,* which reveal a mastery of choral texture equal to that of Brahms.[2]

Parry had not the resilience, the easy inventiveness, the love of stylistic experiments which belonged to his contemporary, C. V. Stanford (1852–1924). The latter's now forgotten oratorio, *The Three Holy Children,* in considerable tracts of which Dr. Walker finds 'French influence, especially that of Bizet', brought him before the public, in company with Mackenzie's *Rose of Sharon* and Sullivan's *Golden Legend,* and therefore a little before Parry's *Judith* appeared.

Up to that time Stanford had been known chiefly as the keen-witted Irishman who had used his position as organist of Trinity College, Cambridge, to awaken that University to the importance of music as a factor in the life of an intellectual community. He had studied in Leipzig in the intervals of his work at Cambridge. He had brought Joachim to Cambridge,

---

[1] The point of view which underlies all this phase of Parry's composition is developed in a literary work, *Instinct and Character,* which Parry completed shortly before his death and left in MS. Copies of it were deposited by his executors in the British Museum, the Bodleian, and the R.C.M. libraries.

[2] That sense of choral texture in Parry was not the outcome of any direct influence from Brahms on him. They had acquired it in the same school. Parry's lifelong devotion to the work of J. S. Bach had stamped itself on his own composition from the early stage of the Duo in E minor for two pianos (1875) onward. It found ultimate literary expression in *Johann Sebastian Bach, the Story of the Development of a great personality* (1909), one of the foundational works of the modern criticism of Bach.

there to conduct the first performance of Brahms's C minor Symphony, had himself, as conductor of the University Musical Society, directed important German works of the newer type, and had raised the level of that Society's performances to heights undreamed of previously in University circles. He was already a member of the teaching staff of the new Royal College of Music, as Parry was; two years later he was to succeed to the Professorship of music in his own University, a post which he held thenceforward to the end of his life.

Stanford at the age of thirty-three was regarded very much as a coming man in composition; his works were eagerly performed but none of the major ones made the decisive impression that Parry's work of the same period made. He was much occupied with opera, and there, as we have seen, the fates were against him, though when ten years later Augustus Harris produced his charming Irish comedy, *Shamus O'Brien*, for a run at the Opéra-Comique in London, its success was sufficient to prove that Stanford had not mistaken his gift for the stage. In choral music he excelled in the lighter style of the choral ballad, the vogue of which in England he largely created with *The Revenge* (1886). He had a special fondness for the poetry of Tennyson, and he set *Carmen Saeculare* for the jubilee of Queen Victoria, and followed the *Revenge* with *The Voyage of Maeldune*.

In these two last-named works first appeared what is the most obviously British attribute of Stanford's music, the gift for writing vividly and breezily of adventure by sea. It was exemplified much later in the choral *Songs of the Sea* and *Songs of the Fleet*, made famous by Plunket Greene's capacity to 'lead the line' of the choralists. Parry was a seaman who sailed his own yacht, preferably in the worst weather and on the most dangerous courses, but Stanford, a landsman, who disliked a channel crossing, was the sea's chief musician, and it was with his music of the sea that he most endeared himself to English singers and audiences.

A second oratorio, *Eden*, made no more permanent mark than its predecessor, in spite of the fact that its book, written by Robert Bridges, was planned to give opportunity for Stanford's skill in the display of what may be described as a series of mystical musical frescoes. Later, he turned to Latin liturgical texts, a Mass for soli, choir, and orchestra, a Requiem in memory of Lord Leighton, the painter, a *Te Deum*, and a *Stabat Mater*, produced at several Birmingham and Leeds Festivals. In these things it is easy to detect influences from various continental sources, more especially that of Verdi in the last-named work. The skill with which Stanford caught the externals of a style foreign to himself and his environment made him suspect of insincerity, but the suspicion was unjust. A strong religious sense animated this phase of his work, and found expression in the worship of fine workmanship, appositeness of line and colour, polish of phrase. The *Stabat Mater*, designed in four vocal movements, with a turbulent orchestral interlude picturing the darkness of the scene on Calvary as centre-piece, is one of the most deeply-felt and original works of the kind, even though it is difficult to remember in listening to it that it is not the direct product of Italian Catholicism.

Equally difficult is it to realize that these monumental works come from the same brain and hand as the several 'services' and the many fine anthems with which Stanford enriched the Anglican Church. He was the only musician of his generation who made a substantial addition to the long tradition of English church music, and in that respect he must be regarded as the successor of S. S. Wesley. But while Wesley's whole artistic outlook was bounded by the cathedral choir, Stanford brought new life to it because he moved in a larger world. His famous *Te Deum* in B flat was spoken of by a contemporary as the first work of the kind which could be called a composition. That is exaggeration, but it points to the fact that Stanford's services were not, as so many of the time were, merely expressive renderings of devotional words. They have musical form in the development of salient themes. The technique of a symphonic structure is applied to them without transgressing the limits of time imposed by the 'short service' of the Elizabethan era.

Broadly speaking, we may say of Stanford's work that the smaller the form the more exquisite is the workmanship. It was that applied to the foundation of Irish folk-melody which made him supreme as a writer of solo songs with piano accompaniment. He and Parry together began a new era in English song. They escaped from the confinement of the Mendelssohn tradition in which Sterndale Bennett had lingered; they despised the debased currency of the 'royalty ballad' to which their contemporaries pandered. They began in every case from the poem, and, without accepting any doctrinaire notions of poetic supremacy, they sought the right music for the particular poem chosen, and discovered it in vocal melody, set off by a piano accompaniment charged with the first duty of supporting the voice and the second of contributing to the expression of the poem.

The bulk of Parry's songs are collected in the twelve books of English Lyrics, the first of which appeared in 1881 and the last two of which were published posthumously.[1] The Leipzig influence on Stanford is declared by a number of songs of Heine and other German poets amongst his early opus numbers, but he was not long in finding his own personal standpoint towards song, and having found it he never left it, but continued to enrich English song with his treasures throughout his life. Such

[1] These and other posthumous works of Parry we owe to the careful editorship of Dr. Emily Daymond. A complete catalogue of all Parry's works compiled by her was published in the 3rd edition of *Grove's Dictionary of Music and Musicians*, 1928.

things as the three Cavalier songs of Browning and the *Child's Garden of Songs* from R. L. Stevenson's *Garden of Verses* show the earlier stages of his gift for setting English poetry to music, but it was after the publication of *Songs of Erin*, a collection of fifty Irish folksongs, that his finest work was done in *An Irish Idyll* (Moira O'Neill), *Cushendall*, and *A Fire of Turf*, song-cycles which contain the gems of his art.

Stanford had two advantages over Parry: his background of native folk-melody and his own greater facility of musical invention. It must be remembered in regard to Parry that the modern cult of English folksong came too late to influence him.[1] The English quality which we recognize unmistakably in *My true love hath my heart*, *When we two parted*, *Love and laughter*, *On a time the amorous Silvy*, indeed all along the line, is something innate both in the poet and the composer, but the exact terms of its expression were not found without an effort sometimes apparent in the result. The best of Stanford's Irish songs are effortless. Such things as *The Fairy Lough*, *Cuttin' rushes*, and *Grandeur* give the impression that not a note could have been differently placed without detriment.

These two pioneers had the satisfaction of seeing their work carried further in the songs of their immediate successors. Arthur Somervell's *Maud* cycle, Charles Wood's *Ethiopia saluting the Colours*, Ernest Walker's *Corinna going a-maying*, Roger Quilter's and Walford Davies's Shakespeare songs, and Vaughan Williams's *Songs of Travel* are just a handful gathered at random of the things which began to make the song literature of England what Dowland had made it three hundred years before, the richest of any country in the world.

Some of these composers were the first product of the Royal College of Music; those who represented the results of reform

[1] The English Folksong Society was founded in 1898, and Cecil Sharp first saw the 'Morris' danced at Headington in the following year.

at the Royal Academy of Music, Edward German, William Wallace, Granville Bantock, Arnold Bax, and many others, began to set their mark on their country's music at about the same time. We may not here follow any of them into the twentieth century in which, together with many other native composers whose early training and experience had been gained abroad, they have built on the foundations described above.

One of this number must be specially named here because of a single work which gained a momentary attention, and ought to have had more, in 1893. Ethel Mary Smyth (born 1858) suffered from two disabilities. She was a woman and she was the daughter of a distinguished gunner officer. She had no right, therefore, to be a composer, or if she insisted on being one she should have been content to remain a modest amateur, like her contemporary Miss Ellicott, who was the daughter of a bishop. But Miss Smyth was neither modest nor an amateur. She insisted on studying her art seriously in Leipzig with Herzogenberg; she made Madame Schumann commend her, a little grudgingly, perhaps, to Brahms,[1] and she achieved a firm footing in the society of that circle. Her Mass in D for solo voices, choir, and orchestra proved her claim not only to seriousness of intention, but to skill in execution and considerable originality in design. It was given at the Albert Hall under Barnby, and though Fuller-Maitland wrote of it later that it definitely placed her 'among the most eminent composers of her time',[2] she was certainly given very little tangible evidence of the fact at the moment. The public was as indifferent as was the performance itself. The critics were condescending. George

[1] 'Tomorrow morning we are expecting Ethel Smyth for a day or two. I am surprised at the progress she has made and even if she has no originality as a composer, I cannot help feeling respect for such ability in a girl.' (Letter from Clara Schumann to Brahms, Dec. 5, 1883. See English translation of *Letters*, ii, p. 86.)

[2] See *Grove's Dictionary of Music and Musicians*, 2nd ed. (1908).

Bernard Shaw used the word 'pretty' three times in one article, and likened Miss Smyth and her Mass to 'a mundane young lady' decorating a church for Christmas. This was very unjust, not because the Mass was a masterpiece, but because it ought to have been clear to a man of Shaw's intelligence that it deserved to be judged by the same critical standards as the other works of the kind, both English and foreign, which at that time he was so eager to demolish.

It was thirty-one years before Ethel Smyth's Mass was heard again,[1] and in the meantime she had compelled admiration for her opera, *The Wreckers*, in both Germany and England, and had written the humorous opera, *The Boatswain's Mate*, for her own country together with a number of other works. But what perhaps most conduced to a change of front in her critics was the fact that during the interval the 'Suffragettes' had paraded the streets of London to the strains of her *March of the Women*, and had won their cause.

Two dates at the end of the century give us the right to include names without which this record would be manifestly incomplete. They are November 11, 1898, when Coleridge-Taylor's setting for tenor solo, chorus, and orchestra of Longfellow's *Hiawatha's Wedding Feast* was first heard under Stanford in the temporary concert-hall of the Royal College of Music, and October 3, 1900, when Richter conducted the first performance of Elgar's *The Dream of Gerontius* at the Birmingham Festival. Each of these dates marks the decisive arrival on the scene of English vocal music of a distinct and fully formed personality.

Samuel Coleridge-Taylor (1875–1912) was of mixed West African and English parentage. He was eighteen years of age when he won a composition scholarship at the Royal College, at which he had already studied for three years. His natural

---

[1] The Mass was revived by Adrian Boult at Birmingham in 1924.

gift of melody appeared in many instrumental works produced at college concerts and his Ballade for orchestra in A minor had attracted favourable attention at the Gloucester Festival in the year of *Hiawatha*. But it was the latter which at once placed Coleridge-Taylor in the first rank at the age of twenty-three. It showed a composer possessed by his subject, pouring out melodies precisely fitted to Longfellow's verse but entirely untrammelled by it, melodies as simple-minded as those of Dvořák which had so captivated English people a generation earlier, but owing nothing to that or to any other known source. The orchestration was as vivid as the situation demanded; the choral writing as competent as was to be expected from Stanford's best pupil, but in neither was there any sign of pupillage. Coleridge-Taylor was to extend *Hiawatha* later into the trilogy of cantatas which has gone through the world wherever the English language is sung. He was inevitably to add to it a long list of choral works ranging from the pretty *Bon-Bon Suite* to an elaborate oratorio called *The Atonement*. His best work, whether for instruments or for voices, would approach the level of *Hiawatha* and his worst fall away from it, but by it all would be judged, because it contained the whole of his genius in its purest form.

The name of Edward Elgar, on the other hand, opens up a long vista, along a portion of which a glance has already been taken. When *The Dream of Gerontius* appeared he was not a young man, and he was not unknown. His mastery of the orchestra had been proclaimed in the *Enigma* Variations and he already had a fairly long list of choral cantatas to his name. The list had begun a little tentatively, but very significantly, with a short oratorio called *The Light of Life*, and had culminated in the successful production of *Caractacus* (Leeds, 1898), a work in which a rare romantic imagination contended with a welcome note of downright British patriotism. It seemed possible that *Caractacus* might succeed *The Golden Legend* in popular favour, but *The Dream of Gerontius* made it quite immaterial whether this happened or not. It was equally immaterial to the future that, owing to an inadequate performance, some ecclesiastical partisanship, and a spice of protestant prejudice against its subject, the work did not immediately take hold of the public. That could be easily rectified by a performance at the Lower Rhine Festival at Düsseldorf two years later. What mattered supremely was that here was a mature artist who had lived with a poem for ten years or more until it had become part and parcel of his own inner nature, and that he had transmuted it into music which revealed his vision of its content completely and finally. It was that which made *The Dream of Gerontius* an epoch-making work.

It is open to criticism of detail like any other. It can be pointed out that in the matter of orchestral texture Elgar's technique is very dependent on Wagner's example, that despite the singular beauty of the 'Kyrie' and the 'Commendation', the handling of the voice parts, particularly in the Angelic hymn, is not always felicitous, that the 3–4 time of the 'Sanctus, fortis' song of Gerontius is in danger of leading to triteness, and that in the dialogue between the Angel and the Soul the musician has evidently found some difficulty in making his music transcend the several points of theological disputation. But these and other such points amount to very little in view of the first-hand invention of the musical ideas, and their coalescence into a single conception: the depth of the insight into human suffering and the height of the vision of Divine glory give to the work its tremendous emotional range of expression.

The unique experience of *The Dream of Gerontius* was not to be repeated. That, taking other literary ground, the inexhaustible sources of selection from the Bible, Elgar was able to re-create something of the same vision in the oratorios of *The Apostles* and *The Kingdom*, showed the extraordinary fecundity of his genius. Into these and later works we shall not here enter. *The Dream of Gerontius* is cited as the last milestone in the path of English music of the nineteenth century.

The aim of this chapter has been to describe the precipitous ascent of that path through fifty years, the energy of the musical impulse in the country asserting itself and struggling uphill without any of the aids in the way of established institutions for music which other countries were accustomed to, the combined efforts of diverse talents and their reward in the occasional appearance of genius. Apart from his personal genius, Elgar's contribution to these efforts was that he persuaded his countrymen to begin a new faith in their musical artists, and that, further, he compelled the Continent to look with increased respect on English music.

The Continent would have been well advised to look earlier, and English people had little excuse for their generally shamefaced attitude before the foreigner. They had every reason to be ashamed of the small encouragement meted out to composers and executants, and there is still cause for shame in that direction thirty years after the date at which this record closes. It is forty years since the Royal English Opera House collapsed and still no permanent home has been found for native opera. It is thirty-five years since Dan Godfrey began his exemplary work at Bournemouth, yet orchestral music outside London still rests on the sporadic visits of the orchestras of London, Manchester, and Glasgow on tour, the bare minimum of provision from municipal authorities in places where such music may be regarded as an attraction to the town,.and on the spirited efforts of amateur performers.

Without some determination to face these problems the artistic benefits which the nineteenth century achieved must be lost in the twentieth, no matter how brilliant may be the talent for music of all kinds which professionals and amateurs alike display. If there is ever any truth again in the saying that England is an unmusical country, it will be, not that she wraps her talents in a napkin, but that she squanders them. The nineteenth century recovered the national heritage in music; it remains for the twentieth to discover wisdom in its use.

INDEX

INDEX